THE DESPERATE YEARS

BOOKS BY JAMES D. HORAN

WORLD WAR II
ACTION TONIGHT: THE STORY OF THE DESTROYER O'BANNON

WESTERN FRONTIER
DESPERATE MEN
DESPERATE WOMEN
PICTORIAL HISTORY OF THE WILD WEST (WITH PAUL SANN)
ACROSS THE CIMARRON
THE GREAT AMERICAN WEST
THE WILD BUNCH

CIVIL WAR
MATHEW BRADY: HISTORIAN WITH A CAMERA
CONFEDERATE AGENT
C.S.S. SHENANDOAH: THE MEMOIRS OF LIEUTENANT
    COMMANDING   JAMES I. WADDELL

NOVELS
KING'S REBEL
SEEK OUT AND DESTROY
THE SHADOW CATCHER

CRIME
THE PINKERTON STORY (WITH HOWARD SWIGGETT)
THE D.A.'S MAN
THE MOB'S MAN

CONTEMPORARY HISTORY
THE DESPERATE YEARS: A PICTORIAL HISTORY OF
    THE THIRTIES

THE DESPERATE YEARS

A PICTORIAL HISTORY OF THE THIRTIES

by JAMES D. HORAN

BONANZA BOOKS   NEW YORK

For Gertrude,
lovely and durable partner
of our Desperate Years.

Acknowledgements

For their cooperation in securing photographs, official documents, surveys, and the results of polls, the author is indebted to Miss Joseph Motylewski in the Audio-Visual Branch, National Archives; Lewis E. Rubin, Chief, Property Liquidation Unit, Office of Alien Property, Department of Justice; Miss Noreen Sherlock, National Broadcasting Company; John Faber of Eastman Kodak; Arthur Rothstein of *Look* magazine; Peter Hunter, Press Features, Amsterdam, Holland; Roy Melchen, United Press International; Harry Williams and Frederick A. Chapman of the Automobile Manufacturers Association, Detroit; Robert Hefty and Ernest H. Barton of the Ford Museum, Dearborn, Michigan; Grace N. Mayer, The Museum of Modern Art; Sid Garfield, Director of Press Information, CBS Radio; Sam H. Day, retired managing editor of the New York *Journal-American* who introduced me to the works of Dr. Erich Salomon; Dr. A. Carlson, New-York Historical Society; William Edelle, World Wide Photos; Paul Feiss, Chief Librarian of the New York *Journal-American's* Reference Room, and James Haberkorn, librarian of that department; and A. Baragwanath, Curator of Prints of the Museum of the City of New York.
(I)

Contents

Contents

Foreword

I HAVE always maintained that the Desperate Years of the nineteen-thirties adhered strictly to the elementary principles of the novel and the play; the period had a beginning, a middle, and an end. It began against the grim backdrop of 1929, reached its peak of great expectations in 1935, and ended in bewilderment and fear in the thunder of Hitler's guns in Poland.

It was a grim period, but in that decade there was much more than the fierce struggle for survival; there was excitement, social revolution, changes in our government which rebuilt our lives, and experimentation in arts and science. Looking back it seems that our domestic disaster made Americans once again aware of their neighbors and taught them to face the cold, brutal fact that only close cooperation could pull them and their nation out of the quicksand of despair.

I remember the thirties vividly. They were my formative years, my unforgettable years. When the bottom dropped out and we lost what we had, I went to college at night and tried to find a job in the daytime. It seems strange now to say it, but there just weren't any jobs. I recall visiting an agency on West Forty-second Street and having the owner shake his head when I asked for an application.

"I've been waiting for three days for a job to come in, kid," he said, "and when it does I'm grabbing it. I haven't paid the rent for three months and next week's the deadline."

The following month I stopped by out of curiosity and found the place closed. The elevator operator told me the owner just locked the door and never returned.

The first job I got was in the New York City office of a small Virginia tobacco company.

I had to deliver packages of cigarettes to small stands the company operated throughout New York City. I hated to spend the nickel for the subway, so while the job lasted I walked all over the city. The supplies were eventually delivered.

I was always writing and determined to get into the newspaper field somehow. One night I wrote a long and intense letter to the editor of the local paper and was amazed to have it returned with a terse note scrawled on the bottom: "Come in and see me tonight."

I can recall the managing editor, surrounded by a world of copy paper, numerous pipes, and a battered typewriter which he pounded furiously. In between pounding and puffing clouds of smoke he interviewed me—only later did I realize how shrewdly. I was hired at the glorious salary of eight dollars a week. But more importantly I was given a police card, which allowed me to pass through fire lines, view dead bodies, and talk to policemen.

It was an exciting time—what thrill can be compared to reading one's first copy in cold, impersonal type?

I resigned, with the editor's approval, to work as a copy boy on the *New York Journal;* it was more money, twelve dollars a week. In 1932 I became a metropolitan reporter and an eye witness to many of the episodes in this book. I can remember how a box of candy for his secretary got me an exclusive interview with Sir Gerald Campbell, then British consul in New York, in which he outlined Britain's plan of economic embargoes against Italy for her Ethiopian invasion. Washington and London confirmed it several hours later.

The ten-dollar bonus was overwhelming.

Then there was Fritz Kuhn, surrounded by his Nazi bully boys, threatening to throw me out of a window because of my paper's Bund exposé; and Dutch Schultz advising me not to split an infinitive a few nights before he was shot in the Newark bar.

There was the impromptu press conference held in the elevator in Penn Station by FDR, and the wild moment when the government agents found the ransom money in Bruno Hauptmann's garage and reporters fought like madmen to capture the one telephone in the nearby beer garden. The Beer Parade, the glorious night of repeal, the exciting One Hundred Days of the New Deal, the blind veteran with the ragged coat covered with medals who led the New York contingent of the Bonus Army down Eighth Avenue and confided to me that he could still smell the gas of the Argonne. There was also the afternoon in the Central Park West apartment-house lobby when an intense Ambassador Dodd tried to describe how dangerous Adolf Hitler had become. And the interview a few months later with the Austrian boy who proudly told how he had helped the underground distribute anti-Nazi leaflets. The interview was in sign language through an interpreter; the Nazis had smashed his voice box. Dodd's words came back then with the shock of a stone thrown in a man's face.

While I was busy learning how to be a metropolitan reporter, my friends, most of whom were fighting to continue in school or attend college at night, were scratching around for jobs. This was before the WPA, so when they couldn't find jobs they demonstrated their Yankee ingenuity. They carted eggs in from the Jersey farms and sold them door to door. One fellow lugged aluminum ware around day and night, cooking free meals, to lure prospective buyers into signing a suspicious contract. He had never cooked an egg in his life but had his mother give him a furious three-day course in cooking one complete meal. He never served anything but that one meal. The sales he made fed his family, paid the rent, and resulted in a new suit. He was the envy of our group.

Another fellow made a deal with a local tailor; for every new customer he received a commission. At the end of the day he delivered an impressive assortment of men's and women's garments to the little tailor, who now had so much work he couldn't even listen to Father Coughlin.

Our amusements were few or self-made. I either went to the dime movies or hiked enough through Palisades Park to satisfy a lifetime. In the company of another young reporter, who

today is a distinguished member of the *New York Times* staff, I discovered the Group Theatre, Orson Welles, the Abbey Players, and Sean O'Casey. Like every other theatregoer under twenty-five, I cheered and raved when the curtain came down on Odets' *Waiting for Lefty*. Frances Farmer, John Garfield in *Golden Boy*—Tallulah Bankhead in *Rain*—all for seventy-five cents!

It was a glorious experience to have been an eye witness to such a vibrant, exciting theatre.

There weren't many luxuries; window ice-boxes were fine in the winter and a ten-cent piece of ice was enough to last the day. The ingenuity of wives was challenged every night at the dinner table. No one bought clothes, you shopped for them, not for style but for durability. How long would it last and would it fade or shrink?

As the shadow of war began to loom over the world, the paramount question was, Are you going into the cavalry or the infantry?

A Model T, black and shiny, was purchased for the grand sum of twenty-five dollars. There were five partners—each contributed five dollars. It carried many a whooping, singing crowd out to the beach. It was so durable I am sure it is still chugging along some New Jersey backroad.

Politics and social issues were violently debated and mostly by the young. One friend became a Communist. I can still see him in his black shirt trying to shout us capitalists down. Today he is the most conserva-

tive of men, living a calm, suburban life as a gray-haired grandfather.

"Hell, I was no Communist as we know them today," he said recently. "There was just a lot of excitement around in those days and I wanted to be part of it."

Excitement, movement, things being done and things being born—that was the thirties. It was a time of individualism, of getting mad at something or somebody. It was a time when tremendous things were happening, and to us—young and undefeated as we were—the hope of accomplishment was the justification for living. None of us thought about defeat or lying down to die. The only thing that worried all of us—in contrast to our elders—was the dreadful thought that perhaps we would be forced to live out dull lives in which nothing could be done and a man would be forced by events beyond his personal control to give up and wallow in black despair.

Those were the thirties as I remember them. In planning this book for those who lived through it and for those who heard about it, I knew that I would have to have both extensive text and a wealth of pictures to bring home the story.

This then is my pictorial history of our Desperate Years.

JAMES D. HORAN

Horan's Boondocks,
September, 1962

Prologue: The Crash

NEW YORK, WEDNESDAY, OCTOBER 30, 1929.
TWO CENTS In Greater New York | THREE CENTS Within 200 Miles | FOUR CENTS Elsewhere Except 7th and 8th Post

Newark Man, 4 Feet 10, Says He Was Smallest in A. E. F.

WASHINGTON, Oct. 29 (AP).—Nicholas Casale of Newark, N. J., wants to be known as the smallest man who went to France with the American Expeditionary Forces.

He has appealed to Representative Hartley of Kearny to establish that fact. Casale recently secured an affidavit from the Veterans' Bureau certifying that he was 4 feet 10 inches tall and weighed 106 pounds when he enlisted. The bureau has refused to declare him the "smallest man," saying it would require months for clerks to scan the record of every man who served with the A. E. F.

It was not explained how Casale secured enlistment when the minimum requirements are 5 feet and 110 pounds.

MISSING AIRLINER BROUGHT IN SAFELY

Pilot Lands Western Express Ship at Albuquerque After Being Forced Down.

WOULD NOT RISK STORM

Passengers Tell of Cold Night in Deserted Ranch House as Snow Swirled Round.

Special to The New York Times.
ALBUQUERQUE, N. M., Oct. 29.—Lost for more than twenty-four hours while marooned on a bleak New Mexico mesa, Western Air Express tri-motored liner 113 escaped today from the snow-swept stretch where it was forced down Monday and landed here with its crew of three and two passengers, chilled but safe.

Caught in a blinding swirl of snow Monday at 10:15 A. M., the plane was forced down near Trechado, [se]veral miles southeast of

STOCKS COLLAPSE IN 16,410,030-SHARE D[AY], BUT RALLY AT CLOSE CHEERS BROKER[S]; BANKERS OPTIMISTIC, TO CONTINUE AID

LEADERS SEE FEAR WANING

Point to 'Lifting Spells' in Trading as Sign of Buying Activity.

GROUP MEETS TWICE IN DAY

But Resources Are Unable to Stem Selling Tide—Lamont Reassures Investors.

HOPE SEEN IN MARGIN CUTS

Banks Reduce Requirements to 25 Per Cent—Sentiment in Wall St. More Cheerful.

Resources of the banking group which was organized last Thursday to stabilize conditions in the stock market were utilized yesterday to break the force of the terrific flood of selling which accompanied the biggest day, from the point of view of volume, ever experienced on the New York Stock Exchange. Despite the drastic decline, sentiment in Wall Street last night was more cheerful than it has been on any day since the torrent of selling got under way. Periodic "lifting spells" which developed between intervals of extreme weakness were cited by bankers at the close of the market, as testifying to the presence of investment buying. The public is in some measure regaining its senses and the unreasoning fear which has [...]

240 Issues Lose $15,894,818,894 in Month; Slump in Full Exchange List Vastly Larger

The drastic effects of Wall Street's October bear market is shown by valuation tables prepared last night by THE NEW YORK TIMES, which place the decline in the market value of 240 representative issues on the New York Stock Exchange at $15,894,818,894 during the period from Oct. 1 to yesterday's closing. Since there are 1,279 issues listed on the New York Stock Exchange, the total depreciation for the month is estimated at between two and three times the loss for the 240 issues covered by THE TIMES table.

Among the losses of the various groups comprising the 240 stocks in THE TIMES valuation table were the following:

Group.	Number of Stocks.	Decline in Value.
Railroads	25	$1,128,686,488
Public utilities	29	5,135,734,327
Motors	15	1,689,840,902
Oils	22	1,532,617,778
Coppers	15	824,403,820
Chemicals	9	1,621,697,897

The official figures of the New York Stock Exchange showed that the total market value of its listed securities on Oct. 1 was $87,073,630,423. The decline in the 240 representative issues therefore cut more than one-sixth from the total value of the listed securities. Most of this loss was inflicted by the wholesale liquidation of the last week.

U. S. STEEL TO PAY $1 EXTRA DIVIDEND

American Can Votes the Same and Raises Annual Rate From $3 to $4.

BIG GAIN IN STEEL INCOME

Earnings for Nine Months Are [...] a Share, Against

RESERVE BOARD FINDS ACTION UNNECESSARY

Six-Hour Session Brings No Change in the New York Rediscount Rate.

OFFICIALS ARE OPTIMISTIC

Mellon Also Attends Cabinet Meeting, but Declines to [Di]scuss Developments.

CLOSING RALLY VIGOROUS

Leading Issues Rega[in] From 4 to 14 Points in 15 Minutes.

INVESTMENT TRUSTS BUY

Large Blocks Thrown on Mar[ket] at Opening Start Third Break of Week.

BIG TRADERS HARDEST [HIT]

Bankers Believe Liquida[tion] Now Has Run Its Cours[e] and Advise Purchases.

Stock prices virtually collapsed [yes]terday, swept downward with gigan[tic] losses in the most disastrous trad[ing] day in the stock market's h[is]tory. Billions of dollars in open mar[ket] values were wiped out as price[s] crumbled under the pressure [of] liquidation of securities which had [to] be sold at any price.

There was an impressive rally ju[st] at the close, which brought man[y] leading stocks back from 4 to [...] points from their lowest points of th[e] day.

Trading on the New York Stock Exchange aggregated 16,410,0[30] shares; on the Curb, 7,096,300 share[s] were dealt in. Both totals far [ex]ceeded any previous day's deali[ngs].

From every point of view, in [the] extent of losses sustained, in [the] turnover, in the number of specula[tors wiped out, the day was the [most] disastrous in Wall Street's his[tory. Hysteria swept the country [...] [sto]cks went overboard for just w[hat they] [w]ould bring at forced sa[le] [...]to [...]stimated [...]

The front page of the New York Times the day following the 1929 Wall Street crash.

BY THE FALL of 1929 most Americans had climbed the peak of Prosperity high enough to glimpse an unlimited plain in the distance glittering wiith motor cars, bathtubs, refrigerators, and console radios—the touchstones of progress in their age. It was a time of plenty. Only a year before, President Herbert Hoover had predicted that the day would soon come when poverty in the United States would be abolished for all time.

The country was at the height of a great industrial development which had begun shortly after the end of the Civil War. Mass production was in high gear.

The middle classes were literally at the bursting point after absorbing an unprecedented quantity of worldly goods; it was a lavish era of silk shirts and two-car garages.

The advertisement-bloated Sunday newspapers that fall reflected the nation's prosperity. Custom cars were selling for $10,000 and a man with the right connections could lease a Park Avenue apartment fitted with gold-plated faucets for a trifling $45,000. The market was booming; there were hundreds of thousands, perhaps millions, of new stockholders, including clerks,

housewives, and truck drivers, and almost every one of them was making profits—on paper. Very few were taking their profits; most of the stock-buying was on margin. But no one worried, certainly not the small investors who had

WORST STOCK CRASH STEMMED BY BANKS; 12,894,650-SHARE DAY SWAMPS MARKET; LEADERS CONFER, FIND CONDITIONS SOUND

FINANCIERS EASE TENSION

Five Wall Street Bankers Hold Two Meetings at Morgan Office.

CALL BREAK 'TECHNICAL'

Lamont Lays It to 'Air Holes' —Says Low Prices Do Not

Wall Street Optimistic After Stormy Day; Clerical Work May Force Holiday Tomorrow

Confidence in the soundness of the stock market structure, notwithstanding the upheaval of the last few days, was voiced last night by bankers and other financial leaders. Sentiment as expressed by the heads of some of the largest banking institutions and by industrial executives as well was distinctly cheerful and the feeling was general that the worst had been seen. Wall Street ended the day in an optimistic frame of mind.

The opinion of brokers was unanimous that the selling had got out of hand not because of any inherent weakness in the market but because the public had become alarmed over the steady liquidation of the last few weeks. Over their private wires these brokers counseled their customers against further thoughtless selling at sacrifice prices.

Charles E. Mitchell, chairman of the National City Bank, de-
that fundament

LOSSES RECOVERED IN PART

Upward Trend Start With 200,000-Share Order for Steel.

TICKERS LAG FOUR HOURS

Thousands of Accounts Wiped Out, With Traders in Dark as

Following the first big slump in October, 1929, the nation's leading bankers assured the country there could be no financial collapse.

taken most of their savings out of the bank or mortgaged all they owned for cash to play the market. Taxi drivers paid as much attention to the stock quotations from Wall Street as to the score in the afternoon ball game.

In every town in America the Babbitts were keeping up with the Joneses. If they didn't have the cash on hand, they used the installment plan. Before the decade was finished, ten million Americans were paying off debts by the month.

It was true that after Christmas of 1928, there had been a slackening of luxury-item sales. The new cars weren't moving as fast as they had been. Gleaming, oak-boxed radios cluttered display windows. Warehouses began to be jammed. This led to layoffs. Yet this slight tremor in the nation's economy was not felt nationally. Manufacturers read reports of overloaded depots and warehouses and shrugged; it was only temporary, it would soon clear up.

Early in September the stock market reached an all-time high. Two days later there was a break, and in the following weeks a gradual slide. But each time the drop seemed to be getting really bad, support came into the

market. Then, on the afternoon of October 24, 1929, the first hammer-blow smashed down on this uncomprehending, surfeited, arrogantly self-comfortable world. A total of 12,894,650 shares swamped the board and rocked the financial district. Hysteria swept through Wall Street like a wind-fanned prairie fire. Brokers collapsed under the strain of trying to keep up with orders to sell.

Huge crowds watched the arrival that afternoon of the titans of Wall Street at the House of Morgan. There were the country's top five bankers: Charles E. Mitchell, chairman of the board of the National City Bank; Albert H. Wiggin, chairman of the board of the Chase National Bank; William Potter, chairman of the board of the Guaranty Trust Company; Seward Prosser, chairman of the board of the Bankers Trust Company; and Thomas W. Lamont, senior partner of J. P. Morgan & Co. For a brief few days it seemed as if these giants of finance, shoulder to shoulder, had averted disaster. After the meeting Lamont issued a cheery statement: "There has been a little distress selling on the stock market. . . . There are no houses in difficulty and reports from brokers in-

Charles E. Mitchell.

dicate that margins are being maintained satisfactorily." He added that it was the consensus of the bankers that "many of the quotations on the Stock Market Exchange do not fairly represent the situation."

STOCK PRICES SLUMP $14,000,000,000 IN NATION-WIDE STAMPEDE TO UNLOAD; BANKERS TO SUPPORT MARKET TODAY

Sixteen Leading Issues Down $2,893,520,108; Tel. & Tel. and Steel Among Heaviest Losers

A shrinkage of $2,893,520,108 in the open market value of the shares of sixteen representative companies resulted from yesterday's sweeping decline on the New York Stock Exchange.

PREMIER ISSUES HARD HIT

Unexpected Torrent of Liquidation Again Rocks Markets.

DAY'S SALES 9,212,800

Nearly 3,000,000 Shares Are Traded In Final Hour—The Tickers Lag 167 Minutes.

NEW RALLY SOON BROKEN

On the morning of the twenty-ninth bankers were prepared to come to Wall Street's aid, but that didn't seem to help.

Yet it had been a hectic, frightening day. The break had been one of the wildest in the market's history, although the losses at the tapping of the three o'clock bell were not particularly large, many having been recouped by an afternoon rally.

The plunge had carried down with it speculators, big and little, in every part of the country, wiping out thousands of accounts. The *New York Times* reported that, had it not been for the calming influence of the five bankers and the subsequent rally, "the business of the country would have been seriously affected." But the wild afternoon had generated many rumors, many of them false. All that afternoon reporters at police headquarters were busy checking with the downtown precincts, trying to confirm a report that eleven brokers had stepped out of windows to their deaths. By five o'clock tension had mounted to such a pitch that a workman outside the upper floor of a Wall Street building found himself staring into the wild eyes of four policemen who were reaching out to pull him inside.

"Don't jump," one cop shouted. "It's not that bad."

"Who's going to jump?" the bewildered man asked. "I'm just washing windows!"

But five days later, on October 29—Black Tuesday—Wall Street was in a real panic. The stock market had collapsed. Sixteen million shares were tossed overboard on the New York Stock Exchange for whatever price could be obtained. Similarly, many millions of additional shares were sacrificed in other stock markets, from the Curb Market in New York to the exchanges on the Pacific Coast. The drop in values of listed shares represented a loss of 30 to 60 billion dollars; no one could compute it exactly. And it included Jones's $1,500 and old Mrs. Smith's $5,000, the grocer's $2,500 surplus as well as Mr. Vanderfosterfewster's millions. Besides the excruciating loss that could be seen and felt, there was the unseen, weakening, undermining impact on the financial structure of the country, on the banks, mortgage companies and investment trusts and funds.

The figures mentioned are 1929 figures. The value or purchasing power of the dollar then was at least three times what it is today, and the number of shares listed on the stock exchanges of 1929 was only a fraction of the number listed today. In relation to today's economic picture the loss was the equivalent of 250 to 500 billion dollars. But the damage to confidence was even more costly. The economic life of the country was smothered in gloom. Faith in the wise men of business and finance was shattered. The people asked for reassurance and guidance.

Secretary of Commerce Robert P. Lamont contented himself with listing the gains for 1929 over the previous year and predicted that prosperity would continue "for the long run." He forgot to say how long that run would be.

In Washington, it seemed that everyone was whistling in the graveyard.

As the long winter went on, the rate of unemployment rose; factories shut down, one after another, and office staffs were laid off. By March several millions were idle. Within three years there would be 14,500,000 unemployed.

The first impact of the Depression was not felt in the country's wage structure. The earnings of millions were slashed by layoffs and reduced work schedules before wage rates were undermined. It was not until the end of 1930 that wage changes would be noticed. The drop was about one cent an hour from the 1929 average of fifty-nine cents an hour.

In some quarters wage cuts were being advocated, but such a measure was opposed by both government officials and industrial leaders, who hoped that the maintenance of wage-earners' income would help to stabilize the market for consumer products and stimulate an economic recovery. But before the year was out, wage cuts became a reality. According to Bureau of Labor statistics, in 1929 four times as many employers reported wage increases as reported wage reductions; in the latter part of 1930, wage increases were reported by 126 firms, while 900 reported decreases. As a rule, the cuts were 10 per cent. By the end of the year, an industrial worker who had received an annual wage of $1,500 was now getting $1,300.

Retail business was still going strong in the early months of the new year. Lowboy consoles were selling at $119, and a Fifth Avenue store reported a brisk sale of cloth coats "trimmed with Manchurian wolf" for $38.50, while karakul coats were selling at $88. Food prices hadn't changed much: bread was still 7 cents a loaf, beans 10 cents a can—two for 15 on sale—and butter 49 cents a pound. And there were even plenty of buyers for the air-cooled Franklins, which went for $2,585.

But there was a great uneasiness in the land. As time went on, it became

Crowds outside the stock exchange, October 29, 1929.

clear to the man in the street that the country's leaders in government, finance, and business, had been badly mistaken or were outrageously misleading him. It seemed that nothing was secure any more. You couldn't depend on anyone or anything. One Fifth Avenue minister warned his congregation: "Our day of reckoning is coming near, prepare yourself. . . ."

Wall Street on October 29, 1929.

Apple-Peddler

IN THE FALL of 1930 appeared a figure that was to become the symbol of the Depression—the apple-peddler. If you couldn't get a job you could at least sell apples and perhaps make enough to buy a meager meal for yourself and your family. Men who had once been engineers, mechanics, clerks, stockbrokers—men who had once owned homes, cars, and businesses—huddled on street corners and sold their polished apples for a nickel. There usually was a small sign:

BUY AN APPLE.
HELP THE UNEMPLOYED.

Sometimes there were no signs: everyone knew what this man was doing standing beside the box. He was trying to survive.

The main apple depot in New York was the Apple Growers' Association,

Fred Bell, nearly a millionaire in the 1920's, like thousands of other Americans was reduced to selling apples in 1931. When this picture was taken, Bell, known in San Francisco as "Champagne Fred," had nothing left of the famous Theresa Bell fortune.

Charles Yale Harrison as a young reporter for the New York American, living the life of an apple-peddler. Harrison later became a well-known novelist.

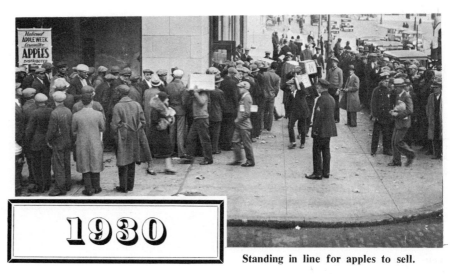

1930

Standing in line for apples to sell.

at West and Harrison streets on Manhattan's lower East Side. Most of the men and women who came there lined up before dawn after a restless night in the Salvation Army's Bowery headquarters, the "Munie" (Municipal Lodging House), or the "cold dock," an infamous East River pier hastily erected as an annex to the "Munie" when the city's unemployment and homeless population began to increase in the latter months of 1930.

Thirty years later a man who once was forced to sleep in the cold dock recalled it as "the most terrifying night of my life."

It was a large dormitory at the foot of East Twenty-fifth Street. I had been in the trenches in World War I, but the cold dock was worse. It was damp and bitterly cold. There was one thin blanket to a man on a rough spring. Outside, you could hear the tugs; inside, you could hear the guys coughing their lungs out. In those days a lot of the unemployed were fellows who had a touch of gas and who could only live by selling apples. About midnight I couldn't stand it. I got out of bed to find half the place was up, sitting around wrapped in their blankets like Indians. I'll never forget the man who sat next to me. He gave me a drag from his butt. Later he told me he was a graduate of Wisconsin. Five o'clock they sounded a gong. It was still dark. We lined up, had a bowl of evil-smelling mush and so-called coffee and went over to West Street for our box of apples.

Charles Yale Harrison, author of *Generals Die in Bed,* then a staff reporter for the *New York American,* was assigned to do a series of articles on his experiences as an unemployed apple-peddler living in the cold dock for a week. He started out with $2.25, the price of a box of apples at the Apple Growers' Association warehouse.

Fight for Work or Wages
Participate in the

Mass Demonstration Against Unemployment

March 6th, 1930, 5:30 P. M. at 4th Ave. and Broadway, Gary

Comrades, Workers!

The increasing unemployment and part time work are getting so bad that even the capitalists are beginning to TALK about relief for the distressed jobless workers. Millions of workers' families cannot afford the bare necessities of life. Millions of workers are working part time and lead a hand to mouth existence.

The State of the capitalists is expending hundreds of millions of dollars for armaments but it won't provide relief for the unemployed. The capitalist corporations made billions of dollars last year by exploiting and speeding up the workers. The workers must force these corporations to provide unemployment insurance from the super-profits.

The Department of Justice and the police are attacking most viciously the leadership of the unemployed workers as represented by the Trade Union Unity League and the Communist Party. Hundreds of working class fighters are arrested, beaten up, and sentenced on inciting to riot and disturbing the peace charges. But in spite of everything the Communist Party and the TUUL will lead the working class in the International Demonstration Against Unemployment.

The oppression in the shops is being intensified. Every worker stands the chance of getting kicked out the next day because of the deepening crisis in the U. S. This should bring to the attention of the employed workers that the struggle against unemployment is of concern to the whole working class.

STRIKE ON MARCH 6th!
FIGHT FOR WORK OR WAGES!
DEMAND FULL WAGES FOR ALL PART TIME WORKERS!
FIGHT FOR THE 7-HOUR DAY!
LONG LIVE THE UNITY OF THE BLACK AND WHITE WORKERS!
DOWN WITH IMPERIALIST WAR!
DEFEND THE SOVIET UNION!

Auspices

Trade Union Unity League
➡ 361

Communist Party
Young Communist League

Labor Day, a cartoon by Rollin Kirby.

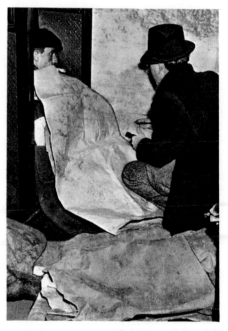

Many homeless men refused to spend a night in the infamous "Munie"–the New York Municipal Lodging House–even preferring to spend a night in a public phone booth.

Above the door was a large red sign: HELPING UNEMPLOYED. Harrison noted that starving men knew no color line; in the block-long queue were black, yellow, and white men. Some had overcoats, some wore two shirts made of burlap as protection against the bitter winds. There was even a one-legged man who dragged his box in a little wagon.

"Nobody cared what you were, who you were," Harrison wrote. "We were all starving together."

Carrying his box, he walked to the subway and bought a bundle of paper bags. At four o'clock he sold his last apple and took stock of his finances. Four apples were so damaged they couldn't be sold; they become his dinner. The box had contained 72 apples, of which he sold 68. That gave him $3.40 gross. He had paid 10 cents for the bags and 10 cents for subway fares. His profit for working almost twelve hours was 95 cents.

On the way to the cold dock that night, Harrison met a fellow apple-peddler, a construction worker who had lost his job and his home. He took Harrison to meet his wife and their two small children. "It was at the tip of 59th Street and the river," Harrison wrote, "where there is some vacant land and some huge rocks. He had placed pieces of odd timber against the rocks and fixed the end of his 'house' with strips of sacking. Inside his floor is more sacking. A little frightened woman and two small children look at us as we push through the sacking door. . . . Overhead the lights of the Queensborough Bridge shine. They talk of only one thing—winter . . . what will become of them in the winter . . ."

As Harrison noted that night on his way back to the cold dock, the jobless and the homeless were everywhere. Shadows huddled in doorways or slept on subway benches. The lucky man with a few pennies sipped a beer and wolfed down the free lunch until he was chased by the bartender. That night in front of the Holy Name Mission, where almost a thousand men were standing in line waiting for the doors to open, he heard a voice muttering, "Damn! I'm never going to forget this year! 1930! I can spit on it!"

Friends of Mr. Sweeny

PROHIBITION was in effect in the year 1930, but the law was disregarded and flouted by most Americans. Anyone who wanted liquor could get it delivered by his bootlegger. If he wanted a quiet drink with friends there was always a nearby speakeasy. Or he could assemble the ingredients and make it at home in his own bathtub. The speakeasy was now an accepted part of the American scene, particularly in the big cities. Dapper Police Commissioner Grover Whalen officially estimated that there were 32,000 speakeasies in New York City. Shortly after he came out with this figure, Maurice Campbell, federal Prohibition administrator, asked bluntly what Whalen intended to do about closing them. Campbell insisted that the police padlock the "speaks" under Section 1530 of the state law after the high courts had ruled that speakeasies were "nuisances" within the meaning of that law.

Commissioner Whalen pointed out that his men had closed 5,000 speakeasies in one year, and Campbell retorted that 5,000 more had sprung up.

Administrator Campbell categorized the varieties of speakeasy in 1930 as follows:

First we have the night club and extravagant "private clubs" patronized by visitors bent on seeing night life or what they think is the gay New York way of living. New Yorkers themselves are too smart to patronize such places. . . . Next in order is the bar patronized by the businessman. Often he thinks it is clever to drink his cocktail in defiance of the law. I am sorry to say that a considerable section of the business community likes a sly drink.

Then we have the bohemian place in the cellar or the garret, supposedly patronized by artists or people who would like to be. After

Hotels with tongue in cheek insisted that guests sign a pledge not to use their ginger ale or club soda for highballs or "rickeys."

NOTICE
The content of this bottle is sold to you as a beverage and with the understanding that it will not be mixed or used with any alcoholic content liquor in violation of the prohibition laws.
By Order of
THE MANAGEMENT
THE NEW YORKER

them there is a great gap in the social order of the speakeasy. New York's working people are not part of this illegal trade. They spend their money on better purposes or put it in the bank, which explains the city's prosperity [sic]. I also like to think they are law-abiding and wish to live with the Constitution.

Finally, there is the criminal gathering of the lowest order. In these places it is possible to buy

any kind of drink, occasionally genuine but generally diluted or poisonous. No matter who says it "just came off the boat," it usually came from some nearby still or bathtub.

Campbell declared his own staff was so small it could not possibly cope with the speakeasy problem, and he passed the buck to Whalen.

The police commissioner also examined the law and came to the conclusion that the high courts had failed to define precisely what constituted a "nuisance." In his opinion, the speaks were a federal problem. He set most of New York laughing when he observed, "The number of speakeasies proves that the distilling and smuggling of liquor is a common practice. . . . Let the federal agencies shut off the flow of liquor at its point of origin and they need not worry about the speakeasies." For the benefit of the New York taxpayers, he pointed out that to enforce the law as Mr. Campbell desired would mean 5,000 more men at a cost of $15,000,000.

Despite their wrangling, federal officers and police officials of the nation's largest cities agreed that speakeasies were not only increasing by the day, but were becoming bolder in their de-

Senator Dwight Morrow of New Jersey, an early advocate of Repeal.

16

For those who couldn't afford the smuggled "Canadian" whiskey, there were the cordial shops which sold malt, hops, barley, and oats, as well as rye coloring and gin extracts.

FOURTH REPORT OF THE
LITERARY DIGEST PROHIBITION POLL

State	For Enforcement	For Modification	For Repeal	Total
ALABAMA	2,797	1,678	1,713	6,188
ARKANSAS	3,447	1,724	1,749	6,920
CALIFORNIA	34,672	38,169	41,451	114,292
CONNECTICUT	9,091	15,739	25,558	50,388
DELAWARE	1,288	867	2,180	4,335
DIST. OF COLUMBIA	2,560	2,998	4,836	10,394
FLORIDA	1,900	1,824	2,558	6,282
GEORGIA	4,884	3,885	4,245	13,014
ILLINOIS	40,619	52,225	78,892	171,736
INDIANA	23,791	17,736	18,096	59,623
IOWA	24,971	17,790	17,036	59,797
KANSAS	21,270	8,119	6,000	35,389
KENTUCKY	6,598	5,526	8,170	20,294
LOUISIANA	916	1,319	2,377	4,612
MAINE	4,116	2,589	4,035	10,740
MARYLAND	4,493	5,632	10,999	21,124
MASSACHUSETTS	19,594	16,723	30,688	67,005
MICHIGAN	24,969	27,782	38,360	91,111
MINNESOTA	23,425	23,506	29,710	76,641
MISSISSIPPI	1,651	1,022	1,540	4,213
MISSOURI	26,193	21,119	36,164	83,476
NEBRASKA	11,551	8,058	7,314	26,923
NEW HAMPSHIRE	3,160	2,279	2,386	7,825
NEW JERSEY	21,023	35,793	58,863	115,679
NEW YORK	57,484	116,453	186,867	360,804
NORTH CAROLINA	6,628	4,195	3,444	14,267
NORTH DAKOTA	3,056	2,681	2,975	8,712
OHIO	41,702	42,826	44,949	129,477
OKLAHOMA	6,687	3,535	3,166	13,388
OREGON	8,510	7,263	5,920	21,693
PENNSYLVANIA	55,484	58,079	106,521	220,084
RHODE ISLAND	1,968	2,582	5,116	9,666
SOUTH CAROLINA	1,885	1,210	1,348	4,443
SOUTH DAKOTA	3,815	2,971	2,439	9,225
TENNESSEE	4,853	2,460	2,240	9,553
TEXAS	7,848	4,236	3,904	15,988
VERMONT	1,959	1,440	1,874	5,273
VIRGINIA	4,859	4,404	7,437	16,700
WASHINGTON	11,517	11,270	10,277	33,064
WEST VIRGINIA	4,942	4,255	4,145	13,342
WISCONSIN	11,161	14,290	21,209	46,660
	553,337	598,252	848,751	2,000,340

The 1930 Literary Digest poll on Prohibition.

fiance of the law. Speakeasies had become a part of the social life of every major city. There was usually a Speakeasy Row—a street on which there were certain to be one or several speaks. (In New York City, Fifty-second Street between Fifth and Sixth avenues was a notable example.) A brownstone front, somewhat run-down, usually concealed a lavish interior with a handsomely appointed dining room, deep red carpets, luxurious draperies, well-trained waiters, a French menu, and a well-equipped bar. There would be music, anything from a jazz combo to a lone piano-player, depending on the size of the place.

The speaks described by Campbell as "bohemian" often had phony cracks in the plaster, walls painted in zigzag style, and candles thrust in wax-encrusted bottles. Artists' smocks and American pseudo-French predominated. Within the walls of some speaks one could find an old-time bar, with men in crisp white coats ranged behind it, asking the age-old question, "What'll it be, sir?" Some had free lunch set out on a counter; others had a chef in a starched cap, his knife poised over a huge, rare roast beef.

But bohemian or plush, the speakeasy always had a gay air. Each was regarded by its regular patrons as a sort of private club where you readily conversed with strangers, male or female, sang college songs, made business deals, and told magnificent lies to the lady you were flirting with. What seemed to weld everyone into a common brotherhood was the knowledge that all present were engaged in a conspiracy to flout a very unpopular law.

Business in 1930 was so lucrative that speakeasies just refused to be closed; in many instances, according to Campbell, a speakeasy, raided and padlocked by federal agents, would re-open for business that same night. "The moment a bartender is seized, a new man takes his place, a new supply of liquor appears, and business goes on as usual," Campbell said sadly.

Although speakeasies were numerous, they were not wide open to the public. You had to be known to get in. But even if you weren't, it wasn't too hard to talk your way in: "I'm a friend of Mr. Sweeney's"—or whatever name was likely to be known at the particular speak . . . Joe, Mike, Otto, etc.

This devious means of admittance added a romantic touch to illegal imbibing. The *New York Times,* in an article on New York speakeasies, reported:

> Introduction by someone who has been there before is usually required. Then there is the business of registering the new patron's

Padlocked!

SH -SH-

SH -SH-

SURE! JUST CALL UP

BEekman 3430

Prohibition liquor list.

name and perhaps the issuance of the card of admittance for his next visit. It is sometimes made even more important-looking by a signature or a cabalistic sign on the back of the card. Many persons about town carry a dozen or more such cards.

The devious means employed to protect the entrances to speakeasies probably adds to the general mystification. Bells are rung in a special way. A sliding panel behind an iron grille opens to reveal a cautious face examining the new arrivals.

But by 1930 the move for repeal of Prohibition was growing stronger. Up to 1928 the Anti-Saloon League, the Women's Christian Temperance Union, the Methodist Board of Temperance, Prohibition, and Public Morals, and the other bone-dry groups were riding high. Their lobbies were all-powerful in Washington and many of the state capitals, and a public declaration

Grover A. Whalen.

against Prohibition was an act of political suicide. Neither of the major political parties had cared to make a stand on Prohibition during the early twenties. By 1928, however, the issue could not be kept out of politics. The Democrats nominated Alfred E. Smith and the public knew where he stood on Prohibition. The organized drys swung behind Hoover and the crushing defeat of Smith was interpreted—by the drys— as an unmistakable warning that the United States would stay dry.

However, Smith's campaign encouraged the wets. The issue no longer could be ignored. In the spring following Smith's defeat, Coolidge had signed the heavy-handed Jones bill sponsored by the drys. In the reaction following, the repeal movement began to pick up speed. In the winter of 1929, three hundred nationally prominent lawyers formed the Voluntary Committee of Lawyers to Work for Repeal.

In January various wet groups, including the Women's Organization for National Prohibition Reform, joined forces to battle the drys.

Then, in the spring, Dwight W. Morrow, former Morgan partner and father-in-law of Charles A. Lindbergh, electrified the country by announcing, as a candidate for the Senate, that he favored repeal and the return of jurisdiction from the federal to the state level. When Morrow was elected, it

The famous figure, created by Rollin Kirby, that appeared in many of his cartoons and became a popular symbol of Prohibition and Intolerance.

19

Speakeasy—de luxe (after a raid), East 58th Street, New York City.

Speakeasy—low-grade (entrance at the right), West 23rd Street, New York City.

was evident that there was no longer any question of the respectability of the wet movement; other public men in 1930 approved Morrow's courageous position; the repeal groups multiplied and by the fall of 1930 they had exerted so much political pressure that the congressional elections swept seventy wet members to the House and four to the Senate.

It was obviously no longer political suicide to stand for repeal, and 1930 was the year that marked the beginning of the end of national Prohibition, which had brought in its wake mounting crime and corruption.

Messages from Another World

Sir Arthur Conan Doyle and Harry Houdini.

DURING THE LAST years of his life, Sir Arthur Conan Doyle, creator of Sherlock Holmes, was more concerned about the spirit world than his detective. In the fall of 1930, he told a *New York Times* correspondent that Holmes was based on a real-life character, a Dr. Bell, a Scot under whom he had studied medicine. "Dr. Bell," Doyle said, "had an uncanny gift of drawing large inferences from small observations. . . . Watson was just an average man—not really stupid, just average." But he added, "Holmes is dead. . . . I'm through with him."

Shortly after this interview, Doyle died. In the flurry of newspaper comment on his passing, the London *Times* observed, "All sincere British mediums are now sitting in the darkness, waiting for a spirit message from Sir Arthur."

Even in the Bronx they were waiting —and receiving. The New York papers had a field day with one medium, decribed as "an illiterate construction worker," who claimed he had heard from Sir Arthur. Before an audience of newsmen and with Joseph Dunninger, the magician, present, he put on a show that included "spirit voices" and a luminous hand floating in the darkness. One cynical reporter wrote, "The voice from the grave had a decidedly Italian accent."

Shortly after Sir Arthur was buried, his widow startled the world by revealing a pact they had made that he was to communicate with her within ten days after his death. In fact, they had arranged a secret code.

A week after the funeral, a crowd of ten thousand packed London's Albert Hall to see Lady Doyle receive what she claimed was a "spirit message" from her husband.

When reporters pressed her for its contents she replied, "It is beautiful and sweet—but private."

Meanwhile, back in New York, Dunninger scoffed at the numerous "Sir Arthur spirit messages" which were being reported by mediums all over the United States. Of one séance he remarked, "I could duplicate the whole thing in a half-hour."

Thousands of London spiritualists paid tribute to the memory of Sir Arthur Conan Doyle in London's Albert Hall. The vacant chair was left for the deceased.

THE CURSE OF KING TUT

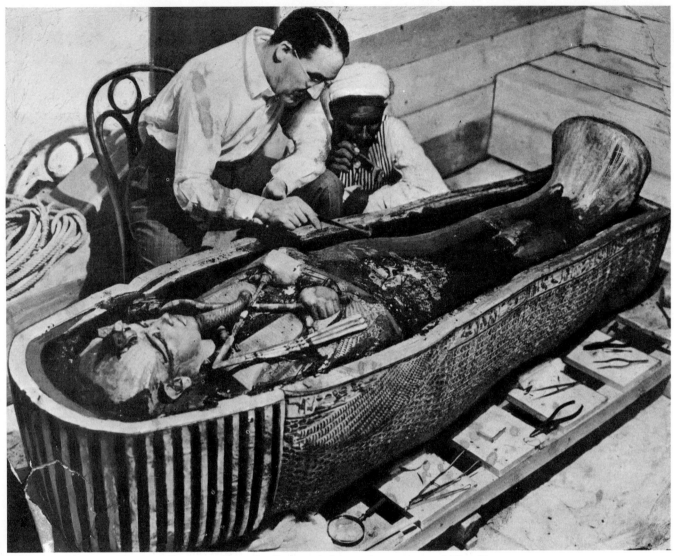

Explorer Howard Carter studying the mummy of King Tut.

AN ANCIENT Egyptian relic with a strange inscription had had an honored place in the spacious London apartment of Lord Westbury for seven years. It had been taken from the tomb of the boy Pharaoh, King Tutankhamen, by Howard Carter, the famous English archaeologist who had discovered and excavated the tomb. The inscription, as translated by scholars, read:

Death shall come on swift wings to who toucheth the tomb of the Pharaohs.

Lord Westbury, father of Captain Richard Bethell, secretary to Carter, made little of the "curse of King Tut," as the newspapers called it, although Captain Bethell had died unexpectedly and his widow had killed herself. "Nothing to it," he told reporters. "Just a lot of superstition."

Then one day in 1930 he stepped out of a seventh-floor window of his London apartment. "The Curse has struck again," London newspapers solemnly declared. Even the innocent were not to be spared from "death on swift

wings." As Westbury's body was being taken to a crematorium, the hearse knocked down and killed an eight-year-old boy. Before the decade was over, fourteen persons connected in some way with the opening of King Tut's tomb had died in some mysterious manner.

But Lady Westbury was undismayed; she told the London newspapers that no one in the family, including her late husband, had ever believed such "nonsense." She herself died in the late 1930's at the ripe old age of eighty-one.

Emperor Haile Selassie I of Ethiopia, under a gold lace canopy following his coronation in Addis Ababa.

The King of Kings

A SLIGHT, BEARDED figure who seemed to have come out of another age, was often in the news during the Desperate Years. Haile Selassie, a small, dark-faced man with melancholy eyes, was known to have a taste for Shakespeare, champagne, and cayenne pepper. On a November day in 1930, he rode amid barbaric splendor through the twisting streets of Addis Ababa to his tin-roofed palace, where he was crowned emperor of an African domain of lions and some three million Ethiopians. He passed down the streets at dawn in a chariot that had once belonged to the Kaiser. His subjects shouted their loyalty, shook their headdresses and ostrich-feather plumes, and held high their hippopotamus shields and curved swords.

The Emperor had more names than an American boxer: His Majesty Ras Taffari, Elect of Kings, King of Kings, etc. Europeans and Americans present at the ceremony found that the Emperor's palace combined the present and the past in a disconcerting way. The service plates had borders of solid gold and the knives and spoons were of gold from native mines, but everything was stacked in common wooden closets "like those in an American farm kitchen." One London newspaperman wrote, "The whole palace is like an enormous roadhouse: pool, movies, theatre, radios, refrigerators, while on the other hand there are odorous camel corrals and slave markets. . . . The Emperor has more than two hundred men watering his garden each day."

Although Emperor Haile Selassie appeared to some Americans to represent a twentieth-century anachronism

23

Haile Selassie's palace.

Judge Crater

that would soon disappear, he proved to be a wise and firm ruler. Soldier, lawyer, statesman, and aesthete, he brought many reforms to his people and won for them the sympathetic interest of the world.

Selassie himself was well liked by the world leaders. He had only one weakness—absent-mindedness. He once ordered a special house built for a visit from the Duke of Abruzzi. Only the day before the arrival of the royal party did he remember that he had forgotten to furnish the house. At the last hour he found and commandeered a brass bed for his visitor from the house of the police captain.

Selassie detested dissoluteness and more than once denounced the liquor-sellers in his country. He was an avid autograph collector; the one he desired most was Field Marshal von Hindenburg's. The marshal, however, detested autograph collectors. Selassie subtly suggested to him that he could select any animal he wanted from the royal zoo—twelve elephants, a lion, and two zebras. Von Hindenburg took the zebras and sent the Emperor his autograph.

The new Emperor was enchanted with a famous Paris chef and, after much negotiation, persuaded him to cook for the royal household. The chef later reported, "I found the palace a tin-roofed affair, with the kitchen in the cellar and a window to let out the smoke. I was reduced to stew and roast lamb. But the trouble was that the kitchen boy was always hungry. When I had a choice joint for the Emperor, I would find my boy eating the meat raw, cutting pieces from the joint with his curved knife and sprinkling it with cayenne pepper, as is the national custom." He declared that he had had to cook meals behind locked doors because of the many attempts on the Emperor's life. But Selassie shrugged off the many assassination attempts. "The sun goes up and the sun goes down," was his reply.

In 1939 Italy invaded Ethiopia, using planes and bombs against spears and camel corps. But Selassie's warriors, painted for war, won admiration for the way in which they defended their land and spoiled Mussolini's timetable of conquest. The slight man with the grizzled beard made a stirring plea before the League of Nations, but nothing came of it. World War II and Italy's defeat would finally restore the King of Kings to his throne in the palace—now roofed with bright red tile.

Thirty-one years ago, a portly middle-aged man wearing a dark double-breasted suit and a Panama hat stepped into a taxicab in front of a restaurant in midtown New York and waved to a friend as the cab drove off. That man was State Supreme Court Justice Joseph Force Crater, then 41. He was never seen again.

What happened to Judge Crater has become an American classic mystery. More than a quarter of a million dollars has been spent in searching for him, but not a single clue to his fate has ever turned up. He has been reported in almost every country in the world, by such diverse persons as a New York iceman, who insisted Crater ran a tavern to which he brought ice, and a policeman in Turkey. On June 6, 1939, Crater was ruled legally dead, but as late as the 1960's they were digging up a Yonkers, N. Y., backyard, looking for the judge's bones.

THE BELOVED AMERICAN

FEW AMERICANS have held a greater number or variety of public offices than William Howard Taft. Yet he ran for office only twice: once when he was elected President in 1908, once when he failed to win re-election in 1912.

A large, fat man with handlebar mustache, he had entered public life under men who had fought at Gettysburg and Shiloh. Over a period of forty-nine years he served in thirteen public offices, to twelve of which he was appointed, beginning as assistant prosecutor of Hamilton County, Ohio, in 1881. In his later years he was finally appointed to the high office of chief justice of the United States.

In some respects the League to Enforce Peace, which he sponsored, was incorporated in the League of Nations. His dream was compulsory arbitration

William Howard Taft with Charles Evans Hughes.

to resolve all international conflicts. "That is the only way we can attain world peace," he said.

On March 8, 1930, the man Teddy Roosevelt had called "the beloved American," died at his home in Washington, D.C.

More than ten thousand mourners passed his bier on a catafalque under the Capitol dome. In the morning the casket was placed on a caisson for the journey to Arlington, where he was

given a soldier's burial, befitting a former secretary of war. Flags throughout the world were at half-mast. In London, the King called him "a man of peace." His grave was in an oak glade not far from that of Robert Todd Lincoln.

For the first time, Americans throughout the country heard, over a national radio hookup, the details of a ceremony marking the last rites for a former President.

Taft and Woodrow Wilson.

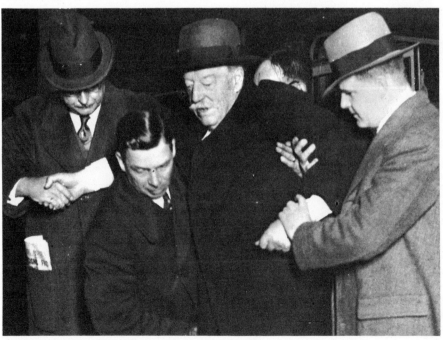

Taft arriving in Washington shortly before his death.

25

"I Fix the Price of Beer in This Town"

ON THE AFTERNOON of June 9, 1930, Alfred Lingle, police reporter for the Chicago *Tribune*, left the Stevens Hotel in Chicago and strolled down Michigan Boulevard. In the *Tribune* city room he glanced over his assignment sheet and told the city editor he was trying to contact the notorious underworld figure, Bugs Moran, to verify a story of renewed gang war. Wending his way through the traffic of the Loop, he paused at the corner of Randolph and Clark streets, known to most Chicagoans as "the corner," a common

Alfred (Jake) Lingle.

Jake Lingle lying on the sidewalk in the railroad station tunnel.

A view of Jake Lingle's funeral. Police estimated the crowd to be 25,000.

instead of a vigorous reporter whose exposés kept the mobsters on the run, Lingle emerged as a confidant of the underworld, a man who lived high, who spent his afternoons not in the fearless pursuit of his profession but at the track. When he died, he was wearing an expensive diamond belt-buckle given to him by Al Capone.

John T. Rogers, staff writer for Pulitzer's St. Louis *Post Dispatch,* ignoring the run-of-the-mill coverage of the sensational crime, dug deep into Lingle's shadowy background. His dispatches, printed also in Pulitzer's New York *World,* revealed the real Jake Lingle.

Rogers showed that the $65-a-week reporter lived the life of a rich man. He reportedly had a chauffeur-driven car, wagered heavily at the track, and was on the "Private Register" at an expensive hotel. The "Private Register" was for those important guests who didn't want to be disturbed for any matter. The *New York Times* came up with the startling information that Lingle's income was in the neighborhood of $65,000. He handled $150,000 in one year, losing about half in the stock market.

It was also reported that Lingle once boasted, "I fix the price of beer in this town."

The Chicago police and State's Attorney Swanson were working around the clock to get his killer, and months later finally nabbed Leo V. Brothers, a curly-haired fugitive who liked fancy suits and fawn-colored spats. He was convicted and given a surprisingly short sentence of fourteen years. But the big question was never answered: why did Brothers kill Lingle?

There were many guesses and a few facts. John Boettiger, a Chicago reporter who was for a while a son-in-law of Franklin D. Roosevelt, surmised that Lingle had been killed on orders from the owners of a padlocked night club and gambling spot, who learned that Lingle had refused to intercede with higher-ups for permission to reopen.

Another unexplained mystery was how Brothers could finance one of the most elaborate legal defenses in the history of Chicago. Although penniless when captured, he had a five-man staff of legal experts, including a top defense attorney brought to Chicago from St. Louis. Who paid for Brothers' defense? Thirty-one years later the question still can't be answered.

meeting-place for the city's gamblers, mobsters and racetrack touts.

Lingle entered the lobby of the Hotel Sherman, chatted with some politicians, then walked down the south side of Randolph Street to catch a 1:30 train to the racetrack. He bought a racing form, then entered the pedestrian tunnel under the boulevard.

Some distance behind him, a tall young man, nattily dressed, pushed his way through the crowd. He seemed to be in a hurry and brushed against several pedestrians, attracting their annoyed attention. As he came up behind Lingle he coolly took a revolver

from his jacket pocket, aimed, and fired. Lingle fell forward and lay still, the glowing cigar still clenched between his teeth.

Lingle's murder was one of the most sensational of the 1930's. At first the *Tribune* and other Chicago newspapers banded together in a shoulder-to-shoulder editorial cry of indignation. No stone must be left unturned in this case of a courageous reporter murdered because of his relentless war against racketeers. The papers posted rewards totaling $55,000 for the apprehension and conviction of his killer.

But then the story began to change:

THE BANK THAT COULD NOT FAIL

IT WAS BITTERLY cold in New York that winter. But snow and ice and fierce winds did not keep anxious men and women from lining up before the branch offices of the Bank of the United States. In early December rumors of disaster began to spread, and the lines grew longer. People huddled outside the closed doors day and night.

In Albany, State Banking Superintendent Joseph A. Broderick read in shocked surprise a report which showed that the bank's surplus had been wiped out. He immediately called a meeting of the officers and advised them that the only way out was a merger. The officers agreed and a conference was held with city banking leaders at Governor Franklin D. Roosevelt's home in New York City, but the proposed merger fell through because of bad "business conditions." Broderick, working to stave off a panic, tried other banks. A few weeks later a conference was held with officials of four of the nation's leading banks. A merger was agreed upon, and the terms were announced at a dramatic press conference held at dawn.

However, this plan, like the others, fell through. Broderick made still another attempt to save the bank. He called for subscriptions totaling 30 million dollars from the member banks of the New York Clearing House Association, in order to put the bank on its feet. But he was informed that the banks could do nothing.

By December 11, runs had already

The Bank of the United States as it closed its doors.

Isidor J. Kresel, after his exoneration by the Appellate Division in connection with the failure of the Bank of the United States.

begun on the bank. Broderick, every other resource exhausted, reluctantly ordered it to put up its shutters. Depositors had taken out 20 million dollars in four days, but thousands of others, mostly small merchants on New York's East Side, refused to believe that the "neighborhood bank" in which they had had such confidence for so many years could fail. But it did.

It was one of the most disastrous failures in the banking history of the country. The collapse carried with it four affiliate corporations, involving an additional 200 million dollars, and more than a million stock units once marketed at the bargain price of twenty-five dollars but now apparently quite worthless.

Men wept as they tried to rush past the police guards and pound on the closed doors; women screamed as they held up their bank books. Crowds refused to disperse and stayed outside the doors for days, hoping that their savings were not lost. There were in-

vestigations and more investigations. There were great plans for reorganization, which never got beyond the planning boards.

Then slowly, day by day, the story became known of how Bernard K. Marcus as president and Saul Singer as vice-president had pyramided a little East Side bank into a multimillion-dollar banking business, with branches in every part of the city. In the process, however, they had skirted the edge of propriety, had made loans, particularly on real estate, that not only went beyond the bounds of prudence but beyond the bounds of the banking laws into the realm of criminal malfeasance.

The two principal lawyers involved, Max D. Steuer and Isidor Kresel, took leading parts in the story as it unfolded. Steuer, a great criminal lawyer and a power in Tammany Hall, was the arch investigator of the bank's operations. Kresel, counsel for Marcus and the bank, had done much to purge his profession of the evil of ambulance-chasers

(Left to right) B. K. Marcus, Saul Singer, and Herbert Singer.

and, at the time, was heading an intensive investigation into the city's magistrates' courts. It was said that these two lawyers had had a long-standing feud.

A grand jury indicted Kresel, Marcus, Singer and others. Marcus and Singer were sentenced to terms in Sing Sing. Kresel suffered a physical collapse and went to trial later on charges of fraud. He was convicted, but the conviction was reversed by the high courts.

His personal fortune gone, his brilliant career at an end, his health shattered, Kresel was finally allowed to settle his share of the $600,000 civil damage suit that had been brought against the bank and its officials for $5,000. To make even that settlement, he was forced to borrow $1,000.

The bank's failure brought great distress, particularly on New York's East Side, where many a depositor was wiped out. But the shock was felt—and remembered—all over the country. Perhaps that memory had some part in the bank runs of 1932, which led to the bank holiday of 1933.

The ironic denouement of the whole episode was that eventually the bank's assets, which had not been sufficiently liquid at the time of the run to pay off its depositors, proved enough to pay off all debts and deposits.

Bernard K. Marcus (left) and Saul Singer (center pair of the four with linked arms) enter Sing Sing Prison.

The Little Brown Saint

Mahatma Gandhi at the start of the 1930 "Salt March."

THE DECISIVE battle in India's long struggle for independence, the cherished goal of her 400 million people, began early in 1930, when, after Britain refused India's demand for dominion status, a frail and ascetic Hindu leading seventy-odd faithful followers set out to march from Ahmedabad by a circuitous route to Dandi on the Cambay coast; his announced intention was an act of defiance of the government. At dawn of April 6, Mohandas Karamchand Gandhi waded into the sea at Dandi, dipped up some sea water and let it dry out, leaving some crude salt. It was illegal to possess untaxed salt, but he held it up boldly. As head of the Indian National Congress, he had opened his campaign for complete independence by an attack on the British-imposed salt tax, a levy that affected every household in India.

Gandhi's son and several followers were arrested that day, but he himself was not taken into custody until May. By that time the crusade had spread widely and there was bloody rioting over the land.

That march centered much greater attention on Gandhi than any of his other efforts had up to that time. The 24-day "march to the sea," through withering heat that caused the deaths of several crusaders en route, added thousands to the column. All this was emphasized by Gandhi's gesture of broadcasting to the world the day and the hour when he would break the salt tax law. That, coupled with the primi-

tive setting of the act itself, appealed to the mystics of India and piqued the Western world.

It was in 1930 that Gandhi adopted the now historic spinning wheel as a symbol of economic independence and began to dress only in homespun cotton. He called homespun a "sacred cloth," regarding it as a symbol of the simple life and a weapon against England's economic domination of India. In a speech to his followers he said that he wished he could introduce a spinning wheel into every cottage. "Then I shall be pleased with this life . . . I could go on with my other plans in my next, if it pleased God."

No mogul or emperor ever had more

power in India than this unpretentious man clad in white loincloth, shawl, and sandals, who, without rank or post, played on the emotions of a people and won their loyalty and support. In 1947, on his seventy-eighth birthday, he would see his country win its freedom. Yet he received the news with bitter diappointment. He had served his cause, spent terms in prison, fasted, always stressing nonviolence; yet at the very hour of independence, he saw his country divided into two hostile parts. Now it was Sikh and Hindu against Mohammedan, and the bloodletting had no parallel in the violent pages of Indian history.

But in 1930 this was still far in the

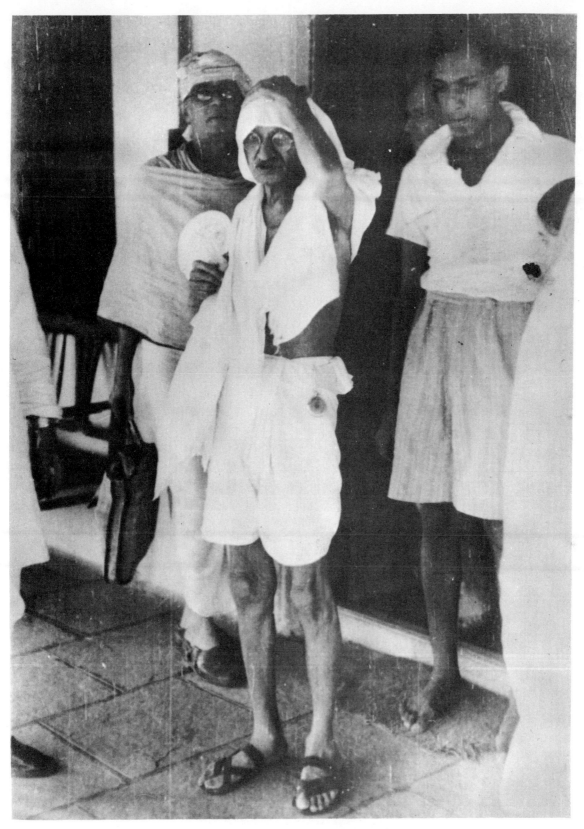

Gandhi in his famous loincloth.

Gandhi leading one of his "defiance" meetings in 1930. He sat on a platform and spun as he talked.

future. Before the year was out, Gandhi was regarded as a saint by his fellow Hindus. The masses of India followed his commands without question. He learned that his hunger-strikes were his best weapon against what he called "British oppression." They usually brought compromises, for the British feared public reaction should he die.

"I always get the best bargains behind prison bars," he said.

Gandhi stepped, as a leader, into the world's consciousness from the role of a promising attorney, educated in London. From London he went to South Africa, where he championed Indians and people of Indian descent in their fight for equal rights. It was there he organized his first civil-disobedience campaigns.

The 1930's showed Gandhi to be a master political artist. His boycotts, whether of salt, fabrics, elections, or of law, were always dramatic enough to earn headlines throughout the world. His public protests by means of fasting, his much publicized policy of nonviolence; his central doctrine of Satyagraha, or "soul force," an uncompromising insistence on truth; his austere diet and dress and his sexual abstinence, all helped to make him one of the world's outstanding personalities.

But it was his philosophy of nonviolence that captured the imagination of the West, particularly in the United States. Once he called off a startlingly successful mass civil-disobedience campaign because of a single act of violence in the obscure village of Chauri Chaura.

To Nehru's question, "Must we train the 300-odd millions of India in the theory and practice of nonviolent action before we can go forward?" Gandhi's answer was a firm "Yes," because, unlike Nehru, he rejected violence for religious rather than practical reasons. As far as he was concerned, to have one weak link in an iron chain was to have no chain at all. One wonders if the nonviolent philosophy of the frail little Hindu could have survived in the turbulent Congo or Stalin's Russia

Although the mantle of Gandhi falls on the "sit-in" demonstrators of the South in the 1960's, no Negro leader has yet attained the stature of the "little brown saint" who, in defying the salt law, enlisted the powers of nature and of humanity to his cause.

Highlights and Sidelights: 1930

THIS YEAR MARKED the end of the silent movies. Sound was to become both king and salvation; without it Hollywood would have suffered a crippling blow from the Depression. Within two years every major studio would be equipped with sound, although it would be some time before the movie-makers learned to use the new technique with full artistry.

Sound did more than bring dialogue writers to Hollywood. Sound technicians were now as much in demand as directors. The new equipment was expensive, and banks, as financing agents, had a voice for the first time in an industry that heretofore had been controlled by individuals and clans. Stars with unsuitable voices fell like meteors after their first sound movie, while a sultry voice or a seductive accent started many an unknown on the way to stellar billing.

With the advent of sound, film cycles began to appear. Broadway musicals, gangster pictures, newspaper pictures, topical pictures, prison pictures—all had

Katharine Hepburn.

James Cagney as he played the underworld king in Public Enemy.

their turn. When one became a hit, other studios rushed along imitations as fast as they could grind them out. The musical extravaganza appeared, with outstanding names, blaring music, glittering backdrops, and scores of pretty girls, arms linked, showing off their legs in the chorus line. As one theatre manager groaned, "You seen one, you seen 'em all."

The gangster-film cycle began with *Little Caesar,* starring Edward G. Robinson. It would soon be followed by *The Public Enemy* and *Scarface.* Imitations of these ran into the hundreds throughout the thirties. However, the early crime pictures had a certain vigor and realism and, above all, reflected the times; to the viewer sitting in a darkened movie theatre, to see James Cagney, Edward G. Robinson, or Paul Muni stagger down the street after being hit by a burst of tommy-gun fire was like seeing the day's headlines come to life.

On Broadway scarcely anyone noticed a thin, frail-looking girl with high cheek bones and freckles, who was playing a maid in *A Month in the Country.* Later, when she joined the veteran Jane Cowl in *Art and Mrs. Bottle,* a few critics mentioned her name. Two years later she starred in *The Warrior's Husband,* and from there Katharine Hepburn went on to Hollywood and stardom.

Edward G. Robinson.

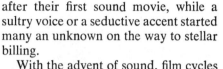

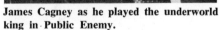

Typical of the nerve of the early 1930 bootleggers was their operation of this lighthouse near New Jersey's Atlantic Highlands. They used its beacon and radio to direct their ships into port.

In Washington, D.C., at the first of the year, the Department of Labor breathed optimism, predicting that after the "public momentary loss of confidence in the stock market, there were signs that the new year would be a splendid employment year." . . . The capital chuckled over a disclosure that Prohibition Director Moran had ordered an undercover agent into the Senate to find out who was selling booze to the senators. When an indignant Senate asked who had given him permission for such an unprecedented act, Moran said the White House—but there

was no statement from Pennsylvania Avenue. . . . In Atlantic City a tea house was padlocked, but a few hours later a sign was up:

Padlocked. No home brew here. But we have neighbors. Ask and ye shall receive. . . .

There was a scandal in New London, Conn., where it was reported that Coast Guardsmen were holding what the tabloids called "orgies" with the whiskey they captured. Washington ordered an "all-out investigation." . . . It was also

the year of one of the biggest car shows in automobile history. At Grand Central Palace, Chevrolet showed its "improved six-cylinder valve-in-head 50-horsepower motor with a gasoline meter on the dash," and proudly announced that official figures showed 1,300,000 Americans had bought the six-cylinder car. The Hulett Car Company unwrapped its air-cooled Franklin, "powered with an airplane-type engine," while full-page ads in the New York papers proclaimed the new Willys, which reached "a speed of 72 miles an hour and maintained a cruising speed

Cadillac V-16 convertible coupe, 1931 model.

Pierce-Arrow, 1931 model, with a Le Baron body.

1930 Jordan roadster.

Oldsmobile's "Companion Car," manufactured in 1929-30.

Rudy Vallee, first of the famous crooners.

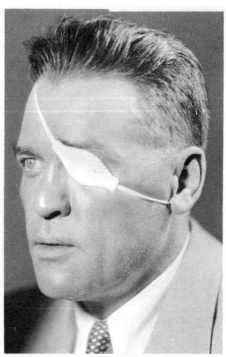

Floyd Gibbons.

"Scarface Al" Capone.

35

of 45 miles per hour." . . . This year also saw the arrival in America of pugilist Primo Carnera. The Italian giant awed sports writers who went down New York's Lower Bay to greet him. Bill Corum wrote: "I have seen Primo Carnera, and words fail me. He came fifty years too late. He is an answer to Barnum's prayer. Even when you see him you can't believe it." Primo's manager solemnly swore that when he went camping he used his fighter's coat as a tent. . . . Actress Jane Cowl caused a sensation by writing an article in the *North American Review* in which she lambasted New York theatre audiences for having the worst manners of any audience in the world. "The banging of seats, the tinker-bells of the lights of the ushers, the horror of the whispered, "Do you want to sit over here?' is enough to drive any actor mad." . . . In Hollywood Rod LaRocque had signed for *Strictly Business,* along with Doris Kenyon. Joan Crawford was billed as the star of *Montana,* which the studio called "one of the big pictures of the year . . . a western talkie." . . . Radio stars Rudy Vallee and Guy Lombardo were sharing honors on WEAF. On the crime front, Alphonse (Scarface Al) Capone was secretly transferred from the Eastern Penitentiary in Pennsylvania to the new state prison farm, thirty-five miles away in Montgomery County, and paroled from there on March 17, after serving ten months of a year's sentence for carrying a pistol. He turned up at Chicago a few weeks later and was warned by police to stay away. He next appeared in Florida, only to be told by police he was *persona non grata.* "Look, all I want is peace," the crime boss told a reporter, "just peace." . . . In September, Jack (Legs) Diamond, a prime target for the hired guns of Dutch Schultz, who was taking over all the rackets in New York, arrived in Antwerp, Belgium, only to be escorted to the border by police as an "undesirable guest." He went to Germany only to be taken to a freighter in Hamburg which delivered him to Philadelphia. The cops of the City of Brotherly Love couldn't find any love for the mobster and put him on a train for New York, where he vanished for a few weeks. But the Dutchman's guns finally caught up with Legs in a midtown hotel and pumped him full of lead. Legs, who seemed to have an incredible capacity for absorbing lead poisoning, survived and left for upstate with the

One of the two Negroes lynched by a mob near Marks, Mississippi. The lynching took place after the pair confessed to an attempted assault on the wife of a plantation owner.

Dutchman's boys hot on his heels. He managed to duck them, but not for long. . . . Throughout the year various mobs fought for the control of bootlegging and the speaks. In the underworld, murder was commonplace; scarcely a week passed that some hood wasn't found garroted, riddled with bullets, or burned to death in the Canarsie flats or the New Jersey swamps. . . . And in this fateful year several Negroes were taken by mobs from jails in southern states and lynched. In Texas there was a double lynching, with the mob shooting at the swaying bodies, then cutting them down and burning them with gasoline.

Joan Crawford in Untamed, her first "talking picture."

Jane Cowl in her famous portrayal of Amytis in Robert Sherwood's The Road to Rome.

A rare picture of New York's Lieutenant Governor Herbert Lehman and Governor Franklin D. Roosevelt as they received news of their party's victories in the 1930 election. The braces on Roosevelt's legs were seldom shown in newspaper.

37

Death of a Hero

THERE IS a story told in Atlanta about the weeping newsboy who looked down at his pile of papers and pushed them into the gutter. "I don't want anyone to read about the Rock," he sobbed. "I want to make believe it didn't happen."

A large part of the nation felt the same way the day the tickers tapped out the news that Knute Rockne was among the eight who died when their plane crashed in a Kansas wheat field.

Rockne, the Notre Dame football coach who had become a legend in his lifetime, was en route to Los Angeles for a business meeting when he was killed. His death stunned the nation. It seemed almost impossible that his rough-hewn face would no longer stare out of the sports pages each fall.

Fate had cut him down at a time when he was reaping more honors than ever before. Only that previous fall his Fighting Irish had been national champions, capping his thirteen years as Notre Dame coach during which his teams had compiled a 105-12-5 record.

Perhaps Rockne will be remembered most for his famous team of the Four Horsemen backfield – Elmer Layden, Harry Stuhldreher, Don Miller and Jim Crowley—and the Seven Mules line of the mid-1920's. But many believe his 1930 team was the most brilliant; it rolled over Southern Methodist, Navy, Carnegie Tech, Pittsburgh, Indiana, Pennsylvania, Drake, Northwestern, Army, and Southern California.

In the Southern California game, the little Norwegian-born coach pulled a master stroke of psychology by convincing the Trojans he had no fullback. Larry Mullins, last of his experienced regulars in the position, had been injured in the Army game. Rock secretly switched Paul (Bucky) O'Connor to fullback, and in one of his legendary pep talks that included mothers, country, flag, and Notre Dame, fired Bucky to his "big chance" and pitted him against the unsuspecting Trojans. The great USC team was mauled 27-0.

Knute Rockne.

Rockne, once a star pass-snagger himself, was voted the All-American coach in the 1931 Associated Press poll. He is famed for creating the backfield shift, although he always gave the credit to Amos Alonzo Stagg at Chicago. As the legend goes, Rockne had seen a musical in Chicago where he had been impressed by the precision of the dancing girls. The next day, in a sudden burst of inspiration, he began to experiment with what came to be known as the "backfield shift."

He was the first football coach to replace the players' cumbersome protective equipment with tight-fitting silk pants and jerseys.

Although Rockne's Four Horsemen, immortalized by Grantland Rice, probably were the finest backfield in the history of football, they also had their off days, such as the afternoon in 1924 when the team was returning by train from a rather dreary win over Iowa. A drunk was moving through the crowded car and, after fumbling about in his pockets, told the conductor he didn't have a ticket.

Knute Rockne on the bench with the players as Notre Dame battled Pittsburgh in the 1930 game.

"Well, then, where are you going?" the exasperated conductor shouted.

The drunk shrugged and gave him a vague wave.

"I don't know, mister—I guess I'm not going anywhere."

Above the laughter rose the voice of Jim Crowley.

"That's all right, conductor, he's one of the Four Horsemen. *They* didn't go anywhere this afternoon. . . ."

1931

Sidelight on Vice

IN THE WINTER of 1931 a beautiful blackmailer and her damaging little black book, and a slender, smiling procurer from Santiago, Chile, shook New York City's Police Department, set its wise-cracking mayor, Jimmy Walker, on the path to ultimate obscurity and disgrace, and brought into prominence a man—Samuel Seabury—whose name became synonymous with law and order and public decency.

The sensational murder of Vivian Gordon was the spark that touched off Manhattan's most famous reform wave. Her little black book, a day-by-day diary, destroyed many men, many homes, and finally her own daughter. The subsequent investigation of the Walker administration by Judge Seabury became a classic of its kind.

It all began years before, when Vivian Gordon, daughter of a modest Detroit family, ran away from a convent school at the age of fifteen. Capable and independent, she worked her way into show business and went on the road with burlesque troupes. This palled, however, and she married John Bischoff, a "traveling man." For several years she and her husband moved about the country. When her daughter, Benita, was born, she left Bischoff to go to New York. Bischoff became an official of a federal penitentiary, and Vivian became New York's biggest blackmailer. She had many lovers, plenty of money, an expensive apartment, little Benita to care for, and a diary in which she listed names and dates. No man's indiscretion was safe.

One day when Benita was six, Vivian failed to return home. A friendly hotel clerk took care of her until her father could come and take her to his home in Audubon, New Jersey.

After a term in Bedford Reformatory for Women on a vice charge, Vivian tried to regain custody of her daughter, although the courts had declared she was unfit to raise a child. There were stormy visits to the Audubon home, passionate charges that the vice

Vivian Gordon.

charge that sent her to prison had been framed. As time went on, Benita became a teenager whose dark eyes had seen much of the shabby, sordid side of life. She was easily frightened, shy and withdrawn.

Vivian Gordon never succeeded in getting her daughter back. This defeat penetrated through all the callousness, the cynicism, the evil that had been part of her life for so long. In one desperate move for vindication, she paid a visit to Irving Ben Cooper, Seabury's young assistant, and gave him extensive evidence on the vice squad and its crooked members. A few days after the interview with Cooper, during which she had arranged for another appointment, her frozen body, clad in a lace-trimmed dress, was found in Van Cortlandt Park. She had been strangled to death.

In her apartment was found the explosive diary containing the names of many men, some of whom were public officials. As the investigators dug deeper, a network of crime and corruption was revealed. Vice cops were found on her payroll; others were listed with an indication that they could be bought for a price.

The sensational crime made lurid

Vivian Gordon in court in 1931.

39

headlines, and Governor Roosevelt acted; he appointed a special investigative body under Samuel Seabury to probe conditions in New York City.

Although teachers and classmates at Audubon High School joined in an effort to shield Benita from the tragedy, the girl read every line of the stories about her mother's death and the revelations that followed, and she became more and more withdrawn. Like her mother, she kept a diary. The February 28th item read: "Mother found dead. Terrible things are being said."

And on March 1, the pitiful entry: "I guess I will have to change my name."

Two days later, while her stepmother was out shopping, Benita stuffed the kitchen-door cracks and turned on the gas. Beside her was her diary with its final entry: "March 3, 2:15 P.M. . . . I'm tired . . . I've decided to give it all up . . . I am turning on the gas."

Vivian's brother, an automobile salesman in Montreal, gazed horror-stricken at the front-page picture of his sister, came immediately to New York, and made formal identification of the body. Less than a week later, he went berserk from grief and shock.

The Gordon murder made headlines for a year. More than two hundred men found that their trysts with her were far from secret. Week after week official heads rolled. Jimmy Walker decided to take a "vacation." The reformers began whetting their knives.

Vivian's murder was never solved, but her place in the headlines was

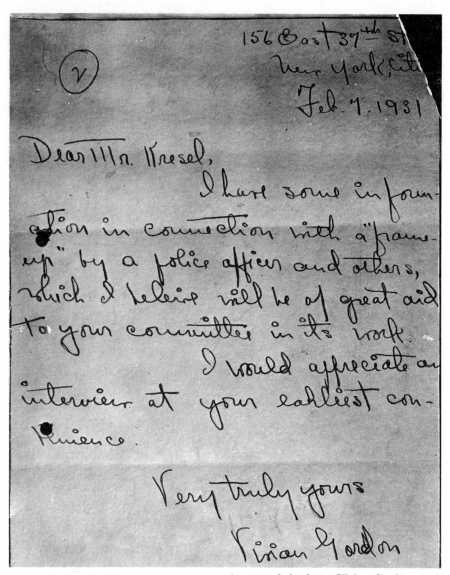

A copy of the letter Vivian Gordon wrote to Kresel offering to give information against crooked vice cops.

taken by Chile Mapocha Acuna, a slender Chilean procurer who named names, dates, and places where he had paid off vice cops. Twenty were fired or dismissed. A "star performer" for Irving Ben Cooper, Acuna later wrote a book entitled *Women for Sale,* the biography of a pimp.

Buried in the archives of the New York Police Department are the day-by-day reports of guards posted by the police commissioner to protect the life of the man who was helping to tarnish its honor. It cost the police department $40,984, including $68.70 for theatre tickets. One of the reports states, "The subject likes the theatre."

Acuna once told a reporter, "You know, I'm like an actor. You gotta be in this business. Down in Santiago the people think I'm a big hero. I'm a crusader."

Vivian Gordon's apartment.

The Dry Messiah

WHEN THE Anti-Saloon League waged its crusade for the Eighteenth Amendment, leading the fight was Bishop James Cannon, Jr., about whose head unprecedented political and ecclesiastical storms gathered in subsequent years.

He first became nationally known during the 1928 presidential campaign, when he led Southern opposition to Al Smith. Many accused him of opposing Smith because he was a Roman Catholic, and after the election the clergyman found himself assailed on all sides, from within and without the church. Senator Carter Glass of Virginia once called him "the Methodist pope," an appellation that was kept alive during the early thirties.

But the bishop was a fighter. He met charge with counter-charge, insisting that he had not opposed Smith for religious reasons but because he was the mortal enemy of Demon Rum. In 1931 Bishop Cannon's personal record was put under scrutiny. When the fact became known that he had dabbled in stocks, his foes were quick to charge him with "gambling." It was also charged that he had "refunded" to himself much of the sixty-five thousand dollars sent him by E. C. Jameson, a New York capitalist, "to elect Hoover." He was summoned before a general council of his church in Dallas, Texas, which demanded that he render a full explanation. In a dramatic hearing the clergyman admitted, "I have made a mistake which shall never occur again and which I deeply deplore." There were tears in his eyes as he made the plea; his oratory was so moving the council exonerated him.

But there was no rest for him. When he returned to Washington he was summoned before a Senate committee interested in knowing how he spent his funds in the Virginia elections. It was a colorful hearing. Cannon, crippled by neuritis, defied the committee and hobbled from his chair while the senators pounded the table and shouted they would cite him for contempt. At

Bishop James Cannon, Jr., of Virginia.

the door he stopped and turned. His face a deep red and his eyes flashing behind his glasses, he declared, "I'll be at my office whenever a subpoena is issued."

Senator Walsh of Montana, famed as a public prosecutor, kept roaring questions, but the little bishop limped out and the committee was left talking to itself.

He next appeared in London, where

he married his secretary, Mrs. Helen Hawley McCallum. He returned to the United States in the winter of 1931 to face additional charges filed against him by four ministers of his church. Again he was exonerated.

He was not yet through his inquiries; 1931 was his busy year with Senate committees. The Senate Campaign Funds Committee recalled him under the Corrupt Practices Act. Testimony showed that he had accounted for only $17,000 of the $65,000 sent him by Jameson. The constitutionality of the committee was challenged by Cannon and a hearing was held in May, 1931. Bishop Cannon reclined in a chair, his crutches nearby, and nodded approval as his former secretary, Miss Ada Boroughs, refused to answer the chairman's questions. The frustrated committee adjourned, threatening to cite the lady for contempt. But nothing came of it.

All through the nation's Desperate Years, Bishop Cannon was Washington's stormy petrel. His list of foes was impressive: Josephus Daniels, Wilson's secretary of the navy, who had been instrumental in bringing Cannon to trial in his own church; Senator Glass, whom Bishop Cannon described as a "mere pawn of Tammany"; Congressman Tinkham of Massachusetts, whom he sued for libel in June, 1931; and Senator Walsh of Montana, his chief inquisitor at the Senate hearings. He went into semi-retirement before World War II and died in 1944.

Bishop Cannon with Mrs. Cannon and his former secretary, Miss Ada L. Burroughs, after Cannon and his former aide were **were acquitted of violation of the Corrupt Practices Act in the Al Smith campaign of 1928.**

41

TWO-GUN

The soft spring air was heavy with the smell of the sea and the Long Island salt marshes. The sky was star-shot and the moon was in its last quarter. It was a perfect night for lovers, Patrolman Frederick Hirsch told his partner, Peter Yodice, as they came to the entrance of Black Shirt Lane near North Merrick, Long Island.

"I think I saw a car back there," he said. "Probably some kids. We better chase them out of there before someone sticks them up."

A few minutes later Hirsch was walking toward the car, the shaft of light from his flashlight bobbing in the darkness. It trailed up the side of the green coupe and framed the thin, sallow face of a teenager who had his arm around a pretty young girl.

"Pretty late to be out, son," Hirsch said as he opened the car door. "Better let me see your license first."

Up in front of the car, Yodice was checking the license. Slowly, nonchalantly, the youth took his arm from around the girl's shoulder.

"Sure," he said. "Sure."

In a moment a revolver was in his hand. He fired three times at Hirsch. The police officer staggered back and fired a wild shot as he slumped to the ground. The youth leaped out, tore the gun from the dying man's hand, jumped back into the car and roared away into the darkness as Patrolman Yodice fired.

For Francis ("Two-Gun") Crowley, it was the beginning of the end, but before the end New York would witness the most savage gun battle in its history. It was a bit of old Dodge City transplanted to the fringes of Times Square.

Crowley, who was nineteen at the time of the killing of Patrolman Hirsch, was already one of the most wanted men in the country. He had engineered a bank robbery, had cold-bloodedly shot down a man in a holdup, had been implicated in the death of Virginia Banner, a dance-hall hostess who had once turned down his partner in crime, Rudy

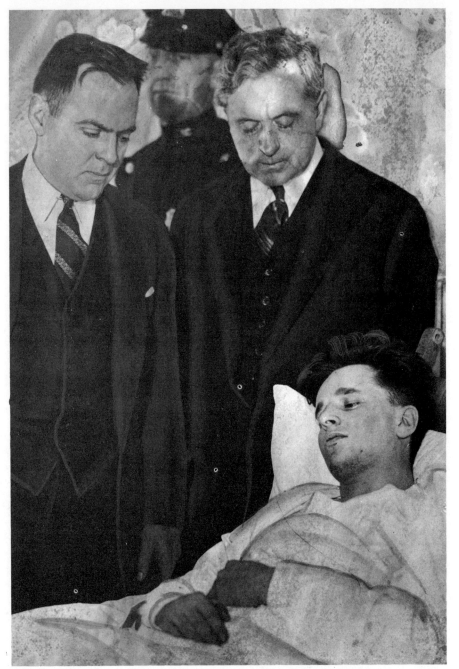

Francis (Two-Gun) Crowley with District Attorney Elvin Edwards and Inspector Harold King.

(Fats) Duringer, and had shot his way out of several holdups. Strangely enough, the police didn't know what Crowley looked like; all the evidence they had was from the microscope of Sergeant Butts, ballistics expert of the New York Police Department. The bullet taken from Patrolman Hirsch's body matched the slugs dug out of the bodies of Crowley's other victims. Now they knew from Yodice what Crowley looked like.

Lights blazed all that night at Police Headquarters and in the district attorney's office at Mineola. Police Commissioner Mulrooney sent out a terse teletype order: "Shoot to kill."

The girl in the car was identified as Helen Walsh, sixteen-year-old sweetheart of Crowley, and the police believed she might have been killed to keep her silent. All that morning police fanned out like African beaters in a tiger hunt to search the salt marshes

"Big Rudolph" Duringer.

named Billie Dunne, a habitué of the Harlem speaks.

Veteran police reporter Joe O'Connor followed various tenuous leads to an East Harlem dance hall where he found a hard-eyed young girl just bursting to tell someone her troubles.

"Do I know where that dirty dog Frankie is? Of course I do. He came to my apartment yesterday with that dame Helen Walsh and you know what that bum had the nerve to say? 'You're through, kid, get out.' Get out of my own apartment! Him and that dame and that fat slob Duringer!"

"Where's your apartment, Billie?" Joe asked innocently.

"Three-o-three West Ninetieth . . . Now look, you're not going to the cops, are you?"

"Maybe I'll pay him a visit myself," Joe said.

for her body, while a police helicopter buzzed overhead.

While the hunt went on, another strange story was beginning. In the office of the New York *Journal,* Assistant City Editor Garry Finley was listening to a girl reporter, Jeanette Smits, who had talked to Crowley's foster mother. She had mentioned a dance-hall girl

Helen Walsh, the sixteen-year-old sweetheart of Two-Gun Crowley, being removed from the apartment by police after they had shot it out with the young killer.

43

Billie shook her head. "You're crazy, Mr. O'Connor, that guy'll shoot his own mother."

Later that day O'Connor met Jerry Frankel, the *Journal's* photographer, and the newsmen settled down to keep a watch on the gray stone building. In the meantime, District Attorney Edwards and Police Commissioner Mulrooney had been informed.

But Frankel fretted as time went on

strapped on his hip and a shoulder holster. Both trouser legs were rolled up above the knee; a gun was strapped to each calf.

Then his two guns blazed and bullets slammed into the wall above the heads of the photographer and policemen. Plaster flew and slugs whined. The door slammed shut. It was splintered in a moment. From behind it Crowley shouted: "Come and get me!"

The gun battle was confined to the top floor of the five-story building. Scores of detectives with drawn guns were perched on roofs, in apartment-house entrances, and behind cars. Other tenants in the besieged building were trapped and huddled in corners, trying to escape the tear-gas. Before long spectators and cops alike were choking and weeping.

The police moved in slowly, foot by foot, fearful that the flying lead would injure the spectators who hung out their windows to watch the battle, using pillows for arm-rests.

Inside the apartment, Crowley had been wounded four times. The Walsh girl and Duringer, a heavy-set man, were both trying to shelter under the daybed. It was Crowley who brought the fight to the police; he darted from window to window, firing, reloading, and shouting threats.

Although he threw out some of the tear-gas containers, many others, hurled through the shattered windows, did their work. When the cops kicked in the door, Crowley was groping like a blind man, his eyes swollen and tearing. He was strapped to a stretcher and removed to a hospital, where he spoke freely of the killings.

Police later found, scrawled on a scratch pad, a letter Crowley had written before the siege. It read:

The bullet-riddled bedroom and kitchenette at 303 West 90th Street where Crowley made his last stand. More than 700 bullets were poured into the suite by 300 policemen.

and there was no sign of police. Photographers are notorious for being impatient when there are pictures to be made. Lugging his equipment, he started across the street for 303, climbed the stairs to Billie's apartment, and knocked.

"Get out of here!" Crowley snarled from behind the door. "We don't want any."

Frankel raised his hand to knock again. Suddenly there was a rush of feet. Detectives who were hiding in the hall grabbed him bodily and hurled him backward. The door jerked open. For a second Crowley was framed in the doorway. The slender teenager was a walking arsenal. He had two guns

The battle of West Ninetieth Street had begun. In the street below, O'Connor was turning in his first bulletin; upstairs Frankel lay on his stomach snapping pictures like mad, while the gloomy stairwell was lit up by the flashes of guns.

Within a few minutes a crowd of more than fifteen thousand had jammed behind the police barricades erected on West End Avenue near the house. The entire area from Ninetieth to Ninety-second had been roped off and the evening rush-hour traffic was creating a massive jam. Now and again came the sharp crack of rifle fire, the dull slam of shotguns, then the nervous rattle of a machine-gun.

To whom it may concern:
I was born on the thirty-first. She was born on the nineteenth. I guess it was fate that made us mate. When I die put a lily in my hand, let the boys know how they'll look. Under my coat will lay a weary, kind heart that wouldn't hurt anything. I hadn't anything else to do, that's why I went around bumping off cops. It's the new sensation of the films. Take a tip from me to never let a copper go an inch above your knee. They will tell you they love you and as soon as you turn your back they will club you and say the hell with you. Now that my death is so near there is a couple of bulls at the door saying "come here." I'm behind the door with three thirty-eights—one belongs to my friend in North Merrick—he would have gotten me if his bullets were any good.

Duringer, when questioned, admitted the murder of Virginia Banner, the dance-hall girl. His explanation, "I

44

May 1931

To Whom It May Concern

I was born on the 13 of Oct and he was born on the 31. If I die and my face you are able to see, wave my hair, make me look pretty and make my face up. Dress me in Black & White in a new dress Do my nails all over I dont use this kind of polish its too dark I use a very pale pink. I always wanted every body to be happy & have a good time — I had some pretty good times my self Love to all but all of my love to Sweets

P.S. Everybody happy & how

Helen Walsh

Helen Walsh's letter, penned in the midst of the famous 1931 "Siege of West 90th Street."

heard she was going to marry someone else . . . I was jealous of him."

Crowley was quickly indicted and placed on trial. The principal witness against him was his sweetheart, Helen Walsh, who winked at him as she left the stand. But Crowley did not wink back. During the trial Crowley's attorney brought out facts that showed the genesis of a killer: a makeshift home, moving from place to place, working at the age of twelve, barely able to write, a consuming hatred for the law, discovery that a gun gave him power and authority over others . . . "A moral imbecile," his attorney called him.

Crowley died in the electric chair after Duringer, who had also been convicted of the Banner girl's murder. He asked the guards as they strapped on the electrodes to "give my love to my mother."

Jesse James or Billy the Kid couldn't have said it better.

Bridge Across
the Hudson

ON THE MORNING of October 24, 1931, the George Washington Bridge, spanning the Hudson River from Manhattan to the New Jersey Palisades, on steel towers 625 feet high, was opened for business.

The bridge was a wonder to behold, and is still considered one of the most beautiful in the world. Unlike the Brooklyn Bridge or any other bridge of its time, it trembled under traffic, moved with the wind. Under the blazing summer sun its great tracery of steel expanded, only to contract in the winter's cold. Its 3,500 feet of roadway could easily accommodate 100,000 cars a day. It had taken four years to build and had cost the lives of twelve men. The years of its building had been marked with controversy as to whether the steel should be covered or exposed. Architect Cass Gilbert wanted masonry on its towers, but O. H. Ammann, the chief engineer, wanted naked steel. He won—with the help of the Depression. Masonry was too expensive and was abandoned—along with plans for a second deck, which was not to be built until thirty years later.

The great bridge had been started in an era of opulence and wild prosperity. On the crisp fall day when it was officially opened, New York was a grim city of fearful men and women, its skyline marked with half-finished skyscrapers which Communist orators were calling the "tombs of capitalism."

A crowd of thirty thousand gathered to watch New York's Governor Franklin D. Roosevelt and New Jersey's Governor Morgan F. Larson open the silver span between upper Manhattan and Fort Lee. By evening 56,313 cars and one man on a horse had crossed. Traffic grew from 5.5 million vehicles in 1932 —its first complete year—to more than 8 million in 1940. By 1958 the traffic had swelled to 35.5 million.

Since that first fall day in 1931, one hundred men and women have leaped to their deaths from the graceful span, and about as many have been forcibly held back.

The George Washington Bridge—viewed from the New Jersey tower.

Hoisting one of the main-span cross-bridges into position on the George Washington Bridge.

46

The Sword
of the Press

ON FRIDAY morning, February 27, 1931, the presses were silent in the green-domed Pulitzer Building at 63 Park Row and men who had once wielded the sword of the press sat at their silent typewriters and talked of the old days so they wouldn't have to think of the future.

The *Evening World,* the *Morning World,* the paper Walter Lippman had called the sword of the press, was dead. Property of the Pulitzers for more than fifty years, it had been sold to the Scripps-Howard syndicate—"not to die but to be born again," in the words of Roy W. Howard, head of the corporation that bought them. But no great promises or plans would ever make it the same. The *World* was dead and a great institution had passed from the American scene.

The paper was snuffed out without having a chance to bid farewell to its faithful readers. The move to kill it had begun a short time before in February, when attorneys for Herbert, Ralph and Joseph Pulitzer, trustees of the *World,*

A view of the city room of the New York World the day it folded.

went to Surrogate Foley and asked permission to sell the paper. Permission was finally granted and in the last issue of February 27, there appeared this page-one notice:

> The trustees of this newspaper to whom Joseph Pulitzer entrusted the duty of carrying on the institution which he had founded, made every possible effort to avoid a sale of the newspaper, but economic conditions have proved inexorable. Had the *World* been nothing more

than a commercial enterprise, a sale might profitably have been undertaken years before; it has now become compulsory. Its publication year after year has brought heavy losses. For forty-eight years it has done its duty as it saw its duty, without fear or favor, without private propaganda or special privilege . . .

A price of 5 million dollars was paid, the highest ever paid for a daily newspaper at that time.

The World

FINAL NEWS EDITION

VOL. LXXI. NO. 25,392—DAILY   Copyright Press Publishing Company (New York World) 1931   NEW YORK, FRIDAY, FEBRUARY 27, 1931   IN TWO SECTIONS SECTION ONE ★★★★ ★   TWO CENTS In Greater New York | THREE CENTS Within 200 Miles | FOUR CENTS Elsewhere

Woman Who Offered to Tell About Vice Framing Found Strangled in Park in Bronx

y of Vivian Gordon, Who d Tried to Aid Seabury nquiry, Shows Signs of a Struggle for Life

NAMED IN DIARY
TAKEN INTO CUSTODY

ear but One," She Had ten; Taxi Driver Chased With Screaming Woman

Strangler's Victim—Her Letter

BONUS IS VETOED; HOUSE OVERRIDES HOOVER, 328 - 79

Tilson Howled Down When He Tries to Rally Support for the President

SENATE BALLOTS TODAY; VETO'S DEFEAT EXPECTED

Mills Says Treasury Is Ready to Seek $400,000,000 for First Payments

By Elliott Thurston
WASHINGTON, Feb. 26—After hearing President Hoover's veto message read this afternoon, scoring the bonus

BANK INDICTMENTS UPHELD BY COURT; NEW DEFENSE PLAN

Judge Allen Rules Stock Held by Grand Jurors Does Not Impair True Bills

SEPARATE KRESEL TRIAL NEW MOVE OF COUNSEL

Probable Acquittal Would Be Favorable to Other Indicted Directors

By Allen Norton
Judge Allen in General Sessions ruled yesterday no illegality was involved in the indictments returned two weeks ago against eight officials

Scripps-Howard Buy World As Court Permits Sale and Pulitzers Fulfill Contract

Statement by the Trustees On Sale of World Papers

The World, The Evening World and The Sunday World have been sold to the Scripps-Howard interests, owners of the New York Telegram.

The three papers will be merged with the New York Telegram under the title New York World-Telegram.

It is the intention of the trustees of the newspaper trust to set aside from the proceeds of the sale the sum of $500,000 to be distributed among employees under the terms of a plan to be announced later.

Surrogate Foley Renders Decision on Plea to Break Will, but Refuses to Pass on Others

THE TRUSTEES SET ASIDE $500,000 FOR EMPLOYEES

Stern and Gannett Bid for Papers—Staff's Fund Wins Public Support

The last issue of the World.

The Great Inventor

WALTER MALLORY looked stricken after he read the brief note.

"My God, Mr. Edison," he told the white-haired man who sat across the room, "Charlotte is worse."

Thomas Alva Edison put aside the tools he was working with. "What's wrong with Charlotte, Mr. Mallory?" he asked.

"She's had this fever for days," Mallory said. "It's getting worse every hour, and the doctors said this heat wave may kill her. I guess all we can do is pray."

Edison stood up and put his arm around his employee's shoulder.

"Let's go over and see what we can do."

Later, both Mallory and his wife watched with some apprehension as Edison began nailing a small, wooden, boxlike affair to the bedroom window. He smiled now and then at the feverish child who tossed and moaned on the bed.

"Now, if you will give me that fan, Mr. Mallory," he said.

"But, Mr. Edison, that's all the relief she gets now!" Mrs. Mallory exclaimed.

"Please trust me," Edison said as he placed the fan in the box. Then he told Mallory to bring in a cake of ice from the ice box. After he had placed the ice in the box with the fan, he had Mallory open the window across the room a few inches.

"With the fan blowing the air across the ice, the room should soon be cooled," he said.

Mrs. Mallory cried, "Why, it's cooler already . . ."

This first makeshift air conditioner was probably the most insignificant of all Thomas Edison's many great inventions. Out of Menlo Park, near East Orange, New Jersey, came the stock ticker, the duplex, quadruplex, and automatic telegraph systems, and incidentally the electric pen, which developed into the mimeograph. His invention of the carbon transmitter, in which compressed lampblack buttons were

Thomas Alva Edison with Mrs. Edison.

used to obtain the necessary variable resistance in the circuit, marked a great advance in the art of telephony and added materially in bringing the telephone into practical use.

Edison's most popular invention was the phonograph or "speaking instrument." Later he invented the "Ediphone" for office dictation. On Oct. 21, 1879, after spending more than forty thousand dollars in experiments, Edison succeeded in making an incandescent lamp. In 1891 he applied for a patent for a "kinetescopic camera" for taking motion pictures on a band of film.

In World War I his genius produced an early sound gear which located submarines by sound waves and helped the

Allies immeasurably. During the twenties the world paid tribute to Edison, but the inventor cared little about speeches and accolades. He also cared little for food or sleep—four hours was sufficient. He lived only for his work.

He numbered among his friends the great men of industry and science of his time. Probably the closest were Harvey Firestone and Henry Ford.

On October 18, 1931, Edison died in his sleep. He was buried just before dusk in the quiet of the little New Jersey town where he had lived and worked for so many years.

As the casket was lowered the nation paid him its final tribute: the Prince of Light was given one moment of darkness.

Andrew Mellon shown as he presented Edison with a medal in recognition of the **electrical wizard's contributions to science.**

The Clay Pigeon Shattered:
The Last of Legs Diamond

THEY FINALLY shot down the clay pigeon. This time his thin, tubercular frame could not throw off the effect of steel-jacketed bullets. Four times he had survived the best that hired guns could provide; after the last time, in a Cairo, New York, roadhouse, doctors had predicted he would live only a few hours. One of several bullets had pierced a lung and it had collapsed.

But Legs Diamond walked out of the hospital, said quietly he would take care of things in his own way, and drove off with his favorite bodyguard, Danny Meehan.

But at 5:20 A.M. on Saturday, December 19, 1931, two gunmen tiptoed up the stairs of a shabby rooming house on Albany's Dove Street, slipped the lock, and walked inside. This time the executioners made sure: they pumped seventeen bullets into Diamond's head, chest, and torso.

The killing came just an hour after Legs had finished celebrating his acquittal on a charge of kidnapping a Monroe County farmer. When he had left the courtroom, he insisted on celebrating. With a large party he took over a local saloon, and liquor flowed freely. At midnight, drunk and reckless, he ordered a cab driver to inform his sweetheart, Follies girl Kiki Roberts, to expect him in an hour. The cab driver found Kiki standing under a street light reading the headlines: "Diamond freed."

"Tell Jack I'll be waiting," she told the driver.

At one A.M. Diamond told his guests and his wife that he was going to attend a "press conference" and would soon return.

In twenty minutes he was in Kiki's apartment. At four A.M. he staggered back into the cab and drove to a rooming house on Dove Street. The driver said Legs hadn't wanted to face his infuriated wife.

Jack (Legs) Diamond.

An hour later the gunmen paid their call.

His funeral was in direct contrast to the usual gangster farewells that had been a trade mark of the twenties; he was buried in an $800 casket.

Diamond was one of the last of the Prohibition-spawned mob leaders who had left their bloody mark on the history of the twenties. He got his start by hanging around Owney Madden's West Side Winona Club and snatching packages from the horse-drawn delivery wagons. Because of his speed on the getaway, Diamond was tagged "Legs" by his admiring friends. At sixteen he was sent to a reformatory, at nineteen he was serving a year and a day for deserting the army. He later became a

hired gun for Jacob (Little Augie) Orgem, the narcotics peddler, and in a gunfight on the lower East Side received his first slugs. Little Augie died but Jack survived three bullets.

He moved up rapidly after that; the mobs hated and feared him. He was a Broadway figure, skinny, meticulously dressed, suave and soft-spoken unless he was drunk—then he was dangerous as a cobra.

In 1930 at his Hotsy Totsy Club he met Marion Kiki Roberts and fell in love. His plump wife, Alice, knew about the romance but continued to stay on. "He's my hero," she once told a reporter. "I can't let him go—I just can't."

It was Alice who clung to the iron bed where the shattered body of her husband lay. Police had to pry her hands free while she screamed, "He's mine! Let me stay with Jack . . ."

On top of the radio in her Brooklyn apartment was a picture of Legs. On it she had scrawled, "My Hero."

Mrs. Alice Diamond.

Dr. Erich Salomon:
King Candid-Cameraman

ONE OF THE most skilled, aggressive, and successful cameramen of the thirties was a soft-spoken, cultured former banker, named Dr. Erich Salomon. His favorite subjects were the leading figures of his day.

When other photographers were barred from the historic meetings at the League of Nations, Dr. Salomon somehow managed to crash the gates, either by ingenuity, imagination, or plain gall.

He "invented" candid camera photography. Although other professional photographers may have experimented with this type of camera art, Salomon perfected it and made it one of the most popular forms of photography in the early thirties.

He would not take a posed picture, even though his subject might be a president or a premier. To get a candid shot at a Hague conference, he hired a window-washing concern's truck and crew.

He had the truck backed up to the hotel and the crew ran up its three-story ladder. With equipment dangling from about his neck, the dapper, slight Dr. Salomon clambered up the ladder, clung like a monkey to its top rung, and clicked away on his camera. Some of the ministers later complained that "it's not nice to use ladders against ministers," but Aristide Briand said, "the hunting season is now open on ministers" and promptly dubbed Salomon

Chancellor Bruening of Germany and his Foreign Minister Dr. Julius Curtius have talks with Mussolini in Rome at the Hotel Excelsior (1931). (Left to right) Mussolini; Bruening; Count Dino Grandi, Italian Foreign Minister; and Dr. Curtius.

Marlene Dietrich.

"King of Indiscreets."

When the delegates to the London Naval Conference were setting out on their historic journey, all photographers were barred from the station and the train. Salomon, dressed like a delegate, selected an ambassador and engaged him in conversation as they walked through the gates. While they waited for the train, Salomon and the ambassador engaged in what appeared to be a confidential conversation. Just as the train pulled out, Salomon led the ambassador aboard.

The guards, who hesitated to question Salomon, because of this seemingly important talk, later found out that Salomon had asked the ambassador his opinion of a then-popular movie.

Once, in Geneva, Aristide Briand tried his best to get Salomon admitted to a highly important conference, but he was refused.

"I'll bet anyone ten francs the terrible doctor gets in," he said. A fellow delegate took the bet. Ten minutes later the doors opened to admit Salomon. Briand cried, "There he is and I win ten francs!"

Salomon, never at a loss with a cam-

French Premier Pierre Laval visits President Herbert Hoover in the White House (Lincoln Study), 1931.

S. M. Eisenstein, noted Russian film director, and Upton Sinclair, Hollywood, 1930.

Laval, in a special train provided by the U.S. Government, on his way to see Hoover, 1931. (Left to right): U.S. Secretary of State Henry L. Stimson; Laval; M. Rueff, Financial Attaché to the French Embassy in London; Mr. Marriner, First Secretary of the American Embassy in Paris, who acted as interpreter.

Arturo Toscanini studies the score as an aide calls out instructions, 1930.

era, took a famous picture of Briand's look of amusement as he pointed to him.

At a historic gathering in Rome when Mussolini was first becoming an important figure in Europe, Salomon had been promised by the foreign minister a picture of the dictator. But when Salomon arrived he was told the plans had been changed. Salomon, however, managed to get into the dining room of the Hotel Excelsior, where he saw Mussolini sitting at a table apart from other world leaders present. Salomon walked up to Mussolini's foreign minister, who was nearby, and demanded an explanation. Mussolini looked up and asked what was wrong. The embarrassed minister explained, and the dictator told

Salomon to start shooting. The historic picture of an early Mussolini, shown here, is the result.

The Salomon picture that attracted most attention in the United States was his candid camera shot of President Hoover and Pierre Laval, then premier of France. Laval, who liked Salomon, promised to try and get Hoover to break the iron-clad rule of the White House forbidding pictures.

After the second day Laval shrugged and said: *"Vous savez que ce n'est pas simple."* It was indeed difficult; Hoover knew that a howl would go up from American photographers. However, in the last hour Laval finally got permission and Salomon was ushered in.

An annoyed aide kept whispering to

the photographer to take his shots and get out. But Salomon took his time. Both men were staring at him. Finally Salomon, in French and English, ordered them to start talking about a subject they both liked.

Hoover and Laval began chatting. In a few minutes they had forgotten Salomon. They were now relaxed and Salomon made his shots.

As he walked out, Laval told Hoover with a shrug: "I told you, Mr. President, that was how it would be. I know his ways."

Besides the pictures shown here, there are several others by Dr. Salomon, showing the Kennedy family, in the AMBASSADOR AND FAMILY section.

Yachts

OFF THE SPANISH coast, W. K. Vanderbilt sat in the luxurious dining room of his famous 264-foot yacht, *Alva,* built with loving care in the Kiel shipyards that spring. To bring it to the United States, Vanderbilt had paid $267,000 customs duty on the yacht's steel hull and furnishings. In July, 1931, he had set out on a round-the-world voyage with a twofold purpose: to collect specimens for the Vanderbilt Marine Museum, and to complete the first round-the-globe voyage under the yacht ensign of the United States Naval Reserve, in which Vanderbilt was a lieutenant commander.

When they reached Spain one day that fall, nearing the end of the east-to-west journey, Vanderbilt had the latest reports of the stock market brought to him.

As he recorded in his diary, "Central has hit 25; it is time to go home." The Vanderbilt family's stock, which once had soared to $250, was now plummeting toward its ultimate rock-bottom price of $10 a share.

Like all millionaire yachtsmen, Vanderbilt had seen the handwriting on the wall; for the Morgans, the Vanderbilts, the Roeblings, the day of the million-dollar yachts had passed. Even J. P. Morgan removed his famed black-hulled *Corsair* from the waters, and a sure sign of the times was when Harrison Williams, the utility magnate, was forced to sell his *Warrior,* built at the cost of more than a million dollars, for a price less than the cost of her launches.

One of the few luxury yachts which went down the ways during the Depression was the *Hussar,* built by Edward F. Hutton, well-known financial figure and husband of Marjorie Post, Postum and General Foods heiress.

Yet there was one yacht that serenely sailed her way through the stormy seas of the Desperate Years. Vincent Astor's *Nourmahal* probably had more history written or discussed on her decks than any other privately owned yacht.

Astor, a firmly established member of President Roosevelt's inner circle, first welcomed FDR aboard his *Nourmahal* in February, 1933. After a ten-day cruise, FDR went ashore at Miami, where the attempt was made on his

E. F. Hutton's barkentine Hussar.

life which resulted in the slaying of Chicago's Mayor Anton Cermak. During the next few years Roosevelt, his son James, and Harry Hopkins sailed many times aboard Astor's yacht.

However, in March of 1935, FDR had Congress pass his "soak the rich" tax program. That ended FDR's cruising days aboard the *Nourmahal.* Like all the other wealthy yachtsmen, Astor found it impossible to maintain a luxury yacht under the new tax laws. That year saw the yachts which their owners had somehow kept afloat scrapped or towed

in drydock. In March, 1938, Mrs. Emily Roebling Cadwalader, wife of Richard McCall Cadwalader, heiress to the Roebling fortune, sold her huge *Savarona* to Turkey as a present for that country's president, Kemal Ataturk. The cost was a million dollars; the yacht had been constructed at the cost of two million and was probably the most luxurious ship afloat. The depression years had forced the Philadelphia yachtswoman to dock the *Savarona* in Germany for five years at an annual cost of about $70,000.

Vincent Astor's 265-foot yacht Alva.

J. P. Morgan's luxurious yacht Corsair, later turned over to the Coast Guard for use by the Geodetic Survey.

W. K. Vanderbilt's yacht Nourmahal.

Highlights and Sidelights: 1931

To START the year off properly, the governors of thirty states met in New York and issued high-sounding phrases and promises. This was zero hour, they said, the battle against the Depression must be won. The AFL, the Association of National Advertisers, the American Legion Auxiliary, and other organizations opened headquarters with the goal of placing one million men in jobs. It all sounded fine but outside the Waldorf, where the meeting was held, were two apple-peddlers. . . . Larry Fay and sixty others were acquitted in a gigantic milk scandal, but the sallow-faced racketeer wasn't long for this world anyway. . . . In Moscow the first of the "treason trials" were starting, and in the Vatican Pope Pius XI was making his first world broadcast with equipment installed by no less than Marconi himself. . . . The fires of revolution were burning bright in Spain with King Alfonso deposed. . . . In Detroit, Henry Ford's assembly line produced its 20,000,000th tin lizzie and Henry himself was on hand to drive it down the

street. . . . In the quiet graveyard in Duxbury, Massachusetts, a lead casket was lowered into a grave. Miles Standish, that gallant Puritan, was being reburied after all these years. . . . They were still digging in New York and this time they finally finished the BMT spur line which ran under Nassau Street. Aboard the first train was Jimmy Walker, who insisted he had stayed up all night to be on hand. . . . And before the year was out New Yorkers were getting a stiff neck staring upward at the huge, silver, cigar-shaped *Graf Zeppelin,* which was making its first trip to the United States. . . . While new stars were born, old stars winked out. David Belasco died this year. George M. Cohan was still on the stage, but his theatre activities were limited. . . . In the world of books, William Faulkner's *Sanctuary* created a sensation. . . . Hollywood momentarily forgot commercial pictures, the ones that would entertain and make money, and almost in spite of itself the film capital brought out a picture of great realism which ex-

posed the wrongs and injustices suffered by Americans because of the Depression. *I Am a Fugitive from a Chain Gang,* based on Robert Burns' shocking experiences, caused such a furor that many abuses in the chain-gang system were abolished. . . . The Radio Keith Orpheum Corporation, which controlled New York's famous Palace, announced it would be turned into a motion-picture theatre. This was the death knell of vaudeville. The first movie to be shown on a two-a-day basis was *The Kid from Brooklyn,* starring Eddie Cantor. The Palace had opened on March 24, 1913, as a music hall and variety house. The opening bill had included a young and upcoming comedian named Ed Wynn in a skit called "The King's Jester." . . . A former stenographer from Astoria named Ethel Merman became an overnight star when critics and the paying customers liked the way she belted out "Edie Was a Lady." She would take Broadway by storm in *Take a Chance* and in *Anything Goes.*

1932 Chrysler Imperial Eight.

1931 La Salle, with its "sensational hood ports and new interior trim."

1932 Stutz Continental Coupe, "mounted on a Safety Stutz DV 32, 134½-inch wheelbase chassis."

1931 Ford Model A "Cabriolet."

Pope Pius XI shortly before his death.

The Duke of Toledo, formerly King Alfonso of Spain.

William Faulkner.

Florenz Ziegfeld.

Henry Ford at the White House.

The Forgotten Man Is Remembered for the 1932 Presidential Campaign

(Left to right) Louis McHenry Howe, Franklin D. Roosevelt, and James A. Farley.

"WHATEVER YOU DO, Jim, is all right with me," was Governor Franklin Delano Roosevelt's reply to his campaign manager, James J. Farley, one January day in 1932 when Farley told him he had put him in the race for the Democratic nomination for the Presidency.

After the landslide in 1930 that had sent Roosevelt back to Albany, there was little doubt that FDR would be a leading candidate. In fact, he told Bronx County boss Ed Flynn, "I have the feeling I can be elected if nominated."

It was the most promising year for the Democrats since the Smith debacle. Conditions were really bad and millions were existing on charity or meager rations. The Republicans were the logical villains: four years before, they had thundered that if Smith were elected

Americans could only hope for soup kitchens. But Smith had been defeated and there were a great many soup kitchens and breadlines as well.

In Washington, President Hoover tried many measures to help the economic situation, such as the Reconstruction Finance Corporation, which allowed federal aid for banks and businesses, and began to yield to party pressure to provide some measure of federal aid for local relief. The RFC was effective and very helpful. By making needed funds available it could stem the tide for a while. But that was not enough.

1932

While Hoover was attempting to move the ponderous federal legal machine, Governor Roosevelt acted. In March, 1930, he set up an emergency unemployment committee, to consider long-range proposals for stabilizing unemployment. Later that same year Roosevelt took steps to expand public works to relieve unemployment. Despite the opposition of the American Federation of Labor to compulsory unemployment insurance, FDR favored such a plan and proposed a state program. In August, 1931, he got the legislature to create an Emergency Relief Administration. Twenty million dollars was appropriated to help New Yorkers get through the terrible winter of 1931-32. As administrator for this program, Roosevelt selected a gaunt, sharp-faced New York social worker named Harry Hopkins.

58

(Left to right) Secretary of State Ed Flynn, Louis McHenry Howe, and Governor Roosevelt at a picnic for state employees Roosevelt gave at Hyde Park.

Roosevelt predicted that the main issue of the campaign, no matter who ran, would be the economic condition of the country. Aiding him in plotting campaign strategy on this basis were two master politicians, as different as butter and curds: James J. Farley, "Jim" to thousands of party workers, county leaders and state and government officials, and Louis Howe, who had been associated with FDR for as long as they both could remember. While Farley was big, jovial, back-slapping, Howe was gnomelike—a superb puller of strings, a Machiavelli in a rumpled blue suit.

By the spring of 1932, Farley and Howe had made their major moves. Between them they had cut up the country for Farley's elaborate journey across eighteen states; his object was to sound out the sentiments of the state chairmen and, if they were not for Roosevelt, to get them to change their minds.

At the end of his tour Farley knew what lay before them. Some were for Roosevelt, some were on the fence, a number were for native sons, and some talked big though whether they would ever deliver was doubtful.

Another thorn to be removed was Tammany. Roosevelt had wisely leaned to the anti-Tammany forces, even to the extent of shocking the sachems by cooperating with the Republicans to appoint a committee to investigate New York City's administration.

Then there was Al Smith, the bitterly defeated 1928 candidate, who still had enormous popularity not only in New York City but throughout the country. There were many who recalled that Smith had predicted some of the crime and corruption which would follow, should the Eighteenth Amendment continue to stay on the books. Yet he had indicated to Farley that he would not be a candidate. Thus it was with some shock that Roosevelt forces later heard he was intending to run. In an interview published in the Atlanta *Constitution,* Smith bitterly condemned Roosevelt for not seeking his advice during his term as governor and for accepting advice from those "damn fools" around him. It was a break in an old political and personal friendship.

On January 23, 1932, Smith formally announced his candidacy. The reasons were simple. To this wily politician, a Democratic victory seemed certain this election year; the Republicans had been caught in the trap of the Depression. Al Smith knew that if he was ever to sit in the White House this was his last and best opportunity.

Harry L. Hopkins.

59

Mayor ("I am the law") Frank Hague and Franklin D. Roosevelt at Hague's home in Deal, N. J.

Now the preconvention maneuvering began in the camps of the various candidates, from John Nance Garner to George White, governor of Ohio. In April, Smith carried the Massachusetts primary and there was gloom in the Roosevelt camp. In late May, in a three-way contest in California, Garner came in first, Roosevelt second, and Smith third. The first-ballot hopes of the Roosevelt supporters began to grow dim.

Roosevelt took to the campaign wars with zeal and relish. He adopted a militant stand on the unemployment situation and in 1932 coined, or at least gave currency to, one of the most notable terms in American politics: "The Forgotten Man."

Smith, in his rasping, East Side–West Side voice, blasted Roosevelt again and again for setting class against class, poor against rich.

The convention opened on June 27,

1932. Roosevelt's chances for a first-ballot nomination appeared slim. The key was held by the midwestern states Ohio, Indiana, and Illinois. Ohio had suddenly shifted to her favorite son, Governor George White, Indiana was for Paul V. McNutt and Illinois declared for Senator J. Hamilton Lewis, whose flaring whiskers and flamboyant clothes earned him the name of the "aurora borealis of Illinois."

Then Senator Huey Long, the Louisiana Kingfish, almost sank the Roosevelt ship. In a wild, arm-waving speech he declared that the nomination this year should be by majority and not by the traditional two-thirds vote. This proposal raised a storm, and the Roosevelt strategists were caught in a pocket. They couldn't fight Long with his powerful pro-Roosevelt delegation, but other delegations from the South were beginning to waver from the Roosevelt cause, because the old two-thirds vote

had favored southern interests. Farley, who had taken pains not to connect FDR with Long's proposal, finally resolved the dilemma by announcing that he was willing to go along with the two-thirds vote but considered it "undemocratic."

Now that party lines were repaired, Jim Farley swung into action to gather delegates. He was everywhere those hot sweltering days, slapping backs, shaking hands, recalling thousands of names with his amazing memory, while in the Tammany delegation Al Smith sat stony faced. The first roll call gave Roosevelt 666¼, Smith 201¾, Garner 90¼, and White 52. Roosevelt was about one hundred short of the two-thirds needed.

Plainly there was no Roosevelt avalanche. On the third ballot he picked up a few more votes, but the Roosevelt charm hadn't reached the sweating, plotting delegations.

Then, late in the afternoon, through the influence of newspaper publisher William Randolph Hearst, Garner gave Representative Sam Rayburn the word that the Texas delegation was giving its support to Roosevelt. On the fourth roll call, William Gibbs McAdoo, Woodrow Wilson's son-in-law and a former secretary of the treasury, who himself had been bitterly defeated by the two-thirds vote just eight years before, came to the rostrum and in a ringing, memorable speech announced that California was casting her forty-four votes for Governor Roosevelt. Then the avalanche came.

Bitter and defeated, Al Smith left Chicago before Roosevelt arrived. Veteran politicians who knew Smith predicted he would campaign against FDR. When he was asked in New York if he would help Roosevelt, the Happy Warrior just shrugged.

As Roosevelt said: "I think he wants to work it out in his own way and in his own time."

Later Smith put party before personal feelings and vigorously campaigned for Roosevelt in Massachusetts and Connecticut. But Al Smith never forgot that Roosevelt had beaten him at a time when a Democratic victory was almost a certainty. It would not be long before the increasing strain and bitterness built up to such a pitch that Smith could no longer disguise his feelings. In the end he became one of Roosevelt's bitterest enemies.

But this was in the future. Now, in Chicago, Roosevelt was proving to his party that he was a phrasemaker: "I pledge you, I pledge myself to the new deal for the American people. . . ."

It had been just another phrase to the speechmakers, and even to FDR himself. But it leaped into the headlines that night and before dawn was a part of the history of our nation's Desperate Years.

The 1932 campaign was bitter, not so much between Democrat and Republican as between Democrat and Democrat. Jim Farley and Louis Howe again did the unconventional by avoiding the party hacks and bosses and getting right to the humble but important party workers. There were tons of ribbons, buttons, flags, banners, and personal letters, sometimes signed in Farley's famous green ink. But in Tammany the sullen sachems sat on their hands. When Jimmy Walker resigned rather than face hearings on Seabury's charges,

there was a collective sigh of relief; the Republicans now had lost their major national issue of big-city corruption.

Roosevelt's target, of course, was the issue he had predicted: the country's economic plight. His picture of Hoover as a cold, aloof man doing nothing in a time of danger, became the popular image. Hoover struck back at what he called Roosevelt radicalism and collectivism, but the voters had eyes only for the twin villains: Depression and the Republicans.

Roosevelt's whirlwind cross-country campaign swelled his growing popularity. But Hoover just sniffed and remarked that the country squire from

vote to Hoover's 15,759,930. He carried 42 states for 472 electoral votes. The new Senate also would be Democratic, by 59 to 37, the House by 312 to 123.

After the election a new, faint breeze of hope seemed to be drifting across the land. Men began to say that the Depression would finally turn Mr. Hoover's "corner" when the new programs of the Roosevelt administration went into effect. But FDR was silent. When Hoover advised him in November that they had better meet over England's proposal of suspension of her debts, FDR adroitly sidestepped the issue and let Hoover "take care of his own baby."

Franklin D. Roosevelt, Farley, and Al Smith at the 1932 Democratic State Convention. Smith said, "How are you, old potato?"

FDR replied, "Glad to see you, Al." Then, "Al, this is from the heart." Smith said, "Frank, that goes for me, too!"

New York seemed like a "chameleon on plaid."

Looking back, one remembers vividly the magnetism of Roosevelt during the first campaign, the newsreels of the huge, silent crowds under the Kansas sun, the wonderfully appealing Harvard-accented voice over the radio, the crowds that ran after his train in New England.

In the end the people spoke. It was almost a national landslide for FDR. He was elected by 22,815,539 popular

Meanwhile FDR cleared up his affairs in Albany, conferred with Secretary of State Stimson, visited his beloved children at Warm Springs, sailed on Vincent Astor's yacht, and generally kept the small army of newspapermen who followed him in the dark as to his next moves and appointments.

He would only captivate the reporters with his grin, tilt his cigarette holder skyward and slyly inform the newsmen they would know all he knew—after March 4, 1933.

61

The Crime of the Century

THE SHABBY, green-painted sedan chugged up a road in New Jersey's Sourland Mountains and stopped near the clapboard mansion, bone-white in the moonlight. A man carefully raised a homemade ladder, climbed it swiftly, and swung inside the window. The child in the nursery whimpered sleepily as he was lifted from the crib. Then came the hurried descent, the fall from the ladder. A few minutes later the car was racing back down the dark roads.

It was the night of March 1, 1932. Charles Augustus Lindbergh, Jr., twenty months old, had been kidnapped.

The crime was perhaps without parallel in the public shock, indignation, and fury it produced. The nation and all the civilized world was appalled. Tiny Charles was the son of an idol, the Lone Eagle who had flown all the way across the Atlantic in 1927, the first ever to do so.

The child's absence was discovered later that night by nurse Betty Gow. Anne Morrow Lindbergh, pregnant with her second child, was preparing for bed; Colonel Charles A. Lindbergh was in the downstairs library reading. Betty hurried from one to the other. Neither had the baby. Lindy rushed upstairs. Just inside the open window, its shutter warped so it could not be tightly closed, was an envelope containing a crudely written note. It read:

> Dear Sir
>   Have 50000$ ready 25000$ in 20$ bills 15000$ in 10$ bills and 10000$ in 5$ bills After 2-4 days we will inform you were to deliver the money We warn you for making anyding public or for notify the pol [rest of the word was blurred] The child is in Gut care
>   Indication for all letters are singnature and three holes

The letter ended with a design of interlocking circles and pierced holes.

Despair and fury shook Lindbergh as he read the note. But with the good sense of a man of fortitude, he told the police, who swarmed over the house

Charles A. Lindbergh.

within minutes, "Please be careful of fingerprints."

At first everyone expected that the kidnapper would be caught within hours. After all wasn't every road and bridge in New Jersey sealed off—every citizen, every policeman on the entire eastern seaboard watching for the car, for clues? He must be caught soon . . . No one foresaw the long, dreary, heartbreaking search that would follow.

There was one wild moment when police found Henry (Red) Johnson,

Betty Gow's admirer, in Hartford after an all-night drive, a bottle of milk in his car. But Johnson was cleared quickly. Then Oliver Whateley, Lindbergh's butler, Mrs. Whateley, Betty Gow, and Violet Sharpe (who later committed suicide under the stress of police questioning), were also cleared.

On March 7, the *Bronx Home News* received a letter from Dr. John F. Condon, Bronx schoolteacher. There was nothing new in this; Dr. Condon had been writing the *Home News* for years on almost every conceivable subject. But in this letter Condon offered to pay one thousand dollars out of his small savings to the kidnapper if he would return the child.

The editors who knew Condon smiled when they read the letter, but someone decided that a brief story should be written on his offer. The letter lay on a rewriteman's desk for hours and was almost forgotten, but a news brief finally appeared in the March 8 edition.

The next day Condon received a letter bearing a cabalistic symbol of interlocking circles in red and blue. He was informed that he had been selected to act as negotiator between the Lindbergh family and the kidnapper. Condon contacted Lindbergh, who asked him to come to Hopewell, New Jersey, at once.

There police experts compared the symbols; they were found to be the same as were used in the original kidnap note. The Lindberghs authorized Dr. Condon to act in the matter, and several notes followed, including messages inserted in a newspaper "personal" column, setting up a meeting.

Today Dr. Condon's ransom negotiations with the famous "John" seem almost unbelievable. They met twice, both times near a cemetery. All the trappings of a badly written melodrama were present: the deep-voiced stranger "John," wisps of clouds trailing across the moon, the night wind moaning through the trees, gleaming tombstones nearby.

At one of their meetings, on April 2, Dr. Condon gave the stranger fifty thousand dollars and a note was turned over by John saying the child was aboard "boad Nelly" near Martha's Vineyard. Lindbergh took to the sky to search for the boat and his baby. He crossed and crisscrossed the area, scanning the fishing boats with powerful glasses.

There was nothing.

But his cup of anguish was not yet filled. In April, Gaston Means, a former Department of Justice investigator who had spent two years in prison and had once been placed on trial for murder, persuaded Washington heiress Mrs. Evalyn Walsh McLean that he was in touch with the kidnappers. Mrs. McLean gave him $100,000 on his promise that the child would be turned over to a priest in Washington.

Again nothing.

When the child was not produced, Mrs. McLean went to her attorneys, who notified police. Means was arrested and indicted.

But there was still another cruel, heartrending hoax. John Hughes Curtis, a socialite shipbuilder whose fortune had been wiped out by the Depression, came to the Lindbergh home with a weird story.

As he told it, he had been driving in Norfolk when a stranger jumped on the running board of his car and asked if he would be the go-between in the payment of the ransom. Curtis agreed, and the stranger then told him the baby was aboard a two-masted fishing schooner. Again Lindbergh believed. He spent two days searching for the boat off the Virginia capes. He returned to learn that the body of his son had

BABY KIDNAPED FROM this ROOM

SUPPOSED ROUTE of KIDNAPERS

Photo diagram showing course taken by kidnapper of the Lindbergh baby.

been found in the woods not far from his home.

When Curtis showed up at the Hopewell house, he was greeted by police. In the early hours of the morning he asked for a typewriter and began typing feverishly.

"At the present time," he wrote, "I am sane. But I honestly believe that for the past seven or eight months I have not been myself due to financial troubles . . ."

Curtis was tried and fined a thousand dollars. Means was sent to prison for fifteen years.

Justice James M. Proctor, who presided over his trial, observed, "The Lindbergh case brought out all the best in the hearts of men, but also gave opportunity to some to display the weakness and wickedness of human nature. . . ."

While state and federal police were methodically hunting for clues to the kidnap-murderer, a sharp-faced New York City detective was put at the head of a team of more than a hundred detectives who were assigned to the case. Lieutenant James J. Finn had been personally selected by Colonel Lindbergh, who remembered the soft-spoken police officer from the time of his hero's welcome in 1927, when Finn had been one of his bodyguards.

Finn's greatest attribute was an infinite patience. He had a theory, almost an obsession as he later called it, that the kidnapper would be caught passing the ransom money. He constructed a large chart of the metropolitan area and with other officers—federal, state and city—started to travel the more than 76,000 square miles on the trail of the bloody money.

The first note had appeared on April 4, in the East River Savings Bank at Ninety-Sixth Street and Amsterdam Avenue. Finn and Treasury agents hurried to the bank, but no one could recall who had handed in the bill. Hundreds of accounts, hundreds of deposits were checked. They yielded nothing.

Every month or so a bill trickled in —a five here, a ten there. In a confidential room at Police Headquarters, Finn carefully stuck colored pins into the map to show where the bills had turned up. A forest of pins began to grow, but like a forest, grew slowly.

While Finn studied his map, a federal expert named Arthur Koehler was matching pieces of wood. Like Finn, Koehler had infinite patience.

Officer pointing to shuttered window of the Lindberghs' nursery.

The white-haired scientist practically lived with the ladder used by the kidnapper. It was in three sections, each seven feet long, expertly joined together but broken in the middle—apparently under the weight of the kidnapper and the child. The nails were cleanly driven, the saw cuts smooth and true. Every rung was even. The three sections fitted perfectly, round pins sliding easily into grooves drilled for that purpose.

Only a man skilled with tools could have made that ladder.

But the two rails caught Koehler's attention as the days passed. Both edges had been planed with a plane not in good condition which had left ridges. The microscope told him that the wood had passed through a planer at 93/100 inch for every revolution of the top and bottom cutter heads, and 86/100 inch per revolution on the side heads.

This meant there were eight knives in the top and bottom cutter heads and six knives on the side head.

For the rest of the year Koehler checked every planing mill from Alabama to New York. Only twenty-five used such a planer. Two were ruled out because they did not dress lumber. Each of the twenty-three other firms supplied samples of dressed lumber; only one bore revolution marks identical to those found on the kidnapper's ladder. That company was in McCormick, South Carolina, and out of forty-five shipments made during the period before the crime, Koehler traced one to a Bronx lumber yard.

Finn's map, Koehler's wood . . . wood and dollars were building a bridge to the electric chair for a man who still remains one of the most enigmatic criminals of the twentieth century.

WANTED

INFORMATION AS TO THE WHEREABOUTS OF

CHAS. A. LINDBERGH, Jr.

OF HOPEWELL, N. J.

SON OF COL. CHAS. A. LINDBERGH

World-Famous Aviator

This child was kidnaped from his home in Hopewell, N. J., between 8 and 10 p. m. on Tuesday, March 1, 1932.

DESCRIPTION:

Age, 20 months	Hair, blond, curly
Weight, 27 to 30 lbs.	Eyes, dark blue
Height, 29 inches	Complexion, light

Deep dimple in center of chin
Dressed in one-piece coverall night suit

ADDRESS ALL COMMUNICATIONS TO
COL. H. N. SCHWARZKOPF, TRENTON, N. J., or
COL. CHAS. A. LINDBERGH, HOPEWELL, N. J.

ALL COMMUNICATIONS WILL BE TREATED IN CONFIDENCE

March 11, 1932

COL. H. NORMAN SCHWARZKOPF
Supt. New Jersey State Police, Trenton, N. J.

Reward poster of New Jersey state police.

The Big Parades

SATURDAY, MAY 14, 1932, was the day of the Big Parades throughout the country. They were not held in honor of great events, famous heroes past or present, holidays or days of tribute; they were held in honor of beer, that cool, foam-flecked, glorious beverage which had been denied Americans for so many years.

Technically the parades were held to establish a point: that taxes derived from the sale of beer could help reduce unemployment, oil the rusted wheels of industry, build hospitals and schools, and in general do good all around.

The idea caught on quickly. Actually it was all part of the growing tide of revulsion against the Eighteenth Amendment which was gathering strength this year.

The parades were nationwide. In Detroit, 15,000 marchers, including 172 labor organizations and hundreds of floats placarded with anti-dry messages, paraded for hours. In Syracuse, more than a thousand persons marched while the chimes in a nearby Baptist church played "Onward, Christian Soldiers." In Princeton, two hundred college students joined the marchers, holding aloft placards "We Want Beer." The marchers in Daytona Beach gave their parade a realistic touch: they served beer to the marchers from twenty-gallon barrels. In villages, small towns, and cities, bands played, marchers held high their messages, and automobiles followed trailing streamers of colored crepe paper.

Of all the parades, New York's was the longest and the most colorful. All day long and through the night, countless lines of marchers paraded up Fifth Avenue, led by Jimmy Walker. No man was kept out for lack of a uniform or a horse. There were hundreds of bands, and when the bands gave out their places were taken by sound trucks. Airplanes circled overhead. The police made various estimates of the marchers and the crowds, ranging from one hundred thousand to "a couple of million."

But if the numbers were in dispute, the feelings of the marchers were not; everyone was interested in beer. At the reviewing stand at Seventy-Second Street and Central Park West, huge charts displayed statistics in black and red of how a tax on beer would help battle the Depression.

The marchers came from every borough in the city. There were professional groups, veterans organizations, and foreign groups. There were signs, some two stories high, proclaiming, "We Want Beer and We Will Pay the Tax."

There were also more somber signs, such as, "We Want Beer but We Also Want Jobs."

That night men and women with tin growlers marched and sang under red-light torches. There was dancing in the streets, particularly when the German-American delegations, more than six thousand strong, many in native costumes, appeared.

Through it all, Jimmy Walker smiled and quipped. At dawn he made a brief speech and said good-night. He had tipped his derby so often it had a hole in the rim.

But in Hoboken, New Jersey, where beer drinkers had little trouble getting their favorite brew, there were no parades. The traditionally wet city saw no reason to bring coals to Newcastle.

Gene Tunney raising his hat in the 1932 Beer Parade.

The Massie Case and the Unwritten Law in Hawaii

Clarence Darrow (center) flanked by (left to right) Edward J. Lord, seaman; Mrs. Grace H. Fortescue; her son-in-law, Lieutenant Thomas H. Massie; and Seaman Albert O. Jones.

THE PRESS tagged it "The Massie Case," and it became one of the most remarkable crime stories of the country, though it took place in what was then the Territory of Hawaii.

The leading characters in the strange case were Lieutenant Thomas H. Massie, a young naval officer stationed in Hawaii; his pretty wife, Thalia; a handsome beach boy, Joe Kahawawai; two teenage sailors, E. J. Lord and A. O. Jones; and Mrs. Massie's mother, Mrs. Granville Fortescue.

The beach boy was one of five defendants charged with criminally assaulting Mrs. Massie. She had left a party to walk down the beach for some air, when the attack occurred. The five were arrested and released on bail, pending a trial.

In the months that went by before the trial, it developed that the main tragedy was not the assault but its aftermath. Gossip insisted that Mrs. Massie had not told the entire story. Suspicion grew so strong that it colored the lives of the handsome, athletic naval officer and his wife. As Massie later testified, "Everyone shunned me and avoided me like hell."

Finally, driven to distraction, he begged his friends to tell him what to do.

"Get a confession from one of them that they assaulted your wife," he was advised.

With this purpose in mind, Massie, the young sailors, Lord and Jones, and Mrs. Fortescue summoned one of the beach boys to Massie's flower-decked cottage. In a manner reminiscent of the South, circa 1830, Massie asked the boy if he had assaulted his wife.

"It is true. We done it," the boy said.

Hearing the words said produced a powerful reaction in Massie. For a moment he seemed stunned. Then he pulled out his service revolver and shot the boy through the heart.

The sailors and Mrs. Fortescue stood stiff as statues. Then, as the beach boy twitched in his death throes, young Jones cried out, "My God, lieutenant, you're a damn fool!"

Months later Massie would recall that at that moment, his uppermost emotion was "resentment" of this from an enlisted man.

What followed was never really explained. The witnesses agreed that "everyone was in a daze." Later, Massie, the two enlisted men, and Mrs. Fortescue were arrested with the body of the native in the rear of their car. They had been bound for Koko Head, a bluff overlooking the sea.

The four were indicted for second-degree murder, and the case drew international attention. In Hawaii, which

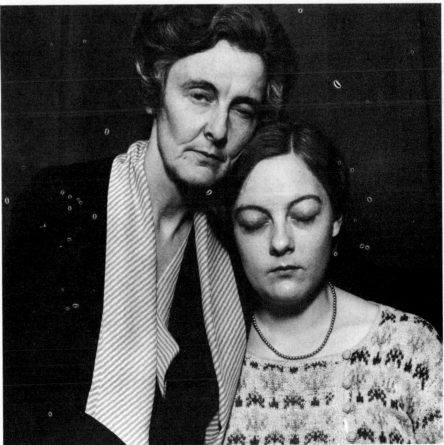

Mrs. Fortescue with her daughter, Mrs. Thomas H. Massie.

had always been staunchly loyal to the States, it touched off riots and attacks on servicemen. As the clashes became more violent, the territorial authorities rushed Massie, his mother-in-law, and the sailors to trial.

Clarence Darrow volunteered and was accepted as defense counsel, and one of the most sensational trials of the thirties got under way.

Massie's testimony was the highlight. He swore that he was driven almost to the verge of a breakdown by the whispering and the gossip that followed the attack. When the prosecutor, John C. Kelley, tried to refresh his memory as to whether he had sought legal advice on the question of the legality of the unwritten law, he was vague.

The trial produced many sensations, not the least being the fact that Massie had discussed the case with the Chief of Navy Operations and the Commandant of Pearl Harbor.

The jury was composed of five native Americans, three Chinese, a Dane, a German, a Portuguese, and a Hawaiian. After eight hours deliberation they found the four defendants guilty.

Congress was besieged with petitions. Governor Judd of Hawaii was swamped by telegrams, delegations, and appeals. Darrow thundered that he would appeal to the Supreme Court. Then the prisoners were unexpectedly ordered brought from Pearl Harbor, where they had been in custody, to the Circuit Court to be sentenced. After they had been sentenced, it was announced that Governor Judd had commuted their terms to one hour each. They served them—sitting in the courtroom as the clock ticked away the sixty minutes. Then Lieutenant Massie, his wife, and her mother, slipped aboard the S. S. *Malolo* for San Francisco.

When they docked, Thalia, her big blue eyes looking larger than ever in a dead white face, told reporters she was sure her husband and her mother would eventually receive full pardon. The full pardons were never granted, but a few days after the family had arrived in this country, Governor Laffoon of Kentucky restored full citizenship rights to Massie.

Lieutenant Massie was transferred to duty aboard the U.S.S. *New Mexico* at Philadelphia, and his wife and mother-in-law accompanied him east. As the months passed and the story faded from the headlines, there were rumors of a rift between the Massies. When he was later sent to California, Thalia did not accompany him.

Thalia finally divorced Massie. When reporters in Reno asked her if she intended to marry again, she quipped, "Of course. I'm going to marry Clark Gable, didn't you hear?"

Tragedy shadowed Thalia's subsequent life. A few hours after the divorce was granted she became critically ill. Her friends said at first that she had poured poison into a cocktail and drunk all of it; the next day both the local sheriff and her companions at her "divorce celebration" denied the story.

On a trip to Italy for her health, she slashed her wrists and was confined to a sanitarium in Genoa. She finally slipped into obscurity where she remained until 1950, when she was sued for ten thousand dollars for attacking her landlady in Los Angeles. News dispatches gave a brief description of the sensational case of which she had been the central figure.

The story rated seven lines. In one large city paper, it was buried on the obituary page.

Mrs. Massie and husband. In the rear are Seaman Jones and Mrs. Fortescue.

PHAR LAP:
The Wink of the Skies

IN SAN FRANCISCO, David J. Davis, the American and Australian sportsman, picked up the phone.

"I wish to send a telegram," he whispered.

"To whom, sir?" the operator asked.

"To the world," Davis said brokenly. "I want to tell them that Bobby is dead."

The telegram that "Bobby" was dead did finally arrive at the office of Harry Telford, a noted Australian racing figure. When he read it he wept, as did most racing fans when the news was made public.

For Bobby, known officially as Phar Lap, was one of the world's great racehorses. Thirty years later trainers, jockeys, and racing fans still talk about the lanky gelding who might have outshone the immortal Man o' War had he lived.

Phar Lap means "The Wink of the Skies," a Javanese expression for lightning, and the horse captured the attention of American fans—like lightning—from the beginning.

Davis, who had spent many years in Australia, bought the horse there for $800 and took his friend Telford into partnership. A disappointment as a two-year-old, the horse with the bright chestnut coat became a world figure in racing as a three-year-old. Known as the Wonder Horse and the Red Terror, Phar Lap won the famous Melbourne cup carrying the high weight of 138 pounds. He lost only one race, and that was another try, as a five-year-old, at the Melbourne Cup in which he was asked to carry 150 pounds.

Phar Lap had just turned six when he pranced down the gangplank in San Francisco on January 15, 1932, as chipper after the rough eighteen-day voyage from New Zealand as if he had been training every day. American turfmen shook their heads in amazement at the chance Davis had taken with such a valuable piece of horseflesh, but they cried out in horror when Davis casually announced he didn't carry any insurance on Phar Lap, "because no sum they could name could ever represent the true value of Bobby."

Everything Phar Lap and his owners did was different. Even Phar Lap's saddle was different; it was made of kangaroo and lizard skin. At Agua Caliente, while the other owners and jockeys pampered their mounts, Billie Elliott, the Australian rider, nonchalantly mounted just before the race started and slipped into his position. Phar Lap won in a walk.

America took the big horse to its heart. Besides being a beautiful animal, Phar Lap seemed to have a sense of humor and a magnetic personality all his own. When he ran crowds flocked to see him. Even the King of England cabled his best wishes.

He easily won all cups and all races. But in Menlo Park, Phar Lap ran his last race. He was found kicking in convulsions in his stall, and died despite the skill of the country's best veterinarians.

Immediately reports circulated that American gangsters had poisoned the horse. Davis ordered an autopsy, which for a time seemed to bear out the rumors. The horse's stomach was badly inflamed and perforated. Members of the Hooper Medical Foundation of the University of California were called in. Two milligrams of arsenate of lead were discovered, but the experts pointed out that this minute amount should have been beneficial instead of harmful.

Further investigation revealed that oak trees surrounding the paddock where Phar Lap had romped had been sprayed with arsenate of lead to kill insects, and dew and rain had probably washed off some onto the grass. The official decision was that Phar Lap had died of perforation of the stomach caused by gastric ulcers complicated with colic resulting from eating too much grass, which had distended the inflamed stomach and smothered the heart action.

Phar Lap's body was stuffed and, after being exhibited at all the major American tracks, was shipped back to his native Australia.

Bobby had come home.

Phar Lap, the mighty Australian racehorse.

69

Death of a Tobacco Tycoon

ALL EVENING, while the guests sang and danced and the ice tinkled in the tall glasses, twenty-year-old Zachary Smith (Skipper) Reynolds, heir to the $30,-000,000 tobacco fortune, seemed distracted. He appeared to be waiting for someone or for something to happen. Something tragic did happen that night in the mansion outside Winston-Salem, North Carolina. At exactly 1 A.M., the crash of a shot rang through the house.

The guests ran toward the sound to find Skipper lying with a bullet in his head on the floor of the bedroom of his beautiful wife, Broadway singer Libby Holman. Libby, her lace-trimmed negligee drenched with blood, was sobbing and screaming, "Smith's killed himself!"

Reynolds was hurried to the Baptist Hospital in New Salem where he died four hours later without regaining consciousness. Police arrived eight hours after the shooting, and at first could not find the .32-caliber Mauser automatic to match the bullet. On the third time round they finally came across the weapon, on the sleeping porch not far from the room where Reynolds had been shot. They also found his wife's lounging pajamas in the room shared by Albert Bailey and Ab Walker, Reynold's closest friends. Coroner W. N. Dalton of Forsyth County delivered a verdict of suicide; Smith's guardian, a high official of the Reynolds Tobacco Company, agreed.

But Raymond Kramer, Smith's tutor, didn't see it that way; he told police Reynolds had not appeared melancholy—"In fact he had looked as if he were expecting someone."

A local sheriff and a Forsyth County solicitor jumped into the investigation and reopened the case. Even the employees of the Reynolds estate got into the act when the local sheriff gave them deputy badges and enlisted their help.

Coroner Dalton suddenly changed his mind and ordered an inquest but barred the press. He had reckoned without the two Winston-Salem newspapers, however; they raised such an editorial fuss that he quickly reversed his ruling and the press was allowed.

Libby, red-eyed but beautiful, told how Smith had called her name as he held the gun, then fell as the shot came. She swore that Smith had

Zachary Smith Reynolds, husband of Libby Holman.

threatened suicide on other occasions, because he was brooding over his inadequacy as a man. However, in the next breath she disclosed she was two months pregnant. The courtroom was plainly puzzled: how could a man consider himself inadequate when he was the father of a two-year-old child by another marriage and knew that his second wife was pregnant?

The verdict finally rendered was "death from a bullet wound inflicted by a person or persons unknown to the jury."

Despite the inquest's finding, Libby was charged with murder and Ab Walker as an accessory. Libby's father, a prominent Ohio lawyer, excoriated the Forsyth County officials, charging them with playing small-time politics and making his daughter the victim of a horrible miscarriage of justice. In midsummer the county grand jury indicted her for first-degree murder, a charge later reduced to second-degree. Walker, indicted as an accessory, was released in $25,000 bail. But the case never came to trial. Smith's uncle and titular head of the clan wrote to Solicitor Carlisle Higgins that the family would be just as happy if the charges were dropped. That fall this was done.

Two months later Libby gave birth to a son, Christopher, who, she hoped, would one day be an aviator.

Echoes of the mystifying death drifted through the legal complications

My Girl has turned me down. Good bye forever. Give My love to Mary, Virginia, Nancy Dick etc. Good bye cruel world, Smith

Reynolds and his "warning of death."

that new decision threatened to eliminate him as an heir.

The bitter contest was finally settled when the courts awarded Christopher, then two, and Anne Cannon Smith Reynolds, age four, daughter of his first marriage, major shares of the Reynolds fortune. Anne received $9,740,625, and Christopher $6,492,750.

But for Libby there were few happy days ahead.

Seven years after the court battle she married airman Ralph Holmes, son of veteran actor Taylor Holmes. Holmes had enlisted in the RAF and later transferred to the U.S. Air Corps, where he served with distinction as a navigator, bombardier, and pilot. They separated, and a month later Holmes was found dead of an overdose of sleeping pills.

But there was still more tragedy for Libby. In 1950 her handsome son, who she once had hoped would be an aviator, was killed while scaling a California mountain.

For Libby, life became a flight from heartbreak. She returned to the theatre and toured the United States and Europe in a one-woman show. Her last professional appearance was in 1954 when she starred in *Blues, Ballads and Sin Songs,* on Broadway. It was scheduled to last six days, but popular demand extended the run.

Christopher Smith Reynolds and his mother Libby Holman and stepfather Ralph Holmes.

that followed in settling the estate, as attorneys for Libby and the Reynolds family tried to establish the status of the newborn child. It seemed that nothing would ever go right for Libby. At the very hour a settlement was being decided upon that would give her $750,-000 and her child about $6,000,000, an old decision by the North Carolina State Supreme Court refusing to recognize Nevada divorces was injected into the battle of technicalities. Because Smith's first wife was divorced in Reno, the state's attorneys declared they could not recognize his marriage to Libby. And although there was never any question about Christopher's paternity,

The palatial country home of Zachary Smith Reynolds.

The Man from the Georgia Chain Gang

FOR TEN YEARS Robert Burns had tried to live in obscurity. In his ears were still faint echoes of the baying of bloodhounds tracking him through the Georgia swamp as he made his escape from the chain gang. He was a veteran of World War I, and his crime had been burglarizing $5.29 from a store; he had been out of a job at the time.

Burns knew that Georgia would never forget. No man ever finally escaped the chain gang except in a pine box.

After his break, Burns had known poverty and ignominy, but he had worked hard and in 1930 he was a $20,000-a-year editor of a national magazine in Chicago. Then one day Georgia authorities appeared with extradition papers; his first wife had located him and notified Georgia authorities.

Burns, who later claimed that the state officials had promised him a quick pardon, voluntarily returned to Georgia, only to be sent back to the chain gang

Robert Elliott Burns.

Robert Elliott Burns as a member of the Georgia chain gang.

and its twenty-pound shackles. His brother, a New Jersey minister, made his case a national issue. A hearing was scheduled in the governor's office but before it could take place Burns, despairing of ever being set free, had escaped again. This time he changed his name and ended up in New Jersey as owner of an antique shop. Then he wrote a series of articles which he later amplified into a book, *I Am a Fugitive from a Chain Gang.* It was sold to Hollywood and Paul Muni made a memorable picture in 1931. It was then that Burns's real trouble began.

An outraged State of Georgia demanded his extradition. The hearing in the Trenton State House before Governor Moore was one of the most dramatic of the decade. Heading his defense was Clarence Darrow and endorsing him were the governors of many states. Hundreds of thousands of petitions were introduced.

The hearing brought out many sensational aspects of the Georgia penal system, which included a "sweat box" —a small barrel with iron staves over the top, into which "insolent" convicts were placed. One convict, who had looked "insolently" at a guard, almost died of the punishment. Will P. Cox,

a member of the Society of Penal Information, exhibited pictures of "prison cages," in which the convicts lived. One was built for eighteen men but held thirty-four inmates.

Moore denied the writ, but still Georgia authorities tried to get Burns back. They telegraphed the police chief in the town where Burns lived, asking him to "arrest Robert Burns, an escaped prisoner." The chief tore up the telegram and Burns remained free.

In 1941 Georgia's newly elected Governor Eugene Talmadge tried again, but Governor Edison refused to return the modern Jean Valjean.

Burns, by then the father of two children and secretary of a state association, was bewildered. "How long will they keep this up?" he cried. "Will I never have peace?"

In 1945, by arrangement, Burns returned and, after a dramatic hearing in the state house in Atlanta, Governor Ellis Arnall, who had wiped out the chain-gang system, commuted his original sentence of six to ten years to the time he had served.

Burns, then fifty-five and gray-haired, returned to New Jersey, this time by Pullman, not cringing in the rear of a bouncing truck. He died in 1955.

Eastman of Kodak

THE SOFT-SPOKEN, bespectacled man of seventy-one years had always been meticulous and methodical, and he saw no reason to change his ways now.

In the study of his Rochester, New York, home he penned a simple note which read:

To my friends. My work is done. Why wait?

G. E.

Then he carefully snuffed out the cigarette, screwed the cap back on his fountain pen, removed his glasses and placed them carefully on the table, picked up the revolver, and sent a bullet crashing through his brain.

George Eastman, chairman of the world-famous Eastman Kodak Company, internationally known philanthropist and inventor, was dead. The news of his death stunned the world. Not only had the industry he founded penetrated to the most remote village of the earth, but his philanthropies of 100 million dollars had been scattered abroad as well as in his native land. At the time of his death he was worth about 20 million. He had given away most of the securities he had owned.

Besides founding the Kodak company, the keystone and now the giant of the photographic industry, Eastman had given lavishly to cultural pursuits which had been closed to him in early life by poverty when he was a boy and a young man. To satisfy a deep yearning for fine music, he had established the Eastman Theatre and the Eastman School of Music, and founded the Rochester Symphony Orchestra.

But his greatest feat was the invention of flexible film, which converted photography from a difficult profession to a popular pastime. Instead of heavy, cumbersome glass plates requiring a sizable camera, the photographer could use a small roll of film in a light, easily portable camera. The flexible film also helped the development of motion pictures by Edison.

By using large-scale business methods, Eastman made his films and cameras available at very low prices.

George Eastman.

Not only did he make photography cheap and easy, but by efficient advertising he made the public aware of it. In his own lifetime he saw his favorite slogan, "You push the button and we do the rest" become a legend in the history of American business.

Eastman had been ill for several years, and close associates knew his dread of a lingering illness and years of uselessness.

He once said, borrowing from motion-picture parlance, "I think it is best that I do a fadeout."

George Eastman with a 1000-lb. bear he shot in Alaska.

The Family that Bought New York

JOHN WENDEL, the first of the Wendels, a former partner of John Jacob Astor, had a firm rule which he impressed on his son, who in turn passed it on to his heirs.

"Buy, but never sell, New York real estate."

And buy the Wendels did, until they owned more New York real estate than any other family in the history of Manhattan. Their mansion at Thirty-ninth Street and Fifth Avenue became a landmark, and a popular sight in the early thirties was Ella Virginia von Echtzel Wendel riding down Fifth Avenue in her 166-year-old carriage. Ella, a 78-year-old spinster and last of the landholding family, died in the house that had been both home and prison to generations of Wendels. Ella was the last of six sisters who had all denied themselves marriage and children, to say nothing of social life and recreation, in order to obey the first John Wendel's warning never to allow the estate to be partitioned among "alien hands."

But the Desperate Years had taken their toll of the huge holdings; real estate values had dwindled until the fortune once estimated at $100,000,000 had shrunk to $36,000,000.

Besides his warning never to sell, the family founder also had another admonition: "Never improve a building—it's the land alone that counts." It be-

came a Wendel working rule, even in the case of their own Murray Hill mansion, built in 1856, which never had a doorbell. Ella and her sisters had lived in rooms as old-fashioned as their own rusty black, stiff-necked dresses.

John Wendel's son, John D. Wendel, had carried out his father's commands literally and passed them down to his seven children. The dominant figure among them was John Gottlieb Wendel, a canny, clever, and most eccentric buyer of Manhattan real estate. Countless anecdotes are still told about him. One reports that, when a broker offered him the present site of the Westinghouse building at Broadway and Liberty streets for $750,000, Wendel went out, stared at the property for a moment, disappeared, and in fifteen minutes was back counting out the purchase price in cash. "Young man, the Wendel terms are cash, nothing but hard cash," he said when the broker protested at having to carry so much money to the bank.

The Wendel purchases moved northward with the growth of the city. Two strong personal qualities ran all through their dealings: a dislike of liquor and a hatred of injury to humans or animals. No sign was ever allowed on the roof of a Wendel building; it might fall down and hurt someone, Ella said. When the neighboring National Repub-

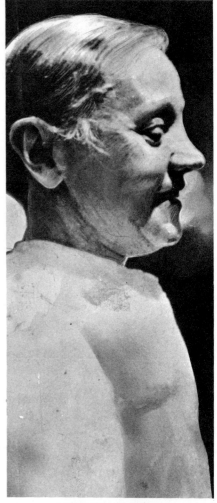

Miss Ella Wendel.

Attorneys filing notices of some 1,000 claimants to shares of the estate of Ella Wendel.

lican Club strung a wire that passed over the yard of the Wendel home, John G. waved his cane and thundered, "That wire must come down!"

Why? asked the GOP heads.

"It might hurt a bird in flight," was the answer.

From 1930 to 1932, Ella assuaged her loneliness with poodles, all named Toby. The dogs had a million-dollar runway in the Fifth Avenue backyard, where Ella hung the family wash.

Her will was an expression of the Wendel sisters' stifled maternal longing and the family hatred of injury and pain. Children's homes, hospitals, the S.P.C.A. were the heirs.

Just after her death, the strange, whimsical drama of the Wendel fortune started to unfold; it was to have an extended run all through the thirties.

No estate in the history of the country ever had more claimants—2,312 in all, from New England to California. Most were distant cousins, who did finally receive a share. The most persistent was Thomas Patric Morris of Scotland, who claimed to have been the son of John Gottlieb Wendel. After a long and desperate fight in New York's Surrogate Court, Morris was convicted of false claims and sentenced to a term in prison.

Real estate experts, after a study of the property holdings, came to the conclusion that if Ella had thrown the parcels of real estate on the market only a few years before her death, 100 million dollars would have been realized. But to the tall, dignified women in rusty black, this would have been unthinkable: a Wendel never sold.

The Fifth Avenue home of Ella Wendel and the courtyard where she exercised her dog Toby daily.

The stairway of the Wendel house showing steps that even the millionaires had to climb. There were five flights and no elevator.

The Match King

THERE WERE two Ivar Kreugers. One viewed the world as a checkerboard, not a habitat of human beings, and analyzed his chances of grand, stolen profits with admirable clarity. The other was an incredibly naïve man who believed that governments would never default on payments and politicians would always keep their promises and renew monopolistic privileges.

Kreuger killed himself in March, 1932. It took the world thirteen years to discover that the man who had been called "The Match King" was actually one of the biggest swindlers of all time. In comparison, Ponzi was a package thief.

Kreuger's suicide shook the international world of finance as few deaths have done. Not long after he was buried, the bankers began to sniff at the truth.

For the next thirteen years investigators for New York's Irving Trust Company worked their way through a fantastic web of forgeries, thefts, fraudulent bookkeeping, and companies that had existed only in Kreuger's imagination.

As trustee of the bankrupt International Match Company, an American concern and biggest of the 140-odd subsidiaries of the huge holding company Kreuger & Toll, Irving Trust made a final 171-page report. It was an incredible document of international thievery.

In brief, Kreuger had swindled the public directly of $560,000,000, of which $250,000,000 came from the United States.

Kreuger, whom John Kenneth Galbraith calls the "Leonardo of the larcenist's craft," was one of the strangest men of his times. To himself he may have appeared as a cutter of corners rather than a swindler, despite his outright forgery of Italian bonds which he kept in one of his numerous safety deposit vaults as an "evidence" of sound security for one of his mountains of debt. He had a peculiar insensitivity to pain, whether to his own or to others'. Dentists could work for hours on the most sensitive nerves in his

Ivar Kreuger.

mouth without giving him novocain. A short, round-faced man, he broke men and companies as casually as he might one of his famous wooden matches.

He first became powerful in the twenties, when Europe, disorganized by a peace that made it impossible to get back on its feet, badly needed capital from abroad. There was only one source, the United States. But American bankers refused.

It was then that Kreuger, using his contacts with sedate banking houses in this country, sold millions of dollars in Kreuger & Toll securities to American investors through American bankers. He then fed the funds to European governments—in return for monopolistic concessions for his match companies.

Kreuger relied on the promises of governments and politicians. They would never default, he told his friends. What this cold, unfeeling man failed to realize was that with the first wind of adversity the American market for securities would dry up, and that when

more cash was not forthcoming, his whole enterprise would fail.

When the Desperate Years closed in and still there was no sign of Mr. Hoover's "corner," Kreuger perpetrated a whole series of frauds. He pledged the same sets of bonds for loans in both Sweden and Germany. He began playing free with the assets of his companies. Finally he could not go on, he could not meet his obligations.

There was only one way out. Kreuger took it that morning in his Paris apartment on the Avenue Victor Emmanuel III.

As financial writer John Chamberlain points out, Kreuger was the prime example of what can happen to probity, integrity, and common sense when governments step in to prevent competition. If anybody and everybody had been permitted to make and sell matches, the whole fantastic bubble represented by Kreuger & Toll, Swedish Match, and the International Match Corporation, would never have come into being.

The Charming Murderess: Winnie Ruth Judd

ONE DAY that fall, a young woman called at the baggage room of the Southern Pacific Railroad in Los Angeles to pick up a large trunk, a small valise, and a metal locker. With her was a young man and they asked the agent to hoist the luggage into their automobile. In handling the trunk, the agent discovered a crimson stain seeping from a crack. There was also a noticeable odor.

"What's in them?" he asked.

In a sweet, gentle voice the girl said they would have to go to the car and get the trunk keys. Moments later the two drove off but not before the baggage man, who believed they were transporting contraband deer meat, had jotted down the license number.

After a few hours' wait he pried open the lids to find the butchered bodies of two women with the faces smashed beyond recognition. The license plate was traced to a terrified student at the University of California, who said the trunks belonged to his sister, Mrs. Winnie Ruth Judd. The bodies were identified as Winnie's friends, Miss Helwig (Sammy) Samuelson, twenty-three, and Mrs. Agnes Le Roi.

A nationwide hunt for Winnie Ruth began while police probed her background. The daughter of an Illinois minister, Winnie was pictured as an emotional, erratic young girl; once she had been found wandering about the countryside in her nightgown. Stricken with TB, she had gone to Phoenix, Arizona, for her health. It was there she became acquainted with the two murdered women, who had worked in the hospital. Later she shared their bungalow. Detectives on her trail found a Phoenix expressman who said he had helped get the trunks to the railroad station for a pretty woman "who was just so sweet you couldn't refuse her anything."

On October 23, Winnie surrendered to Los Angeles police. She told a weird story, saying she had killed the women in self-defense. It was a sad story; she exhibited a bullet hole in one hand and many bruises on her body. Sympathy poured in from all sides—except from the police, who doggedly went over Winnie's hiding places until they found a revealing ten-page letter in her handwriting. Later she confessed that she had shot the two women and dis-

Winnie Ruth Judd.

posed of their bodies.

Her trial took place in the winter of 1932. The verdict was guilty and the sentence was death by hanging. The following April a sanity hearing was obtained. During the proceedings she screamed, shouted, and tore at her hair, and the state's psychiatrists said she was putting on a superb act. National sympathy for her grew, however, and the state finally judged her insane and committed her.

The day of the verdict she appeared to be the old Winnie Judd, smiling, charming, winsome. Even the guards who transferred her to the state hospital were taken in, as were the patients and even members of the staff after a few weeks.

Winnie could have been elected the most popular patient in the Arizona State Hospital had such a contest been held.

But Winnie became bored. One night she fashioned a dummy out of boxes, bottles, and cakes of soap, and let herself out. Another nationwide hunt took place. She was finally found, shoeless and bedraggled. As always, she had

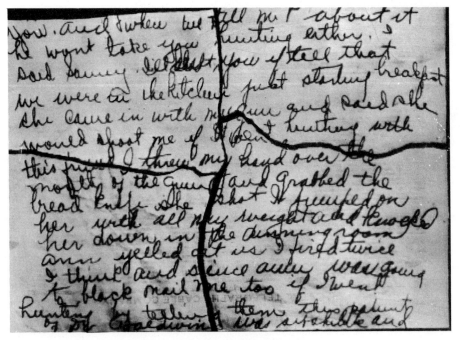

Winnie Ruth Judd's "confession letter."

77

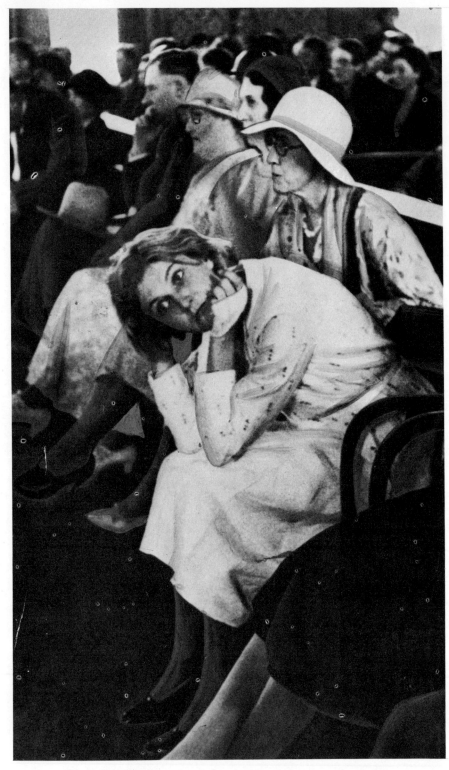

Winnie Ruth Judd in court. *(She escaped again in October, 1962!)

been cared for by strangers, who had swallowed her fanciful stories.

"When she looked at you with those great big eyes brimming with tears, you would believe anything she told you," one witness said.

Another time she got hold of a pass-key and left prison to wander about the state; as usual she had no difficulty in getting people to help her.

More escapes followed—six in all—the last in 1952.* This time she turned herself in to the superintendent of the hospital. A beauty treatment had so changed her that the doctor assumed she had gone to have her face lifted.

She was taken before a grand jury to testify about conditions in the hospi-tal, but then the doctors found another key hidden in her hair and an ejector razor blade under her tongue. Winnie had failed this time.

Curiously, she is still pretty and above all still possesses a strange, evil-like charm that makes most people she meets do things they normally wouldn't do.

The Battle of Anacostia Flats

On a hot summer day in 1932 a contingent of the Bonus Army left New York City for Washington.

FOR TWO MONTHS the Bonus Expeditionary Force, twenty thousand strong, had besieged Washington. During the sweltering days they had streamed into Washington from all across the country. Some were starving, many were dressed in rags, some with shoes patched with cardboard or with no shoes at all.

They were American armed service veterans who wanted Congress to pay their bonus.

Nearly every day another ragged company, flag hanging from a home-made staff, marched into the camp on the Anacostia River flats and settled in tar-paper shacks or huts made of planks and canvas. When Congress adjourned without meeting their demands, the ex-soldiers became sullen. Some moved into some old federal buildings on lower Pennsylvania Avenue, which were being demolished. Others erected huts nearby.

The showdown came at ten A.M., July 28, when workmen came to tear down one of the buildings occupied by a group of veterans. When the men re-

fused to budge, Walter W. Walters, commander of the veterans' group, urged them not to resist. Most of them hooted and jeered him.

An hour later, Washington Police Chief Pelham G. Glassford, a retired brigadier general, who had cajoled, jollied, threatened, and fed the bonus marchers for two months, arrived with a number of policemen and Treasury agents. They removed, sometimes by force, the veterans who occupied the partly demolished buildings. It took just fifty minutes.

Minutes later Attorney General Mitchell ordered evacuation of all veterans from government property in the District of Columbia.

As Mitchell was transmitting the order to Glassford, three veterans carrying an American flag attempted to re-enter a building that had been abandoned. It was the spark that touched off the dynamite.

General Glassford was in conference with his officers when the cry rose, "There's a fight!"

Police, veterans, officials rushed to

the spot. The battle was on. The veterans were hurling bricks; the police had scurried for cover behind the huts, but the veterans' barrage blasted down the flimsy walls and exposed the police to the flying bricks.

Glassford was struck in the head. Police officer Edward Scott, a Medal of Honor winner, went down as he sought to protect his chief, and was kicked unconscious in the melee.

Every police officer in the capital, 660 strong, was rushed to the fight, which now had turned into one of the worst riots in the history of the nation.

Glassford, blood streaming down his face, cried, "Be peaceful, men, be peaceful! You may have killed one of our best officers."

"Hell, a lot of us were killed in France," was the reply.

For hours police and veterans milled about the buildings in a thick haze of dust. For a time there was a lull in the battle. Then Glassford heard of a fight on the second floor of one building and sent two of his men to stop it. The veterans opposed the entrance of the officers. One was hurled down the stairs and the other hit with a garbage can.

Then the first shots rang out. Others followed. For three minutes police guns crashed. Veteran William Haska toppled dead from an upper floor. Two others writhed in agony from wounds.

General Glassford shouted to his men not to use their guns and to get back. Slowly the embattled police moved back under a shower of rocks, garbage cans, and other debris.

By now the situation was out of hand. Veterans who tried to exert leadership were hooted down or even stoned by the homeless, hungry, enraged men. When the news of the riot spread, thousands of other veterans began hurrying toward the battle ground.

At three P.M. President Hoover acted. At his orders the cavalry rode out of Fort Myer to get the situation under control. An hour later General MacArthur was told to take over with tanks and troops.

The south side of Pennsylvania Avenue between Third and Sixth streets, Northwest, extending southward to Missouri Avenue, was a warlike scene as the troops moved in with drawn bayonets to drive the rioters back to the Flats. Tear-gas bombs exploded, veterans clawed at their swollen, weeping eyes and staggered down Pennsylvania Avenue, the troops in battle gear prodding them along with bayonets. The cavalry in advance, the infantry behind, and after them the tanks and machine gunners. All the veterans had were rocks, a sullen stubbornness, and epithets.

Down toward Anacostia the troops and veterans went, a sad and bruising affair all the way, with men swinging blows at the passing troops, the cavalry wielding sabers.

The shacks around the old federal buildings were in flames. They were not

Veterans parading toward the White House.

The main camp of the Bonus Army at Anacostia.

The Bonus Army bank, erected in the hope of doing a flourishing business if Congress passed the Bonus Bill. It didn't.

much as habitations, but the sight of their simple homes burning to the ground made the veterans more stubborn and the drive to Anacostia became harder.

All afternoon and into the evening the retreat went on. A thousand more troops were summoned from camps in the Third Corps area. When they reached the Flats, both sides joined in battle. More gas bombs exploded over the area, more rocks and bricks were thrown, and more than one soldier went down. But the troops surrounded the area and moved in.

Then the tent city was put to the torch and by midnight the sky was tinged with red. In the garish light thousands of veterans left the desolate flats, a pitiful throng of refugees going they knew not where.

In scenes reminiscent of Civil War days, cavalry troops stood guard at bridges leading across the river to the camp. Some of the veterans departed in broken-down automobiles, their few be-

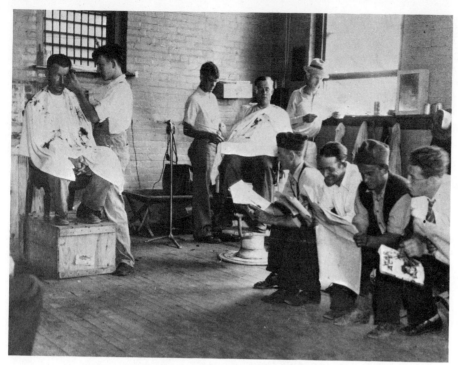

The barbershop of the Bonus Army.

longings tied with rope to the sides and roofs; others were on foot, weighed down with blankets, tin pots, and mattresses.

It was a hot, sweltering night and the haze of tear gas and smoke that hung over the flats and for blocks around was so thick residents were forced to keep their windows sealed despite the heat.

Ringed by tanks and machine guns, the veterans seemed broken in spirit. Leaderless and aghast at the army action (they had thought that no soldier would go into action against them), they left with their women and children to take to the highways. Walters, the titular head of the B.E.F., made a bitter statement, charging President Hoover with responsibility for the death of Haska and the injury to many others.

Of William Haska, it was learned he had gone to Washington because he couldn't find a job. "He just couldn't stay here without a job," his brother said in Chicago.

Haska was buried on one of the green-clad slopes of Arlington National Cemetery, a quarter of a mile from the tomb of the Unknown Soldier. As his coffin was lowered to the melancholy call of taps, another grave was dug nearby for Eric Carlson, a wounded veteran who had subsequently died.

It was a sad day with a gray drizzle falling on the small company of mourners. Ironically, Haska's honor guard was a squad from the Third U.S. Cavalry,

who only a few days before marched with gas masks and drawn bayonets to drive him and the rest of the tattered army from Anacostia Flats.

Kingsbury Smith, Pulitzer-prize foreign correspondent and now publisher of the New York *Journal-American,* wrote of that sad morning: "They buried with simple military honors William J. Haska, the penniless Chicago veteran, who lost his life in the strangest of all wars—the attempt to collect from his government the bonus he felt was his due."

All that week the remnants of the tattered army moved away. Some of them came finally to Johnstown. There it was the same story of makeshift huts, sleeping in rain and mud, and existing on charity. There was also strife and discontent, a threat of an outbreak of typhoid. On August 3, the Baltimore & Ohio offered to take eight hundred veterans and children back to Chicago and points west. Some of the leaders refused to disband, but cooler heads prevailed. In Waterbury, Maryland, other groups moved out after the state police gave them a deadline. Week after week groups straggled home, until finally the B.E.F. was only a sad memory.

But if the B.E.F. vanished physically, the ugly shadow of that hot July day hung over Washington and national events all that year. In a report to President Hoover, Attorney General Mitchell charged that 1,069 of the veterans had criminal records and 829 of these were proved communists. He also stated that the troops were called out only because General Glassford had asked for federal help.

Glassford bitterly attacked Mitchell's statement, denying he had asked for help and pointing out that there were only twelve actual criminals among the twenty thousand veterans, and only a few communists.

The Republicans began to grow concerned. The American public was re-

Police and veterans battle at Anacostia Flats.

Soldiers with gas masks drive veterans from their makeshift shacks in the Bonus Army battle.

General Douglas MacArthur, chief of staff of the Army, eating emergency rations with his troops after they had burned three downtown camps of the Bonus Army.

A veteran wields a lead pipe as police move in on the Bonus Army.

fusing to believe the B.E.F. was a motley band of reds and criminals. Then came word that the American Legion was preparing a resolution censuring the President. The politicians agreed that something must be done quickly. Thus began the attempt to discredit the Bonus Army. F. Trubee Davison, assistant secretary of war, went before the American Legion convention in session at the Hotel St. George, Brooklyn, and told the legionnaires the Secret Service had discovered a band of counterfeiters turning out false credentials for the B.E.F. As one man the legionnaires booed so vigorously that Davison finished his speech with great difficulty.

The Democrats were openly gleeful at the sudden and unexpected turn of events. Their strategists pointed out that the actions of the Hoover administration had so thoroughly outraged the rank and file of American veterans that Governor Roosevelt could now feel free to take an anti-bonus stand without fear of alienating any large section of the veteran vote. Up to the moment when the troops moved down Pennsylvania Avenue, the bonus problem had been one of the biggest flies in the governor's ointment.

Will You Love Me in December?

THE SMILE New York usually wore when she viewed her wisecracking, dandified, vote-getting mayor, James J. Walker, was beginning to wear a trifle thin by mid-1932, when it became evident that his administration belonged in musical comedy rather than City Hall.

The Seabury investigation was in full swing, and even the most sophisticated citizens were aghast at some of its revelations. By putting the spotlight on New York City corruption, the investigation drew attention to municipal corruption generally, and the progress of the Seabury inquiry was followed avidly all over the country.

Finally the day of reckoning came for Walker. Jimmy was summoned to take the witness stand before the Hofstadter Joint Legislative Committee to Investigate the Affairs of the City. It was a sensational day in which the slender, dapper mayor sparred constantly with the stolid Seabury, counsel to the committee. Before long Seabury had Jimmy on the ropes. At one time Walker admitted that he had shared a joint bank account with a broker, who had deposited $246,692 in cash, supposedly the profits from stock trading, though there was no evidence of this. Walker had later transferred the money to a safe.

"Not a tin box," he emphasized with a grin. What happened to the money? He and his wife had "just spent it."

He vigorously denied that Russell T. Sherwood, described as his financial agent, was his front. Seabury had brought out that Sherwood, who could not be located, had banked $700,225 while he was only a small-salaried accountant. Seabury also proved that Sherwood had once withdrawn $263,838 just before Walker had sailed for Europe. All in all, the embattled mayor was forced to admit he had banked $432,677 in four years.

After the conclusion of the hearings, Governor Roosevelt called on Seabury to press charges against the mayor. This Seabury did, but as a private citizen, not as a representative of the legislative committee.

After Seabury placed the charges on FDR's desk, the governor demanded that Walker answer them. After lengthy hearings, it became clear that the next step would be an order from the gover-

Mayor James J. Walker as he took the stand for questioning by Samuel Seabury, counsel for the Hofstadter Committee. Thousands of New Yorkers fought for seats and brought box lunches.

Samuel Seabury.

nor removing Walker from office. On September 1. he resigned, explaining his act as a protest against the "unfairness" of the hearings. Roosevelt dismissed the hearings without comment. Joseph McKee, president of the Board of Aldermen, became acting mayor.

While the pot boiled at City Hall, Walker took off for Europe. He would later be joined by his favorite girl friend, Betty Compton, dancer, whose credits included *Oh, Kay!* and *Fifty Million Frenchmen.* Their romance wasn't exactly unknown. They had danced to Leo Reisman's orchestra at the Central Park Casino, munched hot dogs to the smack of Babe Ruth home runs at Yankee Stadium, and first-nighted the boom-time musicals, which often ran the mayor's plugs in their theatre ads.

In 1935, after the heat of the investigations had cooled, Jimmy and Betty returned home as man and wife. It was typical of the whimsical New York voter to forget Walker's silly-corrupt administration. Still popular, Walker half-heartedly practiced law while his wife ran a flower shop. He conducted a short-lived radio program in the thirties and finally looked around for a full-time job.

Mayor La Guardia gave it to him, as $20,000-a-year czar of industrial and labor relations for New York's giant cloak-and-suit industry. But Betty had had enough.

Mr. and Mrs. Jimmy Walker (née Betty Compton).

THE MAD DOG: Vincent Coll

IN THE ANNALS of bloody crime, the name of Vincent (Mad Dog) Coll stands out with a peculiar horror all its own.

He was the original baby-faced killer, one of the most ruthless gangsters the country has ever known, a man whose murders finally aroused revulsion in the underworld itself, and it rose and killed him. He was then just twenty-three.

Coll cared little for his own life or any other human life. Police officers who had trailed him, who had spoken to his associates and girl friends, claimed he was half demented, a swaggering sadist who from his earliest years had delighted in the pleas or screams of his victims.

Modern psychiatry might label Coll as a man obsessed with a death wish. He invaded the gangster empires of Dutch Schultz, Legs Diamond, and Owney Madden as nonchalantly as he had stolen apples from the peddler's wagon in Hell's Kitchen. He kidnapped the underworld big shots, hijacked their beer trucks, killed their best guns, raided their speakeasies, in short did everything a sensible hoodlum would know he couldn't do and stay alive.

Coll had seventeen arrests in twelve years. The first was as a "disorderly child." The record then showed that he was born on Eleventh Avenue and West Twenty-fifth Street of parents who had immigrated from County Kildare. For this first offense he was sent to the Mission of the Immaculate Virgin.

After his release from the Mission, a series of arrests followed—for theft, grand larceny, breaking and entry, and finally violation of parole, which sent him to Elmira. When he came out, he was changed. He wanted out of Hell's Kitchen. He and his brother Peter began carrying a hired gun for Dutch Schultz at $150 a week.

He wasn't content with that; in three months he was demanding a cut of the Dutchman's percentages. When the outraged Schultz said "No," Coll and his brother started a rival organization.

It was about this time that the first killings were placed at his door. Police claimed, but couldn't prove, that he had gunned down a rumrunner named Vincent Barelli and his girl friend, Mary Smith. The legend, still repeated in police circles, had Barelli working for Schultz and refusing to leave to join Coll. The Coll brothers and Mary's sister, Carmine, had gone to grade school together in Hell's Kitchen. On the strength of this bond, Vincent got Mary to bring Barelli to a meeting at Inwood Avenue and 170th Street. When Barelli still refused to leave Schultz, Coll killed him and the girl.

The story may or may not be true, but Coll was charged with the double killing. There was no proof and the case against him was dismissed.

His next move was to set up a speakeasy on Brook Avenue in the Bronx, near Schultz's headquarters, to recruit the Dutchman's killers and strong-arm men. Before a few months had passed Coll had lured more than half a dozen of Schultz's best men.

Schultz retaliated. His first victim was Coll's brother, Peter, whose body was found in the doorway of a Harlem speakeasy. Coll's answer was swift and ruthless. He hijacked Schultz's beer trucks, kidnapped other gangland figures and held them for ransom, muscled in on Schultz's policy racket, and openly defied the Dutchman as a "yellow rat." All he needed was a dusty street in a western town, a six shooter, and Wyatt Earp as the cowardly sheriff to complete the scene.

Coll also cut down some of Schultz's best men. In midsummer of 1932, he was gunning for Joey Rao, Schultz's policy boss. One July afternoon Rao strolled out of a building on East 107th Street, two bodyguards tailing behind. The three men walked down the crowded sidewalk, threading their way through baby carriages and small children playing in the sun. Nobody paid any attention to the automobile at the curb nearby.

Vincent (Mad Dog) Coll and his attorney, the famous criminal lawyer, Samuel Leibowitz.

Coll and his gangland court: (left to right) Arthur Palumbo, Peter Coll (killed in 1932), Lottie Kreisberger, and Coll.

When Rao appeared, the car had started moving forward, slowly, foot by foot. Rao had just come abreast of a group of whooping, shouting children when the machine guns opened.

After the first blast there was a dead silence, then the screams of wounded children ripped the warm afternoon. Five-year-old Michael Vengalli lay writhing on the sidewalk, bullets in his stomach. Four other children, from two to four years old, lay screaming in pain and hysteria. One seven-year-old had five bullets in his back. Rao and his bodyguards escaped.

Two hours later Michael died.

The biggest manhunt in the history of New York followed. Rewards rose to thirty thousand dollars for information leading to the arrest and conviction of the killers. The order went out to bring in Coll "dead or alive."

Coll wasted little time in acquiring the money for his defense; he kidnapped Owney Madden's top aide and made Madden pay thirty thousand in ransom. Police finally caught up with Coll and his new sweetheart, plump Lottie Kreisberger, in a raid on a West Side apartment.

He and his chief enforcer, Frank Giordano, were placed on trial for the 107th Street shooting, but were acquitted after Coll's attorney, famed criminal lawyer Sam Leibowitz, proved that the state's chief witness was an ex-convict who had starred as "chief witness" in a similar trial in St. Louis, and who had been judged "subnormal" by psychiatrists. Coll, now free, joined Lottie. They were married a few days later.

Schultz's mobsters tried to kill Coll four different times following his marriage, but each time they failed. Then they found that Madden was again being shaken down by Coll. One day as Madden was talking to Coll on the phone, a gunman appeared, stuck a gun in his ribs, and said softly, "Keep talking, Owney."

Within minutes the call was traced to a West Twenty-third Street drugstore. Coll was still in the booth when three men drove up in an automobile. One took a station at the door outside, the other guarded the inside, and the third walked up to the booth and sprayed it with a machine gun.

The autopsy showed fifteen steel-jacketed bullets had struck Coll in the head, chest, and stomach.

In his room police found exactly $101. As the investigation continued, it became known that after his acquittal Coll had been reduced to the role of guarding a crap game. In desperation to get back to the top of the caste-conscious underworld, he had been planning to kidnap another underworld big shot.

Dutch Schultz had once said, "Get Coll off my back . . . get the Mick off my back . . ." Eventually the whole underworld felt the same, and now Coll was off their backs.

TEN OUT OF SIXTY

Three generations of Rockefellers. (From left to right) John D. Rockefeller 3rd, John D. Rockefeller, Nelson A. Rockefeller, Laurance S. Rockefeller, John D. Rockefeller, Jr. This picture was taken in the early twenties.

NOT ALL fortunes were lost in the Great Depression. In 1932 at least some of the sixty big United States fortunes had survived. The three greatest—Rockefeller, Morgan and Mellon—had come through nearly intact, as well-known financial writer Leslie Gould disclosed in the fall of that year.

The Rockefellers, ever since the 1870's when John D. and his brother William were hitting their stride, were always large-scale and successful market operators. The two branches of the family were still carrying on in 1932, with William's line, in the person of his nephew, Percy, probably making the better showing. Percy, at this period, was rated as one of the biggest traders in Wall Street and one of the most successful market operators. Like the John D.'s he suffered large paper losses on his long-term holdings, but they were largely offset by his hedge and other market operations. By 1932 he was rated as one of the richest men in the world, with a fortune reported even greater than John D.'s.

Outside of paper losses, the biggest losses of the John D. Rockefellers were in real estate. But in market operations

in their own stock, Standard Oil, they had an uncanny way of picking the bottom. In the 1929 crash they made their famous bid for Jersey common at $50 and reportedly sold at a much higher price. They duplicated this performance in the summer of 1932, when they put in a big bid for Jersey at around $21. While Wall Street scratched its head, the stock steadily climbed and by October it stood at $30.

This year Percy Rockefeller's fortune was estimated at from half a billion to a billion dollars; that of John D.'s family was slightly lower. The John D.'s in 1920 had had an annual income of between fifty and sixty million; by 1932 they were down to between thirty and thirty-five million.

The Morgans didn't fare so well in 1929; their stocks were the hardest hit in the panic. However, by 1932 they had turned and were again at the head of the Wall Street table.

Another fortune that had survived by 1932 was the Harrimans'. A handsome, slender, and dynamic young member of the family, William Averell Harriman, had merged his small investment house with the old banking firm of Brown Brothers, with young Harri-

man as the leading figure in the combine. This year he also stepped into the chairmanship of the Union Pacific, his father's old road.

The Astor fortune, founded on beaver skins when the West was still unmapped, also came through intact. By 1932 its main losses were mostly on paper, due to the tremendous deflation in real estate which largely made up the fortune.

The Baruch fortune, far from faltering, had increased by this year. Bernard Mannes Baruch, the founder of the fortune, had no peer in the market unless it was his friend, Percy Rockefeller.

The Ford fortune was mostly intact, because of the policy of Henry Ford, who, after his famous battle with Wall Street bankers, insisted on keeping on hand large holdings of cash and government bonds. The fortune had been slightly pared by losses in plants.

Although most of the big movie fortunes had either collapsed or been badly dented by 1932, one had come through. William Fox, who had been forced out of his own company at what was a handsome price, had increased his fortune through shrewd market plays.

JACK SHARKEY, whom the sports writers called a "fine fighting machine," won a decision over Max Schmeling. . . . In Boulder City, Nevada, a fifty-foot hole was blown in the Grand Canyon wall to divert the course of the Colorado River temporarily so workmen could start on Boulder (now Hoover) Dam. . . . Sam Insull was indicted in Chicago. . . . An official of the North German Lloyd Steamship lines testified before the Seabury committee that he had paid a Tammany politician fifty thousand dollars to get a North River pier lease. . . . John J. Raskob released the findings of his national poll on prohibition: the figures showed 93 per cent of the answerers wanted the Eighteenth Amendment abolished. . . . The M-2 British submarine with fifty-three men and officers sank in the English Channel. It was later found that the British sub had come to rest near a German U-boat sunk in World War I. . . . Paul von Hin-

Vannie Higgins (right) as he was arraigned on a gangland murder charge in 1931.

Noted playwright Philip Barry, his wife, and sons (left to right) Jonathan and Philip, Jr.

Greta Garbo and John Barrymore in Grand Hotel.

89

Fred Allen.

Jack Pearl, a popular radio comic.

This is what Babe Ruth called his biggest day. Here he shakes hands with Lou Gehrig, after hitting a home run in the fifth inning of a World Series game against Chicago, October 1, 1932.

The Babe took two strikes, then pointed to the bleachers to tell the crowd and Cub players where the next pitch would land. It landed just where he had pointed. The Cubs' pitcher was Charlie Root.

denburg, the aging and feeble president of Germany, was again elected to the presidency over Adolf Hitler by 2,-235,000 votes, but Hitler's tremendously vigorous campaign indicated that there was trouble ahead. . . . Mrs. Amelia Earhart Putnam left Harbour Grace, Newfoundland, and in 13 hours

and 13 minutes, with 2,026.5 miles behind her, became the first woman to fly the Atlantic. Her goal had been Paris, but she was forced down by engine trouble in England. London, Paris, and New York (with ticker-tape) gave her parades. . . . Charles Van Wyck (Vannie) Higgins, the bootlegger,

Fanny Brice in her most popular radio role as "Baby Snooks."

Amelia Earhart Putnam on her way to Hoover after her epochal Atlantic flight in Washington to be honored by President 1932.

The day Germany voted for the new Reichstag—November 6, 1932. Here is a giant placard the Hitler Nazis placed in front of the Angriff, Hitler's leading newspaper.

Japanese troops entering Harbin in northern Manchuria.

The 1932 English Derby being televised.

was shot to death outside the Brooklyn Knights of Columbus Hall. . . . Japanese troops took possession of Harbin in northern Manchuria. . . . Babe Ruth added to his chapter in baseball history in a World Series game on October 1. After taking two strikes, he pointed to the bleachers, showing the crowd where he was going to hit the next pitch—and he hit it just where he had pointed. . . . Television passed a milestone when on June 1 scenes from the Derby at Epsom Downs were telecast. . . . John Barrymore and Greta Garbo starred in *Grand Hotel*. . . . Fred Allen, Fannie (Baby Snooks) Brice, and Jack Pearl ("Vas you dere, Sharlie?") starred on radio. . . . Among the hits on Broadway were Leslie Howard in *The Animal Kingdom,* Ina Claire in *Biography,* and *Dinner at Eight*. . . . Banks were having a hard time. There were runs on many of them and there was an extraordinary number of bank failures. . . . New Year's Eve was celebrated gaily (though not by those whose money was lost in closed banks), for the New Year would bring the New Deal. . . .

The Bullet that Might Have Changed History

THE YEAR turned, the bread lines were long, unemployment figures were mounting: there were now 15,000,000 jobless. More than 85,000 small businessmen had gone bankrupt during 1932.

Across the seas dictators were on the march, crushing life and freedom. On January 30, 1933, President Hindenburg of Germany dismissed the chancellor and put Adolf Hitler in his place. The new chancellor dissolved the Reichstag, ordered an election, arrested leaders of opposition parties, and shook Germany with terror and panic. A weak League of Nations was debating what to do about Japan's invasion of the Manchurian province of Jehol in March, 1933. Austria had begun to hear the hobnailed boots of marching fascists armed by Mussolini's Blackshirts. South America was not free of discord: revolutions and palace upsets were sputtering in Latin American countries like so many time bombs. It was a period of deep concern both here and abroad. The world was in a tailspin, economically and spiritually.

The brow of any President-elect should have been furrowed, his face worn—but not FDR's. All during the months preceding his inauguration he was cheerful, buoyant, and completely imperturbable. Reporters followed him day and night, and while he joked with them he refused to issue any statements on policy or his plans.

In February Louis Howe did announce that Roosevelt was traveling to Miami in the company of Chicago's amiable mayor, Anton J. Cermak. They would arrive February 15.

One man in Miami, a former New Jersey mill hand, read the news avidly. He bought every edition of the local newspapers and read the stories line by line in his drab room on the second floor of a Miami boarding house.

On the morning of February 15 he rose early. Most of the night he had walked the floor almost bent double with stomach cramps. Just before noon he bought a bottle of medicine for his "indigestion" from a neighborhood drug store. He drank half the bottle, then removed a revolver from a bureau drawer. He carefully spun the cylinder, loaded it, and left.

Joseph Zangara walked rapidly down

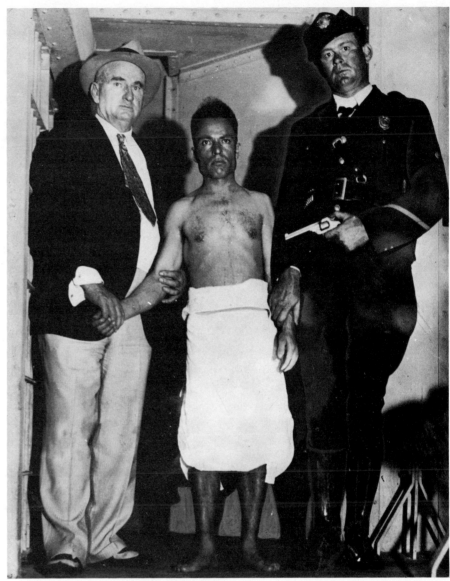

Guiseppe Zangara at a Miami police station after he tried to kill President-elect Roosevelt.

the street; he was in a hurry to kill Franklin Delano Roosevelt, President-elect of the United States. In the last few weeks it seemed that FDR's popularity had increased. That warm, reassuring voice, that ready grin and tilted cigarette holder, had reached out to touch millions of his forgotten men; they were ready to follow him no matter where he wanted to go.

The car moved slowly down the palm-bordered boulevard. FDR and Mayor Cermak smiled and waved. The

crowd moved in; the car could only inch its way. Zangara pushed desperately through the mob. Men and women who started to protest his shoving were silenced by his dark, burning eyes.

"It was like he was going to explode," a man later recalled. "I was going to belt him but something made me stop. He was like a nut."

Finally Zangara was near the automobile. Shouting, "There are too many people starving to death!" he fired shot after shot at the President-elect.

A woman's quick move knocked the gun upward. The bullets hit several bystanders and mortally wounded Cermak.

Despite the screaming and pande-

1933

93

FDR in the motorcade procession.

monium, FDR never faltered. He kept his poise. In his memoirs, Raymond Moley, later FDR's assistant secretary of state, wrote, "There was not so much as the twitching of a muscle, the mopping of a brow, or even the hint of false gaiety."

On March 21, 1933, Zangara marched into Florida's execution chamber at Raiford, shouting vituperation against the "capitalists" and expressing disappointment that no news cameramen were permitted to take pictures of his execution.

"Good-bye, adios to the world," were his last muffled words as the switch slammed down.

Later an autopsy showed that Zangara's brain was "normal on gross examination." The medical men insisted that his actions as he walked into the chamber indicated "proper understanding of his surroundings and he realized fully the nature of the punishment about to be meted out to him for his crimes."

The autopsy also showed that, "while he suffered from chronic indigestion, he was a healthy, well-nourished individual."

Just before Zangara died, Florida Commissioner Mayo visited him in his death cell and asked him if he had any alliance with organized anarchists or gangs.

According to Mayo's report, Zangara replied, "No. I have no friends. It was an idea of my own."

Mayo also said Zangara showed no remorse over Mayor Cermak's death.

When asked how he felt about having hit a woman, a mother of five, he said, "She shouldn't have got in the way of the bullet."

As for FDR, Zangara said, "If I got out I would kill him at once."

It had been a close call, both for the United States and for history.

FDR as he addressed the huge Miami throng.

THE BANKING CRISIS

THE NATION was at its lowest ebb in the winter of 1932-33. Farm prices had slid steadily downward along with factory production, retail trade, and stocks and bonds. There wasn't a city in the nation that didn't have long lines of unemployed, of homeless, of starving men, women, and children. The number of unemployed had skyrocketed to fifteen million.

Throughout the land, occupations and duties that once were scorned suddenly attained popularity. Only two years before, citizens were still shying at jury duty. John Doe and Richard Roe, summoned to serve on a jury, thought of all sorts of excuses. They called upon their ward leaders and their lawyers to get exemptions for them, and when their efforts were rewarded they sighed with relief. But now things were different. From New York to Los Angeles halls of justice were jammed on court days, and there was a plentiful supply of talesmen, for jurors got several dollars for every day they served.

Once the average American had his shoes shined in an established bootblack parlor, paying ten cents with a nickel tip. But now, in this terrible, unforgettable winter, Americans of every age, from every walk of life, had become shoeshine "boys." In New York City, the *New York Times* in a survey counted nineteen shoe-shiners on one block. In Detroit, San Francisco, and other big cities, police reported shoe-shiners ranged from children of ten to men of seventy. An army of new salesmen had also turned to the streets, peddling everything from pins and needles to cheap neckties, trying to eke out a living.

In the farm country, men patrolled their land with shotguns to prevent foreclosure. In Washington a weary Congress bickered over domestic issues but, lacking a leader, did nothing.

In mid-winter, what had been only a rumor became a shocking reality: the bank situation in the United States was rapidly approaching a crisis. Frantic bank officials, working around the clock to check withdrawals, wondered

FDR in conference on his special train with financier Jesse H. Jones and Senator Cordell Hull.

whether their banks would survive another day. In Washington the Treasury Department was begging the governors of New York and Illinois to close their banks and prevent fatal runs.

On March 1, as President-elect Roosevelt was leaving Hyde Park for his inauguration, more than twelve states had closed their banks. Slowly but steadily the nation's credit structure was crumbling. In Wall Street as in homes all across the country, people watched fearfully—helplessly it seemed —for what was coming next.

On March 3, the Federal Reserve

Board reported that a quarter of a billion dollars in gold had left its vaults within a week. In New York it was expected that the banks would close any moment. When Hoover asked FDR to join him in proclaiming an emergency, the President-elect replied that the President was still free to act on his own.

On Saturday, March 4, almost all the nation's banks were closed. Cities were defaulting on payrolls, and thousands of municipal workers were being dropped from their jobs. Public anxiety was rapidly rising to hysteria. It was now a national nightmare. . . .

The President-elect with "Barney" Baruch at Warm Springs.

The Inauguration

THE INAUGURATION of President Franklin Delano Roosevelt took place before the Capitol rotunda on a day that, appropriately enough, was raw, cold, and overcast. The crowd was large but apprehensive. Across the land millions of fearful Americans bent closer to their radios as the clear, calm voice declared that the nation was asking for action—"and action now." More than one man swallowed hard when the words came through the meshed speaker: "Our greatest primary task is to put people to work . . ."

He announced a foreign policy based on good-neighbor relations, but it was the jobless and hungry at home who must come first . . . the dreadful problem at home was his first concern.

His people had asked for direct, vigorous action, for leadership. "In the spirit of the gift, I take it," came the words, clear and precise like bar iron striking an anvil head.

". . . First of all, let me assert my firm belief that the only thing we have to fear is fear itself—nameless, unreasoning, unjustified terror which paralyzes needed efforts to convert retreat into advance. In every dark hour of our national life, a leadership of frankness and vigor has met with that understanding and support of the people themselves which is essential to victory. I am convinced that you will again give that support to leadership in these critical days. . . ."

In the next few days, Washington sprang from its lethargy. The air was electric. On Thursday, March 9, Congress convened in a special session. Both houses rushed through a banking act to meet the President's demand that the resumption of banking be controlled and that he be given broad powers over the nation's currency. The bill was signed the next morning. The next day, after bitter wrangling, Congress passed a bill giving the President powers to maintain the country's credit.

On March 12, FDR sat down before a microphone and gave the first of his famous "fireside chats," beginning, "I want to talk for a few minutes with the people of the United States about banking . . ."

Those who heard him will never forget the warm, reassuring voice describing in simple layman's language the intricate banking situation.

The first inauguration of Franklin Delano Roosevelt, 32nd President of the United States. Chief Justice Charles Evans Hughes administered the oath. Former President Hoover is at the extreme right.

The Cabinet

President Roosevelt and his Cabinet. (Left to right, seated) Secretary of War, George H. Dern of Utah; Secretary of State, Cordell Hull of Tennessee; President Roosevelt; Secretary of the Treasury, William H. Woodin of New York; and Attorney General Homer Cummings of Connecticut. (Left to right, standing) Secretary of Agriculture, Henry Wallace of Iowa; Secretary of the Interior, Harold Ickes of Illinois; Secretary of the Navy, Claude Swanson of Virginia; Postmaster General, James A. Farley of New York; Secretary of Commerce, Daniel Roper of Washington, D. C.; and Secretary of Labor, Frances Perkins of New York. Not long after this photograph was taken Woodin's post was filled by Henry Morgenthau, Jr.

NEVER BEFORE had there been a cabinet representing so many points of view. There were Democrats from both left and right wings of the party. Republicans also were represented. There were conservatives, progressives, isolationists, and inflationists. There was a Wilson idealist and a former Bull Moose nationalist. Business, industry, agriculture, and labor were not ignored. nor were the Protestants and Catholics. Geographically they represented South, North, Midwest, Far West. There was also a woman.

Cordell Hull, a graying Tennessean just turned sixty, was his choice as secretary of state. The soft-spoken Southerner would remain with FDR until the end. William Woodin, a hard-headed, realistic industrialist, became his secretary of treasury. FDR first wanted Senator Thomas J. Walsh of Montana, a superb crusader against crime and corruption, as his attorney general, but the Montana senator died

in a plane crash and Homer S. Cummings from Connecticut, who had been slated for governor general of the Philippines, was selected. Governor George H. Dern of Utah took over as secretary of war, and Senator Claude Swanson, the friendly Virginian whose wing collars and frock coat were Washington trade marks, became his secretary of the navy.

Daniel C. Roper, who had been close to Wilson, was appointed secretary of commerce; genial Jim Farley, who had helped engineer FDR into the White House, became postmaster general.

FDR also broke tradition when he appointed Frances Perkins, New York's industrial commissioner, as secretary of labor. Henry Wallace took over the post his father had once held as secretary of agriculture, Harold L. Ickes, a pugnacious, stormy Republican petrel from Chicago, took over as secretary of the interior.

It was not a cabinet to carry out one single, determined program, as Professor James MacGregor Burns points out in his excellent biography *Roosevelt: The Lion and the Fox*: "The only principle in the cabinet's makeup was, in short, its lack of essential principle. Roosevelt had no rounded program; hence he could not recruit his official family along programmatic lines. The only real significance of the cabinet lay in Roosevelt's leadership role. He could count on the loyalty of his associates; almost every one was 'FRBC'—for Roosevelt before Chicago—and not a single one had been an important opponent in the 1932 convention."

It was a family that FDR could dominate by his magnetic personality and his obvious role of being the right man in the right time. It would make history, but only under the leadership of the man who had brought them together.

The Bank Holiday

ON SUNDAY night, March 5, President Roosevelt informed the nation that the next four days were to be holidays for all banks and financial institutions in the nation. This was to permit an examination of their soundness before their gradual reopening. He also prohibited the hoarding of gold, the export of gold, and all dealings in foreign exchange. All gold—bars, coins, certificates—was to be turned in for exchange. The man he had selected to guide the nation's eighteen thousand banks past the shoals of disaster was William H. Woodin, the chipper financial genius whom FDR had plucked from his successful business of manufacturing railroad equipment to serve

President Roosevelt signing the Emergency Banking Relief Act.

A 25-cent scrip certificate issued by merchants of Clear Lake, Iowa, used in the purchase of farm products. The scrip was guaranteed by cash in the local bank, to purchase 22,000 bushels of corn from farmers at 25 cents a bushel. The farmers had to spend the scrip in local stores within 24 hours.

as secretary of the treasury.

The record shows that from 1930 to 1932 a total of 773 banks had failed, involving deposits of more than seven million dollars, and 3,604 state banks, with deposits exceeding two billion. Depositors were frightened and uneasy. Rumors of national disaster had resulted in wave after wave of withdrawals. Panicky Americans no longer trusted banks; they were taking their cash and placing it in safety-deposit vaults, trunks, even in the traditional mattress. It had become so bad that several cities were printing their own currency or scrip. The Treasury estimated that $1,212,000,000 had been withdrawn from circulation. The American dollar had dropped drastically in value; in Canada, for example, it had fallen to thirty-five cents within twenty hours.

There was some confusion following the banking decree. Next day Secretary Woodin, his gray toupee set firmly in place and his startlingly blue eyes twinkling, called in the press and clarified the situation:

All banks were allowed to make change to relieve the shortage of small bills and coin.

All banks were permitted to make loans for food, for both humans and animals.

All holders of safety-deposit vaults were to be given access to their vaults.

Scrip issued by the Greenwich Village Barter Exchange. Business and professional people in the Village agreed to accept the scrip, backed by notes of West Side businessmen and merchants.

All Postal Savings Banks would remain open.

All banks could cash checks drawn on the United States Treasury.

All banks were permitted to receive payments due to them.

All banks were forbidden to pay out in gold or gold certificates.

The four-day bank holiday didn't faze America. In all parts of the nation ingenuity and a sense of humor solved a lot of problems. Scrip, IOU's, cash, credit, integrity, and a smile took care of things.

In El Paso the First Baptist Church arranged to accept IOU's in the collection plate.

In Milwaukee the West Allis Presbyterian Church provided free gas and oil to all worshipers and tucked the collection baskets in an obscure spot "to avoid embarrassing those without small change."

An Akron newspaper paid off its employees in scrip which they had arranged with merchants to accept. The merchants in turn used it to pay their advertising bills.

In Queens, Borough President Harvey was down to his last dime—and wondering whom he could touch for a loan until the banks reopened—when in came a process server. Harvey took the summons—and the usual dollar.

In Hartford, Connecticut, the nickel-back-on-the-bottle became big business. Housewives and husbands dug deep in their cellars and returned hundreds, getting merchandise in return.

In Philadelphia the libraries declared a moratorium on book fines.

In federal court in Utica, New York, all bankruptcy petitions were held up because the petitions had to be accompanied by checks. It seemed the government would deal only in cash.

The Internal Revenue Department cheerfully announced that all accounts in banks that would not open could be charged as bad debts on the next income-tax return.

In New York a Broadway sports store began accepting crates of vegetables for merchandise. In Pennsylvania Station a man tendered a clerk a thousand-dollar bill and asked for a round-trip ticket to Newark. He didn't get the bill changed.

For the four days of the bank holiday the country was somewhat bewildered but still cheerful. Railroads announced that business had not decreased although they were still running on a cash

Scrip valued at $2,984,000 issued by the city of Detroit.

People returning gold to New York's Federal Reserve Bank.

99

basis. Steamships and airplane lines were accepting "reasonable" checks from customers. Chain stores reported increased sales and plans were being made to issue coupon books redeemable for food. The books would be distributed to industrial and commercial concerns and would be issued to employees as part of their pay.

With the bank holiday came the "Gold Rush of 1933." During the four days Americans hastened to comply with the government strictures against hoarding gold by turning bars of gold, gold coins, and gold certificates into banks which were open from dawn to dusk.

In every large city lines of men and women waited in the windy darkness before dawn until the first lights went on in the banks. Men with drawn guns or with bags chained to their wrists walked up to tellers' cages to deposit their hoarded yellow metal. In Chicago federal authorities estimated that gold was pouring back at the rate of $2,000,000 a day; in Philadelphia more than $1,500,000 was received in five hours, in St. Louis $636,000, and in Richmond $500,000.

In St. Louis a man said he had been saving his gold coins for thirty years. It took a teller with a chisel to pry some apart. In New York one man turned in $35,000 of the precious metal. He was escorted by three men, all armed. Behind him came three

Sacks, canvas bags, shopping bags, and even children's wagons were used by people returning gold to the Federal Reserve Bank in New York.

young men; two had bags chained to their wrists and the third walked between them, a hand held menacingly in his coat pocket.

In Newark a chauffeur drove up with a shoe box containing $10,000 in gold coins.

"Madam said she would bring in the rest tomorrow," the man told the teller.

As fast as the gold was received it was transported under heavy guard to the Federal Reserve Bank on New York's Liberty Street, guarded by one hundred men, mostly former marines, under Colonel Hiram Bearss, winner of the Croix de Guerre and Distinguished Military Cross. Guard mount was held every morning during the five days, as well as arms inspection, drill, and practice. The walls of the central office were ringed with machine guns, teargas bombs, and other small arms. On one wall was a large board with many colored lights that flashed a warning if a door so much as opened an inch. As Colonel Bearss told reporters, his men needed only one qualification, to be a crack shot.

The following Monday the names of all persons in the United States known to have withdrawn big sums in gold or gold certificates were reported to the Treasury by the Federal Reserve Bank. Unless their hoards were returned, action was taken against them under the new Federal Anti-Hoarding Gold Act.

By midnight of the last day, Washington announced that more than $200,-000,000 in gold had poured back into the Federal Reserve Bank.

It was the biggest gold rush since '49.

Official of New York's Empire Trust Company, attended by guards, stores $35,000 in gold coin brought in by one man.

The Hundred Days

FDR signing the historic Farm Measure. Behind the President (left to right) are Representative J. Bayard Clark, Representative Wall Doxey, Representative H. P. Fulmer, George Peek, Representative Jones, Representative John Raber, Senator E. D. Smith, Henry Morgenthau, Jr., and Secretary Henry Wallace.

THE HUNDRED DAYS, the most magnificent chapter of the New Deal, opened with a barrage of terse presidential messages to Congress.

On March 16 Roosevelt asked Congress to pass the Agricultural Adjustment Act, the most dramatic peacetime farm bill ever placed before Congress. The bill provided for crop curtailment to reduce surpluses, in an attempt to establish pre-war parity for farm products, and for refinancing of farm mortgages.

Five days later the President asked Congress to authorize a Civilian Conservation Corps, which would give young men reforestation work by early summer. They would help build dams, fight forest fires, build highways, and in all this relieve the unemployment situation. The bill passed with a resounding voice vote.

On the same day FDR asked for federal grants to the states to relieve unemployment, a move Hoover had cautiously approached in the last days of his administration. Roosevelt's proposal was the biggest welfare program in the history of the United States.

FDR asked that the Volstead Act be modified at once to allow for the sale and distribution of beer and light wines, with federal taxes to be applied to such sales. On March 22 the "Beer Bill" was passed.

The Federal Emergency Relief Act, passed on May 12, authorized the Reconstruction Finance Corporation to give 500 million dollars to states in need.

On March 29 FDR asked for federal supervision of information on new investment securities to be sold in interstate commerce. Under the provisions of the bill, the government could

FDR signs the Railroad Reorganization bill on June 16, 1933. The President, referring to the bill and to the Recovery and Bank bills, all signed on the same day, said that more important legislation was signed into law that day than on any other day in American history. Senator Dill of Washington is at left, Representative Rayburn of Texas at right.

prosecute any who failed to give full and accurate information for transmission to prospective investors.

On April 10 FDR asked Congress to create the Tennessee Valley Authority, which would develop the power resources of the Tennessee River and its tributaries, and use them to build up the economy of the whole area. This was an old dream of statesmen like Senator Norris of Nebraska, who had fought long and hard to prevent the government from selling the Muscle Shoals dam to private utilities. Now FDR presented the exciting prospect of an intensive federal investment to develop a vast and almost untouched land for public use. The bill was signed on May 18.

On April 13, the President asked a bill to save homeowners from mortgage holders. This was one of his most popular bills. Homes were being snatched from unemployed heads of families at a high rate this year. FDR wanted a bill that would establish lower interest rates and postpone interest and principal payments in cases of extreme need.

On May 4 the President asked for powers to appoint a coordinator of transportation, who would crack down on duplication of services of public carriers, prevent waste, and in general encourage reorganization of the financial structures of railroad companies. In early June this bill was passed.

On May 17, Roosevelt asked Congress to shorten the work week, to get employers to pay a decent minimum wage, and to prevent overproduction and unfair competition by means of fair-practice codes for each industry. He demanded unprecedented powers to set up a huge employment program, with an estimated 3,300 million dollars to be invested by the government in all sorts of public construction. This proposal was badly mauled in Congress, but a version of the bill eventually staggered through the Senate gantlet to reach FDR's desk on June 16, when he signed the National Industrial Recovery Act.

After the New Deal's historic and exciting Hundred Days, most lawmakers and members of the public sat back and eyed the dazzling record. FDR was the first to admit that sometimes he had been playing by ear. Many were confused by the mixture of bills, some deflationary, others authorizing expense of government money. But it was a desperate time, and fresh minds were producing new ideas to deal with the crisis. It was no time for the scoffers who were mumbling about socialism or the cautious who were eyeing the government budget.

The CCC

THE MOST pressing problem in the momentous month of March, once the banking crisis had passed, was the stark one of relief and unemployment. There were now fifteen million men and women without jobs; more than six million were on state or municipal relief rolls. President Roosevelt had proposed three measures which would relieve this problem· emergency grants to states to feed and clothe the homeless and the hungry, a program of durable public works, and government enterprises which would recruit workers from the ranks of the jobless.

In the last category was the Civilian Conservation Corps, which became the most popular of all the New Deal agencies. Jobless youths working in the outdoors, teen-agers building roads in the unpenetrated sections of the Far West—the prospect caught the public imagination. It also impressed business men. They later showed a preference for hiring a man who had been in the CCC, and the reasoning was simple: employers felt that anyone who had been in the CCC would know what a full day's work meant and how to carry out orders in a disciplined way. Their experience gave them manual "know how" and self-confidence.

In this age of the Bomb, millions of mature, graying, and paunchy Americans have fond memories of a grim but quieter time when they were cutting down trees in the West, building dams in New England, or even wielding a shovel and pick on the windy stretches of the New Jersey Palisades as members of the Civilian Conservation Corps. The Supreme Court could wring the neck of the NRA's Blue Eagle, but the CCC lasted until a year after Pearl Harbor.

It was among the first measures of FDR's historic Hundred Days and was initially known as the Civilian Corps Reforestation Youth Rehabilitation Movement. In July of 1933, Congress officially made it the Civilian Conservation Corps. Both House and Senate approved an appropriation of 350 million dollars to carry on the work under Robert Fechner, the director appointed by the President.

The idea was FDR's, conceived in

The first CCC recruits in New York City line up outside the Army Building.

the dark winter of 1933 as a means to provide useful employment for the many young men caught in the Depression, unable to find work and faced with the possibility of the street corner, the hobo camp, or riding the rails as a tramp. It was the President's dream that they could be put to work conserving the country's natural resources under army officers and forest rangers.

In Boston hundreds of young men thronged the Federal Building seeking CCC enrollment.

It was the first relief agency to go into action. Thousands of young men from coast to coast lined up in front of army induction centers to file their applications and pass a physical. Then they were sent to military posts and then to various states where the camps were set up—often by their own hands.

One aging enrollee recalls, "I was sent to Utah. I'll never forget the ride up the mountains in this battered old truck. We had an old grizzled army sergeant in charge. When we got to the area, it was just thick woods. 'Where's the camp?' I asked. The sarge waved his hands around the trees. 'This is it. Break out the axes and chop like hell if you don't want to sleep on the ground.' We chopped and built cabins and even a mess hall. For the next three years I grew up, physically and mentally and spiritually, in that beautiful country. It was one of the most rewarding experiences of my life. Before I left I was offered a job as a ranger. To this day I wonder whether I was a fool in turning it down and coming back east. A large number of the CCC's stayed on. Some own ranches today."

The Army feeding CCC recruits at New York City's South Ferry.

A guitar-playing CCC recruit and his buddies on their way to Missoula, Mont.

104

The first batch of CCC applicants reaches Fort Sheridan, Ill.

CCC recruits working at the federal tree nursery, Wind River, Wash.

This writer vividly recalls covering the first day of enrollment at army headquarters in downtown New York when the first applicants arrived. Most of them, in thin summer clothes with no overcoats, had lined up before dawn. The first boy accepted was from the lower East Side. He was dancing a jig to celebrate when reporters told him he would probably be sent to the West. He stopped jigging and a newsman asked if anything was wrong. The boy scratched his head and said very seriously, "What the hell are we going to do about those Indians?"

Each enrollee was to receive thirty dollars a month pay, of which twenty-five dollars was to be sent to his family. This was necessary because none of the federal relief agencies was then in operation, and state, county, and city relief had broken down because of lack of funds. Preference was given to applicants from families on relief, but other young men were permitted to enroll. If the boy's family was not on relief, then the money was deposited in an account for him until the time when he completed his enlistment.

By 1937 the CCC, originally started as an experiment for unemployment relief, was a huge government-operated "concern" owning 100 million dollars worth of equipment and with programs mapped out for years ahead. It performed major functions for four government departments—War, Interior, Agriculture and Labor. More than 2,500,-000 youths had served in the CCC.

There were three hundred major types of labor performed by the enrollees in the corps, scattered all over the country on thousands of different projects, from the building of the great dam on the Winooski River in Vermont, for control of flood waters that in the years past had cost many lives and millions of dollars in property damage, to the building of a small pond in Yellowstone Park to protect a nest of two trumpeter swans that had settled in the brush. At the time there were less than a hundred of those birds in the country and the youths on the project, many of whom had never heard of a trumpeter swan, spent the season protecting the two rare birds from coyotes and other predatory animals.

In between these projects were the

CCC boys working at reforestation, Luray, Va.

vast number of improvements in national and state parks, the enlarged trail systems, the new camping grounds, improved park structures, high bridges and countless miles of stone walls from New York State to the old Illinois Central Canal country. In the Jamestown area, where the first English settlers had arrived, the corps helped archaeologists in restoration work. CCC camps sprang

up from the Skokie Lagoon section of Illinois out through the Black Hills of Dakota, down into Texas, and across to the West Coast.

Besides reforestation and improvement of natural resources, the CCC helped to eradicate the Dutch elm disease, which was threatening to wipe out the eastern elm as a similar blight had destroyed the chestnut twenty years before. Thirty million acres of timber were treated.

In four years the CCC enrollees planted 1,500 million trees. If that many trees were planted ten feet apart in a line, they would form a shelter belt three times around the circumference of the earth. In two years 3,500,000 check dams were built to control erosion, not to mention the thousands of bird sanctuaries that were set up—many still in existence—and the thousands of streams that were stocked.

The CCC's also fired the last shot of Gettysburg. In 1934 a group of boys working on the national park there dug up a Civil War shell. The army commander in charge decided it was too dangerous to be sent to a museum, so he arranged with the Ordnance staff to set it off. With due ceremonies the shell was exploded.

But beyond the material benefits the country derived from the corps was the mental, spiritual, and physical help the lost youth of the Depression received from the CCC. From problems they became assets to their country and their

An arithmetic class in a Georgia CCC camp.

106

CCC boys learning auto mechanics in Washington, D.C.

community. In the beginning rangers and army personnel found the majority of the enrollees, with no previous work experience, were undernourished, badly clothed, bitter, resentful, hostile. Within a month the plain but wholesome food, the outdoors, the comradeship, the regular hours, the work, and the feeling they were useful and helping their families, restored the enrollees to the high morale which has always characterized American youth.

In the National Archives in Washington the yellowing records of the corps give a vivid account of the work of the Education Unit of the CCC; according to the 1937 report, 50,000 illiterates were graduated from grade schools set up in the camps; 400,000 received high-school education and more than 40,000 college courses.

As President Roosevelt said in 1933: "Our program is twofold: conservation of our natural resources, and conservation of our human resources. Both are sound investments for the future of our country."

There is little doubt those investments were among the finest the New Deal ever made.

CCC boys in aviation mechanics class at camp in Fredericksburg, Va.

CWA

IN THE PREDAWN darkness of a November day in 1933, hundreds of thousands of men—young, middle-aged, bitter, hopeful—lined up in front of armories, state employment offices, schools, YMCA headquarters, and many makeshift offices in every large city in the country to try for a job in the newly created Civil Works program set up by President Roosevelt to get the jobless back to work.

Harry Hopkins had announced in Washington that the government was appropriating 400 million dollars for an emergency program and that the President wanted fast action by the states. As Hopkins pointed out, so eager was the government to aid the jobless that "if a state does not transfer people from its relief rolls there will be no government work in that area."

The states rushed to do Hopkins' bidding. In every state capital, lights burned late as the new program, dubbed CWA, swung into action.

There was a little hope and less uncertainty for the coming winter. Hadn't FDR said he wanted the first checks out in time for jobless Americans to have a Thanksgiving dinner?

In Washington, General Frank T. Hines, director of the Veterans Administration which had been designated as the disbursing agency for CWA, announced that 400 million dollars would be paid to CWA workers by February. Even new check-writing machines were rushed to statehouses to get the checks rolling. A small army of disbursing officers was dispatched to states where the payrolls could not be established quickly.

"The idea is to get the checks out fast," General Hines announced.

In New York, Chicago, and St. Louis, ten thousand men waited as long as fifteen hours to sign their applications. Governors in many states ordered armories opened so the men could sleep on the floor. It was not unusual for newsmen to find men in the lines who had not had a job in three years.

Meanwhile in Washington Louis McHenry Howe, secretary to President Roosevelt, announced that thousands of teachers would be employed on the CWA in a national war on illiteracy. Howe explained: "It works this way. Say

Mounted police escort job-hunters to New York's 69th Regiment Armory, which had been opened on orders of Governor Lehman.

for example an unemployed group wants to learn carpentry, geography, arithmetic, grammar—anything. There's always a teacher to teach them. These classes will be organized and the teachers put on a salary. It won't be much but it will be something. That means a teacher has a job and Americans are learning."

And that same day FDR told the nation: "I am very confident that the mere fact of giving real wages to four million Americans who are today not getting wages, is going to do more to relieve suffering and to lift the morale of the nation than anything undertaken before."

On the heels of the President's statement, Harry Hopkins declared that 16 million poor Americans would be cared for in the coming winter. The gaunt-faced man was proving to be a quiet but highly efficient dynamo. After one week in office he had distributed 100 million tons of pork, 15 million pounds of canned beef, and 2 million pounds of butter.

"What else do I intend to buy?" he replied to a reporter. "Coal before the winter gets cold, clothes and shoes for those who don't have any, and maybe even pay the rent for those who don't have any money. . . ."

Jobless who waited all night to register for the CWA.

The Blue Eagle

THE HAPPY, beaming President looked up at the Congressmen who encircled his desk. "Gentlemen," he said, tapping the paper before him, "history will undoubtedly record the National Industrial Recovery Act as the most important and far-reaching legislation ever enacted by the American Congress. It represents a supreme effort to stabilize for all time the many factors which make for the prosperity of the nation. . . ."

And then dipping his pen into the ink well, he scrawled "Franklin D. Roosevelt" at the bottom of one of the biggest pieces of legislation he had received from Congress. It was June 16, and the act, creating the National Recovery Administration, was another achievement of 1933's amazing Seventy-third Congress. The new laws were desperate measures for the nation's Desperate Years, bulwarks against a tidal wave of economic demoralization. Important as all the measures were, none of them compared in might, majesty, and magnitude to the National Industrial Recovery Act. Into that measure had been packed the greatest public-works program ever attempted by any nation and the largest peacetime powers over industrial wages, hours, and prices ever given to one man in the United States. It was FDR's do-or-die attack against the Depression.

He had given his countrymen his estimate of it in these words: "The law I have signed was passed to put people back to work—to let them buy more of the products of the farms and factories and start our business at a living rate again. This task is in two stages: first, to get many thousands of unemployed back on the payroll by snowfall; and second, to plan for a better future for the long pull. As in the great crisis of the World War, it puts the whole people to the simple but vital test: must we go on in many groping, disorganized, separate units to defeat, or shall we move as one great team to victory?

"While we shall not neglect the second, the first stage is an emergency job. It has the right of way."

To guide this massive program FDR

C. T. Coiner, Philadelphia, Pa., creator of the NRA eagle.

appointed a board of public works, composed of the secretaries of Interior, War, Agriculture, Commerce, and Labor, the attorney general, the director of the budget and Colonel George R. Spalding, an Army river-and-harbor engineer.

These were the main features of the historic measure which injected new life into America's sluggish industry:

It gave President Roosevelt and his administrators wide power to promote self-regulation of industry under federal supervision as a means of curtailing overproduction and disastrous price-cutting, improving wages, shortening hours, and thus increasing prices and employment;

Authorized a 3,300-million-dollar bond issue to finance construction of federal, state, local, and public-benefitting private projects to create new employment;

Invested the President with authority to work out codes of fair competition to be accepted by industry voluntarily, with additional power to compel compliance with the codes and to subject violators to a fine;

Provided the President with power to license an industry if necessary to force unwilling companies into line.

The bond issue required 220 million dollars annually for financing. To meet this cost the following new taxes were provided:

A tax of .1 per cent on corporation net worth, with a 5 per cent additional assessment on earnings above 12.5 per

cent; a 5 per cent tax on corporation dividends to be deducted at the source; an increase of half a cent in the refiners' gasoline tax; three-year extension of corporation consolidation return privileges with addition of 1 per cent to the income-tax rate on consolidated returns, instead of the .75 per cent levied the previous year.

Extended for one year were all special excise taxes voted by the last Congress, and changes were made in the tax law to prevent carrying over into subsequent years stock and bond losses exceeding the gains in the year they occurred. These applied to both corporations and individuals.

Another New Deal venture, the Public Works Administration, was set up under the same act, with an initial appropriation of 3,300 million dollars. The PWA, as it was soon dubbed by headline writers, was designed to stimulate heavy industry by sponsoring public works that required huge quantities of heavy material. This new and stimulating giant was placed in the care of Secretary of the Interior Harold L. Ickes, who was noted for his cautious use of the federal dollar. It was Ickes who told reporters he would "never hire a grown man to chase tumbleweeds on a windy day."

The program stipulated no special project but included, among other general work, the following:

Construction, repair and improvement of public highways and parkways,

General Hugh S. Johnson (center), Grover Whalen (left), local head of the NRA program, and Governor Lehman reviewing NRA parade in September, 1933.

erection of public buildings, conservation and development of natural resources, prevention of soil or coastal erosion, development of water power and transmission of electrical energy, river and harbors improvements, and flood control, low-cost housing and slum-clearance projects, dry docks, naval vessels permitted under the London Treaty, and technical construction for the Army Air Corps.

The Public Works administrator—the Senate amendment specifying a board of three had been eliminated—was empowered to make grants to states and municipalities for construction and improvement projects up to 30 per cent of the cost of labor and materials.

NIRA also authorized the President to institute proceedings before the tariff commission and to embargo or limit imports where they interfered with the purposes of the act in raising wages and prices.

Finally, it authorized 100 million dollars for distribution by the Farm Relief administrators.

The highway-construction administrator was given thirty days in which to distribute 400 million dollars for new projects, which had to be started at once.

"I want a million men working by autumn," he was told.

"In my inaugural," said President Roosevelt, "I laid down the simple proposition that nobody is going to starve in this country. It seems to me to be equally plain that no business which depends on paying less than living wages has any right to continue. By 'business' I mean the whole of commerce as well as the whole of industry; by workers I mean all workers—the white-collar class as well as the men in overalls; and by living wages I mean more than a bare subsistence level—I mean the wages of decent living.

"Throughout industry the change from starvation wages and starvation employment to living wages and sustained employment can, in large part, be made by an industrial covenant to which all employers shall subscribe."

Though he was letting down the bars of the anti-trust laws so that industries might get together to regulate prices and wages, the President promised to "stand firmly against monopolies that restrain trade, and price-fixing which allows inordinate profits or unfairly high prices. . . . I am fully aware that wage increases will eventually raise costs, but I ask that managements give first consideration to the improvement of operating figures by greatly increased sales to be expected from the rising purchasing power of the public. That is good economics and good business. . . . If we now inflate prices as fast and as far as we increase wages the whole project will be set at naught. . . . If we can . . . start a strong upward spiral of businesss activity, our industries will have little doubt of black-ink operations in the last quarter of this year."

The man who was to rally industry into line as NRA administrator was General Hugh Samuel Johnson, West Pointer, lawyer, boys' book writer, associate of Bernard Mannes Baruch, and originator and administrator of the wartime draft.

Key men were drawn from the ranks of economists, businessmen, and labor leaders to make up advisory boards. The Industrial Advisory Board appointed by Secretary of Commerce Roper included: General Motors president Alfred Pritchard Sloan, Jr.; Walter Clark Teagle, president of Standard Oil of New Jersey; General Electric president Gerard Swope; Chairman Edward Nash Hurley of Chicago's Hurley Ma-chine Company; Louis Kirstein, vice-president of Filene's, Boston department store; Austin Finch, president of the Thomasville (N.C.) Chair Company and chairman of the Southern Manufacturers' Association's committee already at work in connection with the recovery act.

To the Labor Advisory Board, Secretary Perkins appointed: economist Leo Wolman; President Frey of the International Boilermakers Union; William Green, president of the A.F.L.; Father Francis Haas, president of the National Catholic School of Social Service; Rose Schneiderman, secretary of the Woman's Trades Union League.

Next to be named was a Consumer's Advisory Board representing the public. As outlined by President Roosevelt, the

The National Recovery Administration Board. (Left to right) Walton Hamilton, Chairman of the Advisory Council; Leon Henderson, Director of the Division of Research and Planning; Blackwell Smith, Assistant General Counsel; S. Clay Williams, Chairman; Arthur Whiteside, former Divisional Administrator; Leon C. Marshall, Assistant Administrator for Policy; and Sidney Hillman, member Labor Advisory Board.

George Creel, Assistant District Director of NRA, addresses a noontime crowd at San Francisco's Lotta's fountain.

whole system would work like this:

When a trade group thought it had settled its wage, price, and output problems, it would apply to General Johnson's office for a hearing. The advisory board would designate officials to find out if the trade group was representative of its industry. Other officials would consult with representatives of labor in the industry, still others with consumers of the industry's products. The combined findings would be handed over to the NRA administrator, who would finally take them to the President for approval. Recalcitrant companies in the industry would be firmly kept in line by a system of licenses which the President could put in operation for one year and which, if screwed down hard, could put them out of business.

In the marble halls of Herbert Hoover's monument, the new Department of Commerce Building, both phases of the Recovery Act were administered. Pert young clerks by the score inked up rubber stamps and, like hungry buzzards, Congressmen scented out the headquarters of the government's newest and grandest handout.

His pockets bulging with papers, like those of a country lawyer, General Johnson left the White House as soon as the President had signed the measure. Unofficially he had been talking to industrialists for weeks about the Recovery Act. That evening he was scheduled to speak to harassed soft-coal men in Chicago. When his plane was grounded by fog at Pittsburgh, General Johnson addressed his audience by radio. He strongly urged his distant hosts to "put into effect provisions which you find necessary to protect the willing and the forward-looking among your members from the racketeers and price-cutters and those who are willing to take advantage of the unselfishness and public spirit of other men."

At Bryn Mawr, Secretary of Labor Perkins predicted the Recovery Act would "outlaw the sweatshop."

Racketeering in labor was attacked on another front when New York's Doctor-Senator Copeland left Washington with a committee to investigate hoodlumism in New York, Detroit, and Chicago. The Recovery Act could also be used as a weapon against labor racketeering since an industry's labor would, like its management, be obliged to make a clean breast before the Industrial Recovery Administration.

First to submit a model code was

An NRA rally in Madison Square Garden on September 12, 1933.

the cotton-textile industry, through a committee said to represent two-thirds of the textile millers. The code provided a minimum wage of $10 a week in Southern mills, $11 in the North, a 44-hour week, and acknowledgment of the employees' right to collective bargaining. The coal men in Chicago were preparing a code. The American Petroleum Institute was also doing spadework in Chicago, while the independents sent their own recommendations to Washington. At Bloomfield, Indiana, thirty Indiana limestone producers agreed on a code.

Wage increases were taking place all over the country. In Akron, where Newton Diehl Baker was trying to bring harmony to the embattled rubber industry, Goodyear, Firestone, General, and Mohawk all announced 10 per cent raises. Seiberling upped pay 5 per cent. The Pittsburgh Coal Company was paying 10 per cent more to eight thousand workers. Amoskeag Manufacturing Company, largest cotton-textile manufacturer, announced a 15 per cent raise at Manchester, New Hampshire.

Other textile mills soon swung into line. Then canning factories in Florida, a Philadelphia handbag maker, a Suffolk, Virginia, candy maker, upped their employees' pay, while Sears Roebuck rescinded a 10 per cent pay cut.

Optimism, a sense that perhaps the country was beginning to emerge from the dreadful, grim woods, was on the rise throughout the land.

Still there were problems, notably in the rubber industry, where fluctuations of prices in crude rubber were controlled by overseas conditions. The copper industry was discovering cheap, foreign copper and it would be unwise for Washington to erect high tariff walls. The automobile industry was hinting that perhaps it might request a standard 36-hour week since during its rush months of April, May, and June the factories usually went on a 48-hour week but tapered off in the autumn and winter to much less than that.

There were other major problems that had to be solved, so in the autumn General Johnson—popularly known as Old Iron Pants—packed his work in boxes and valises and took off for action all around the country. His name was on Room 3053 of the old Commerce Building, but for the life of the NRA he was never there; when he wasn't travelling, he and his blue eagle were down the hall in an unmarked office.

The President Who Walked

Gerardo Machado, shortly before he was deposed as President of Cuba.

BORN OF a family noted for its sacrifices in the cause of Cuban independence, General Gerardo Machado had derived a peculiar satisfaction when he was elected fifth president of the Republic of Cuba. His parents, Colonel Gerardo Machado and Señora Ludgarda Morales de Machado, were members of Cuba's most prominent families, long identified with the movement to free Cuba from Spain. General Machado first took the field against Spain when he was twenty-two and fought bravely until his country was free.

After he entered politics he ran for many offices, among them secretary of the interior. But he left government services to form a new liberal party, which paved the way for his first election in 1925.

During his campaign he adopted a revolutionary formula; Cubans had always been used to candidates appearing on a fiery horse to appeal to the imagination of the voters. But Machado eliminated the horse and adopted the campaign slogan *"a pie"* meaning "on foot." It became one of Cuba's most popular campaign slogans and rallied many supporters.

In 1928 the President's four-year term was made six, thus extending his tenure of office to 1931.

After his election Machado visited the United States many times, and regarded it as a personal achievement when the Pan American Congress met in the Cuban capital.

But in 1933 General Machado was ousted as president by a riotous populace that stormed his palace, burned parts of the city and did its best to destroy every vestige of his regime.

Machado fled to the United States with his official party and landed in New York. But the new Cuban government charged him with murder and misappropriation of funds, and demanded that he be returned.

It became a game of hares and hounds, with government agents seeking the former president, who skipped about the country. Once it was reported he was ready to surrender in Easton, Pennsylvania, another time in Chicago.

Machado finally turned up in Canada and later in Europe. Meanwhile a new strong man, a former army colonel named Batista, took over. Seated on the curb of the Prado, watching the army march past and the tanks rumble by, was a youngster with dark hair and black eyes.

His name was Fidel Castro.

Depression Layette

IT COST a mother in those Desperate Years just $7.70 to buy a Depression layette for her baby. In April, 1933, according to the *New York Times,* the Homemaking Department of New York University reported that its students had collected a 61-piece layette which was put on display in the school. Here are the prices:

2 binders @ .20	$0.40
3 shirts @ .20	.60
2 dresses @ .20	.40
2 slips @ .20	.40
2 flannelette slips @ .20	.40
2 flannelette wrappers @ .20	.40
2 flannelette nighties @ .20	.40
24 diapers	2.10
1 bath towel	.20
1 turkish towel	.05
2 washcloths @ .05	.10
2 quilted pads @ .10	.20
1 stockinette rubber sheet	.10
2 wrapping blankets @ .10	.20
1 flannelette sacque	.20
1 rubber diaper	.10
2 pr. bootees @ .20	.40
3 cards safety pins @ .05	.15
1 box Q-Tips	.10
2 pr. woolen stockings @ .20	.40
2 crib blankets @ .20	.40
61 pieces	$7.70

When the *Times* man questioned some of the students who had conducted the survey they said wistfully they would like "better things," if they could afford them, for their own babies.

Death of the AKRON

The Akron crossing the Potomac in 1931.

The remains of the Akron as it was hauled up out of the sea by the salvage crew of the U.S.S. Falcon.

THE FRAGILITY of the beautiful dirigible airship *Akron,* which sailed so surely and serenely in the sky, resulted in things being constantly spliced aboard her — girders, frames, wires. Some broke, some snapped under strain.

For example, on one trip to the West Coast, two longitudinal girders buckled in the section of the ship just aft of the bay. The *Akron* came home, 2,300 miles, with the buckled girders held by timber backing.

One night in April, 1933, the *Akron,* with seventy-seven men and officers aboard, rode out a storm off the Jersey coast. Suddenly she began descending rapidly. Ballast was jettisoned and when the big silver dirigible reached eight hundred feet the order was given to abandon ship. The *Akron* hit the heavy sea, nose first, and swiftly broke up.

Some of the officers and men managed to swim free and were picked up by tankers, but when the final count was made only three had survived. Numerous hearings were held by the Navy and all sorts of theories were advanced, but it was evident from the testimony that the *Akron,* beautiful, serene on the outside, had been jerry-built inside.

Labor's Mixed-Up Giant

IN 1933 a new voice made itself heard across the nation. It belonged to a mixed-up giant who became a monument in American labor, but there were times when he would act like a man two inches high. During the Desperate Years he had enormous successes, abysmal failures; he was loved, hated, despised, feared, and respected.

John L. Lewis, a titan of American labor, had tremendous impact on the nation's economy. In 1933, along with the National Industrial Recovery Act, Lewis entered the main stream of American labor history. After the passage of the Wagner Act, which gave workers the right to organize and required employers to bargain with them on wages and working conditions, Lewis had a great dream: he would organize the millions of unorganized unskilled industrial workers. The American Federation of Labor, interested only in craft unions, turned thumbs down on Lewis' plan. Lewis quit the AFL and formed the Congress of Industrial Organizations. The drive that followed and its towering success was one of the landmarks in the history of labor.

A man of iron will, Lewis fought the captains of industry and even the government itself in a never-ending, relentless battle to obtain bargaining rights and wage benefits gains for workers in one industry after another.

Lewis broke with FDR when he was attempting to organize the steel workers. He had expected help from the White House, but Roosevelt instead voiced a "plague on both your houses" to both Lewis and the steel companies.

"Labor, like Israel, has many sorrows," reported Lewis in one of his most famous speeches. "Its women weep for their fallen and they lament for the future of the children of the race. It ill behooves one who has supped at labor's table and who has been sheltered in labor's house to curse with equal fervor and fine impartiality both

John L. Lewis when he flayed Donald Richberg of the NRA as an enemy of labor.

labor and its adversaries when they become locked in deadly embrace."

In the thirties Lewis proved himself a liberal and a conservative and a colossal egotist who had to be humbled in public. He was a great actor and an enormous ham. He fought American businessmen for one thing: a good part

of their profits for the worker. When he had his own way Lewis was fine; when he didn't he sulked like a small boy. He led his miners to back FDR after the NRA was established and backed Roosevelt in his 1936 campaign. But in 1940 he switched and came out for Wendell Willkie. He made his biggest

116

John L. Lewis lecturing a Senate labor sub-committee.

mistake when he said he would quit if FDR was re-elected. He had matched his popularity against FDR's and when there was a Roosevelt landslide Lewis quit the CIO.

The crowning contradiction of his life came in 1959 when, after he announced his plans to retire from the presidency of his powerful United Mine Workers, the coal barons expressed their sincere regret and gave him an eighteenth-century, fifteen-volume set of Shakespeare, whose works Lewis had quoted many times in his blasts against them.

Lewis' great mane of hair and thick, bristling eyebrows were a common sight for newspaper readers of the thirties. He was notable for colorful phrases such as "He who tooteth not his own horn, the same shall not be tooted."

But when Lewis paused for breath, other men blew his horn for him. Hoover called him the "ablest man in American labor." Huey Long complimented him with "Lewis is the Huey Long of Labor." FDR said, "He is a man whom I respect, a man of honor, intelligence, and good will."

At the height of the Depression his

union wanted to double his $12,000-a-year salary. Lewis refused. Once during a contract crisis in the thirties he told a rank-and-file meeting: "I have pleaded your case from the pulpit and from the public platform, in joint conference with the operators of this country, before the bar of state legislatures, in the council of the President's cabinet, and in the public press of the nation—not in the quavering tones of a feeble mendicant asking alms but in the thundering voice of a captain of a mighty host, demanding the rights to which free men are entitled."

The New Chancellor of Germany

Currying favor, Adolf Hitler bows obsequiously to President von Hindenburg in 1933.

ALL GERMANY was electrified when, on the afternoon of January 30, the news spread that President von Hindenburg had summoned Adolf Hitler to the Chancellery in Berlin. Hitler was the fuehrer (leader) of the National Socialist (Nazi) Party, an aggressive, violent, strictly disciplined and highly regimented organization that stood for extreme nationalism and a totalitarian state. It was rabidly anti-semitic and anti-communist.

Large crowds were gathering on the streets. There was no jubilation, no demonstration, only an air of tension and expectancy. On Saturday, General Kurt von Schleicher had tried to persuade several Reichswehr generals to join a monarchist "putsch," but the generals declined; the rash proposal was futile, it would be better to wait. All over Germany men and women were waiting for announcement of what role would be played by the man who had begun his march to power in the ill-fated beer-hall putsch in Munich ten years before. Hitler had entered the Chancellery only when his party's swastika flags began to break out all over the city. But there were no flags, no demonstrations in front of the grim building where every German knew the fate of his country was being decided.

Then suddenly, dramatically, the announcement was made that Adolf Hitler had been made chancellor of Germany, after a reconciliation with the aging president who twice before had refused him the post.

The nationwide frenzy of fear and enthusiasm that swept through Germany that fateful afternoon was comparable only to that of August, 1914, at the start of the first World War.

At seven P.M. Hitler, in his first broadcast to the people of the fourteen-year-old republic, made it clear that while he was not yet a dictator he would be very shortly.

To temper Hitler's dictatorial ambitions, Von Hindenburg announced that he would insist on a "nationalist front" cabinet that would contain only three Nazis, two nationalists and six Junkers, the latter under his direct influence.

He also announced the appointment of his protégé, ex-Chancellor von Papen, as vice-chancellor and premier of Prussia, key state of the Reich. But Von Hindenburg, Germany's greatest war hero since Frederick the Great, was now a tottering, feeble old man, and these measures were plainly inadequate.

After his announcement, Socialist Reichstag members met to decide whether they should call a general

strike. But this protest was lost in the thunderous acclaim for Hitler's appointment. Behind the former Austrian house-painter and corporal was an army of six hundred thousand Nazi storm troopers, who most experts expected would be made into a national militia or a Steel Helmet organization.

At eight P.M. they staged a gigantic torch parade past the Chancellery. They came by the thousands, down Unter den Linden through the central arch of the Brandenburg Gate, formerly reserved for such as the Kaiser and Von Hindenburg. The old president, bareheaded and wearing an old dark overcoat, stood in a window of the old Chancellery as the Nazi legions marched past, the night shaking with their roars of "Heil Hitler" and "Hoch Hindenburg." In another unlighted window, in the new section of the building, stood Hitler, also bareheaded, his eyes flashing and with his well-known lock of dark hair hanging over one eye. Occasionally he answered the roars, thrusting out his arm in his party's salute.

For four hours the marchers pounded past; once Von Hindenburg smiled when a band stood beneath the window and with blaring horns and booming drums crashed into "Deutschland Ueber Alles." Crowds, cheering and whooping, started dancing in the streets. The old man leaned over slightly and waved.

In northern Berlin the picture was different. Truckloads of Communists shouting "Down with Hitler" roared through the streets, to be booed by the Nazis who lined the sidewalks. Mounted policemen fought the crowds back to the curbs and prevented a riot.

In another section of Berlin, Dr. Joseph Goebbels was sitting quietly with Charles Flick, a veteran foreign correspondent. Since the announcement of Hitler's appointment most correspondents had been trying to get an inkling of his governmental program. In that quiet room Flick got his answer. The small, club-footed propagandist told him: "Within sixty days Germany will be a fascist state. Today is the fulfillment of a thirteen-year battle. Now we have pierced the lines. It is only a question of a short time before we roll them back completely."

There were other statements, other predictions that night. Dr. Hjalmar Schacht, former president of the Reichsbank, Germany's central bank of issue, was telling a reporter what a wonderful thing this appointment of Hitler was. He said Hitler was the "surest guarantee that all German debts to America will be paid to the last."

Hitler, he said, was a man of peace "who someday would be a boon to the entire world."

Goebbels and a Hitler poster.

Vice Chancellor von Papen votes on March 5, 1933, for the new Reichstag.

The Fire

Ruins of the Reichstag.

THE MOST devastating fire in the history of Germany was discovered on the evening of February 27, 1933, less than a week before the March 5 elections which were to be a test of Adolf Hitler's power in Germany.

The fire reduced the Reichstag building, a symbol of free Germany, to a charred skeleton. It also aroused public hysteria, which in a few days' time destroyed all effective opposition to the Nazis and paved the way for the persecution of Jews in Germany, the offensive against Austria, the occupation of Czechoslovakia, the invasion of Poland and, inevitably, World War II.

In the flames and smoke vanished the old Germanies of Bismarck, William II, and the Weimar constitution; in its place rose the monster of the Third Reich.

As Douglas Reed wrote afterward about conditions of the Third Reich:

A man's home was no longer his castle. He could be seized by private individuals, could claim no protection from the police, could be indefinitely detained without preferment of charges; his property could be seized, his verbal and written communications overheard and perused; he no longer had the right to foregather with his countrymen, and his

newspapers might no longer freely express their opinions.

The facts of the fire were simple; in the evening flames were seen shooting from the windows of the Reichstag, located near one end of the Unter den Linden. By the time the fire companies arrived the impressive brick building was an inferno. There was no doubt it was the work of an arsonist; the fire had been started in at least twenty places.

Goering and Hitler arrived together and denounced the blaze as work of the Communists. Hitler was obviously overjoyed: "A sign from heaven," he said as he watched the building crumble in the flames.

Why was Hitler overjoyed? At the time he needed a sweeping victory in the March 5 election to claim Nazi victory in the Reichstag. As it was, before the fire he had only three Nazi cabinet votes as against eight belonging to Von Papen. Things had not been going the way Hitler would like, and Hindenburg distrusted him. The Nazis feared they might lose the election, for they needed a majority of six hundred deputies in the Reichstag, and could claim only two hundred and fifty at present.

The fire did exactly what the Nazis needed done: Germany rose with an angry roar against the Communists for setting the fire. Raids took place. More than a hundred Communist deputies were arrested overnight. Liberty and freedom were suppressed. There were cries that the Communists planned a national uprising. In this haze of fear, distortion, and lies, Hitler's Nazi party took over.

A Dutch half-wit named Marinus van der Lubbe was arrested after police found him in the smoldering ruins. Although the Nazis, particularly Goering, denounced him as a Communist arsonist, the case developed weird twists and turns. The police had traced Van der Lubbe's movements of the night of the fire and found that he had been virtually a hobo wandering about the country-

side. The police found it difficult to explain how a wandering half-wit could have been trusted by the Communist Party to perform this dangerous and important work of arson.

Later the police naïvely told reporters that the moron had had helpers and that these helpers had entered and escaped through a little known tunnel leading from the Reichstag basement to the palace of the speaker of the Reichstag—none other than Hermann Goering—just across the street.

As the evidence piled up, there was little doubt that the Nazis themselves had set the fire. Arrested with Van der Lubbe was Ernst Torglet, chairman of the Reichstag's Communist bloc, who gave himself up to police when he heard the public announcement that he was wanted in the "conspiracy." Later three Bulgarian Communists were arrested, Dimitrov, Popov, and Tanev.

The trial was, as John Gunther put it, "neither a farce nor a frame-up." As the days passed it was clear the state had no case; it was plainly a matter of public hysteria. But Teutonic justice plodded on.

The star of the historic trial was Dimitrov. He tore apart the testimony of the countless cranks and phoney witnesses. When the judges charged him with making Communist propaganda,

the Bulgarian firebrand pointed to Goering in the witness dock and roared: "But he's making Nationalist propaganda!"

Of Lubbe he said with pity: "This miserable Faust! Who is his Mephistopheles?" Lubbe just yawned.

In the end the court was forced to acquit Torglet, Dimitrov, Popov, and Tanev. Van der Lubbe was convicted and sent to the headsman.

In 1946 Allied Intelligence officers found a copy of a letter to Von Hindenburg in which the writer said he was one of the last of twenty-two storm troopers who had been assigned by Captain Ernst Roehm to start the Reichstag fire. The letter described in detail how the fire had been started in twenty-two spots with gunpowder and strips of celluloid, and revealed that Van der Lubbe had been assigned to set fire to an anteroom. What Lubbe did not know was that there would be other arsonists. While the half-witted Dutchman was setting his charges, the main body of storm troopers fired the main hall after Roehm had made sure Van der Lubbe was "still jumping about in the anteroom."

The Intelligence officers in Munich said they were satisfied that the letter was genuine, but they refused to disclose how they had found it.

Marinus van der Lubbe as he was sentenced to death for his part in the Reichstag fire.

The Fabulous Phoney

THERE IS little doubt that Michael Romanoff, variously billed as Prince of All the Russias and son of Czar Nicholas II, was in reality the phoniest phoney of the thirties. However, while he was the grand impostor of his time, a mountebank prince who passed countless bogus checks, achieved numerous swindles and spent time in assorted jails, it was generally agreed by those who knew him that he was a likable rogue.

In the late twenties Mike had been exposed as a bogus prince by West Coast newspapers, but in 1931 was back on the coast, being Rockwell Kent, Romanoff, and a Captain Chitterin of the British Army. This was nothing startling, since Mike had by this time used as many as eighteen aliases.

Once he dropped into a Hollywood book store and signed the visitors' album Rockwell Kent. The owner welcomed Mike and had him to dine and meet other authors. He not only autographed books but also agreed to illustrate them—as Rockwell Kent, of course. He was widely entertained in Hollywood, and later the real Kent said admiringly, "My books never had such a run in California before."

Then the Los Angeles *Examiner,* which had exposed Mike in 1927, again caught up with him. Mike departed for the East, leaving a trail of bogus checks. He was picked up in Salt Lake City on the charge of issuing a phoney check for $386. But iron bars never could hold Mike, and in a few days he was on his way back to New York.

With the police on his heels, he stowed aboard the *De Grasse* of the French Line, armed with a letter stating that he had the authority to stow away in order to write his memoirs; the letter was signed by a well-known writer. But Mike didn't have to use the letter. In a few weeks he was at his old stand, the Ritz bar in Paris. He had just started to sip his drink when he was presented with a bill dated 1922..

"You can't stay here until this is settled," he was told.

Mike drew up his five feet three inches to resemble a ramrod. "Sir," he thundered, "are you not aware that all bills in France are outlawed after seven years?"

The Ritz bar bowed to Mike's su-

"Prince" Michael Romanoff in 1935.

perior knowledge of French law.

When Mike returned to New York he again traveled as a stowaway, but this time he was discovered. When he was asked for his cabin number he answered haughtily, "The whole ship is my cabin."

In April, 1932, Mike was returned to Ellis Island, from which he had es-

caped in 1922. It was a return to Elba for the phoney prince.

His charm was irresistible, and when he asked to return to Manhattan to get some clothes, the island authorities let him go accompanied by an immigration guard. The quest for Mike's wardrobe turned into an inspection of New York's speakeasies. Once one of his friends whispered, "Who's your friend?" and Mike whispered back, "My traveling companion."

After a few quick drinks in one of the most popular bars, Mike said he had to go out and pay off the taxi driver. He stepped outside, paid off the driver, and returned. The guard never knew he had left.

Mike was being treated like royalty returning out of exile. Friends pressed funds on him and urged him to flee, but Mike, with a sad but proud look, said he couldn't, he had given his *parole d'honneur.*

At last both Mike and the guard were incapable of any more inspections. The guard wandered away while Mike continued to stay with his friends in the dollar-a-drink speaks. The next day, to make sure the authorities understood, he called the island to tell them that he was in good health and not to worry.

The Immigration authorities were really mad. An expeditionary force was sent after Mike; scouts trailed him from speakeasy to speakeasy. At last he was taken, with a highball glass in one hand, and was returned to Ellis Island.

After a hearing he was shipped back to France, where he served time for stealing an American passport. Paris saw him after he was released, and from then down through the thirties, newspaper readers here and abroad read about Mike's adventures with the law or with his nemesis, the Immigration Bureau.

In 1940 Mike moved to the West Coast and proposed to his friends that he open a restaurant. A corporation was formed with backing by John Hay Whitney, Joseph Schenck, Robert Benchley and other celebrities. Mike soon demonstrated that he had one of the world's most cultivated palates, trained in the best dining rooms of Paris, New York, and London. His knowledge of service was excellent, as was his taste in wines. His restaurant was a great success.

The Little Flower

ALL THE returns for New York's 1933 mayoralty election were in. The scandal-tinged Democratic Party had been dismally beaten by a stout little man who wore a black sombrero-type hat. His name was Fiorello La Guardia and he left a lasting impression not only on New York but on the nation.

A measure of the man was what he said on election night. The crowds were cheering and whooping for him as he pushed his way through the crowds and climbed on the platform. He glowered down at them and told them in his high-pitched voice, "I don't owe you a thing and you're not going to get a thing." These words foreshadowed his entire administration, which lasted to 1945; they also made him the city's undisputed moral leader.

La Guardia took over the job—traditionally the nation's toughest task of administration outside the presidency—in a time when New York City was on the verge of bankruptcy, when its bread-lines were the longest in the country, when there were apple-peddlers and Hoovervilles in the shadow of the brand new Empire State Building. The city's millions, so used to misrule, crime, and corruption, never expected any forth-right action from City Hall and were startled when they got some.

Right after he was sworn in, La Guardia became a twenty-four-hour-a-day mayor. There were no obstacles that he couldn't conquer. He wanted only the best men in his administration, so he lured men such as Dr. John Rice, who came from New Haven to head his Department of Health, and Austin Mac-Cormick, who left the Federal Prison Service to become his commissioner of corrections. Robert Moses was appointed head of the Department of Parks, and S. S. Goldwater became commissioner of hospitals. It was typical of Fiorello to pick Lewis J. Valentine as his police commissioner; Valentine had excellent recommendations: he had been assigned to the sticks and demoted for raiding a Tammany clubhouse.

La Guardia had a fierce sense of justice, a hatred of corruption, and a love of fine government. Those who recall him will never forget the high-pitched demands that the "tin horns" and "punks" and "dirty chiselers" be driven from the city.

No mobster's life was serene in those days; Valentine was just too happy to raid their clubhouses and harass them off the streets with a disorderly-conduct arrest.

La Guardia was undoubtedly the country's most colorful mayor; pictures of him in a fireman's hat and coat were printed not only in America but throughout Europe. He conducted bands, led panting reporters on "inspection tours," roared around town in his big black limousine equipped with a two-way radio, and was loved by the big city's eight million.

Mayor Fiorello La Guardia on the steps of New York's City Hall.

Mayor La Guardia and his Police Commissioner, Lewis J. Valentine.

Chief Magistrate Abraham Block said, "It seemed as though the town had been invaded by an army of small, plump men in big hats; he was everywhere."

Out of his administration came such towering projects as the Triborough Bridge, the Henry Hudson Parkway, the West Side Highway, Grand Central Parkway, and the Whitestone Bridge. He erected public housing, schools, and made the World's Fair rise like a phoenix from a sprawling dump.

To sum up: Fiorello La Guardia was the right man for the right time.

La Guardia at his favorite sport—smashing $200,000 worth of slot machines.

La Guardia pitching in a few.

"Hizzoner" Butch La Guardia opening an air compressor valve in the new Queens-Midtown Tunnel in 1938.

Mayor La Guardia wielding a baton at Parents' Day in Central Park in 1936.

124

Theatre Collection

STARTING IN 1925, Florence Van Damm was recognized as Broadway's unofficial photographer. There was hardly a Broadway play she didn't shoot: the count is more than a thousand. Her lens had captured the great from the Barrymores to Bobby Clark, and the unknowns who later rose to stardom. To preserve this historic record of the American stage, Mrs. VanDamm placed her collection in the Theatre Collection of the New York Public Library. These pictures are taken from that collection. Another of her pictures, of Mary Martin and Gene Kelly in *Leave It to Me*, will be found in the 1938 section.

One of the 1930 flops was Penny Arcade. Two players in it were James Cagney and Joan Blondell. Warners bought the play for the movies and wisely asked them to repeat the rowdy, wacky roles of a killer and dizzy dame. This marked the start of two vivid, brilliant screen careers.

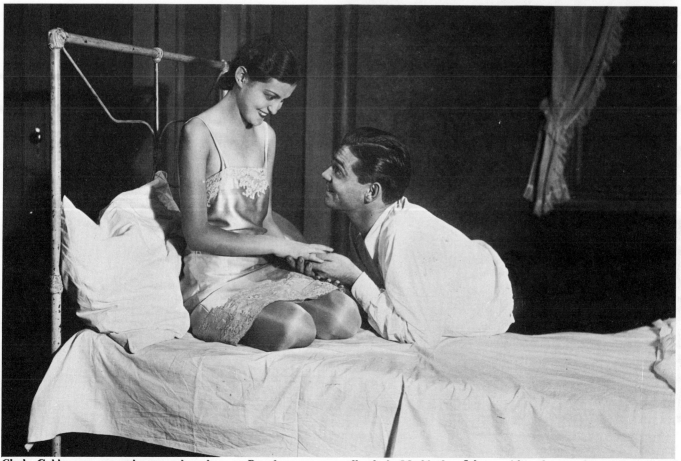

Clark Gable was an unknown when he turned to Hollywood in 1930. His only part on Broadway was a small role in Machinal. He was the lover; the leading lady was Zita Johann. After the run he went west and never returned to Broadway.

Spencer Tracy's brilliant performance as grim Killer Mears in The Last Mile, a 1930 hit, brought him an immediate invitation to Hollywood, where his star rose rapidly. He left Hollywood only once, in 1945, to do The Rugged Path on Broadway. In this scene from the 1930 play, Mears starts the prison revolt when he seizes the gun and keys of the guard.

James Stewart and Judith Anderson in Divided by Three, 1934.

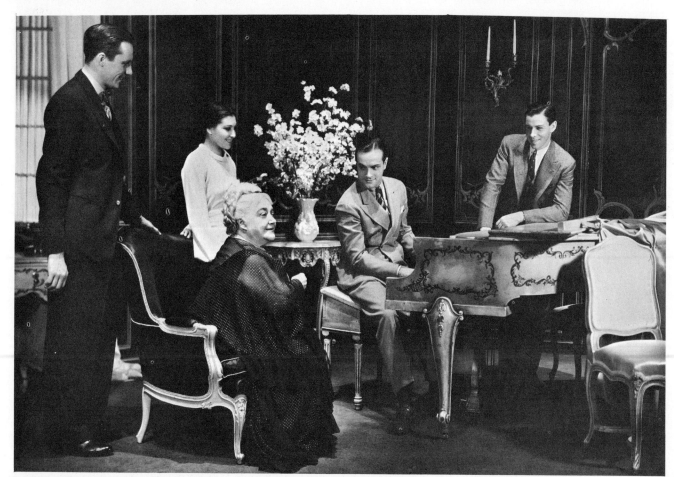

Crowds flocked to the 1933 musical Roberta, not so much for the play or the cast, but to listen to a timeless song, "Smoke Gets in Your Eyes," a song which will always be identified with the thirties. Besides the song, there was a slim, ski-nosed young actor named Bob Hope, who the critics said gave the play a light touch. A few years later, radio made Hope a star. Also in the 1933 musical were Tamara, left; Fay Templeton; Ray Middleton, left; and George Murphy, right.

126

The two children of high society in the 1932 play Chrysalis were unknowns, Humphrey Bogart and Margaret Sullavan. Miss Sullavan caught the eye of the critics but Bogart didn't seem to be making it as a well-dressed juvenile. In 1935, when he played the part of the ill-fated gangster in The Petrified Forest and repeated it in the screen version, Bogart was well on his way to a great career.

Intermezzo, the screen success, had started Ingrid Bergman on her way to success, but she won new acclaim when she played the gentle Julia to the Liliom of Burgess Meredith in the revival of Liliom, which reached Broadway at the end of the decade. Elia Kazan made one of his last appearances as an actor as the wicked Sparrow. Today he is one of the country's best-known directors.

Highlights and Sidelights: 1933

The midget on J. P. Morgan's knee.

RUSSIA'S FIRST five-year plan ended with a drastic food shortage, but Premier Stalin promised the people of the Soviet Union that the second five-year plan would triple the amount of foodstuffs. . . . In January, former President Calvin Coolidge was found dead on the floor of "The Beeches" at Northhampton, Massachusetts. He was sixty-one. President Hoover and the Cabinet attended the simple funeral services. Coolidge was buried with his ancestors in the hillside cemetery at Plymouth, Vermont. . . . Communist riots rocked Spain as the Reds tried to set up a government in Valencia. Police found nine thousand bombs. . . . Electric service was started over the Pennsylvania Railroad system from New York to Philadelphia. . . . The sergeant at arms of the U.S. Senate was fired after he wrote in a sensational article that some senators sell their votes. . . . Ernest Schaaf died in February after a fight with Primo Carnera. An autopsy showed he had had an inflammation of the brain when he entered the ring. . . . In Berlin an emergency decree signed by President von Hindenburg suspended all constitutional provisions guaranteeing private property, personal liberty, and freedom of the press. . . . A two-day earthquake rocked Hollywood, Pasadena, and nearby locales, resulting in eighty-three deaths, five in Los Angeles. . . . Mass rallies were held in New York, Chicago, Boston, and other cities to protest Nazi atrocities against Jews in Germany. . . . Beer and wines—later hard liquor—appeared in the United States legally for the first time in thirteen years. Prohibition ended on December 5, 1933. . . . At Decatur, Alabama, Haywood Patterson, considered the ringleader of a group of Negro youths, was sentenced to death for their alleged attacks on two white girls in a freight train near Scottsboro, Alabama. It was Patterson's second trial. The U.S. Supreme Court had already set aside his first conviction. Two months after his second conviction a federal judge reversed the death sentence again. The subsequent court actions would make headlines for years as the "Scottsboro Case." . . . George Bernard Shaw, on a trip around the world, stopped off at New York long enough to take a taxi ride about Manhattan and advise Americans to scrap the Constitution and their war debts. . . . British Prime Minister MacDonald and his daughter paid a visit to the White House. . . .Farmers at LeMars, Iowa, rioted over farm foreclosure. They invaded a courthouse, dragged a judge from his bench, and almost lynched him.

At Berlin, Chancellor Hitler announced a compulsory work program for every German youth, "high born or low.". . . New York police were faced by one of the most baffling murders in local history when they found the bodies of Edward Ridley, 88-year-old wealthy recluse, and his secretary. In the same dingy room a year before another of Ridley's secretaries had been murdered, as had Ridley's brother some years before. . . . The Senate Banking Committee began an investigation of American banking with J. P. Morgan as the star witness. The highlight of the hearings came when a midget climbed up on his knee—the world chuckled at the expression on J. P.'s face. The whole affair was believed to be a publicity stunt by the press agent of the circus in which the midget was appearing. . . . The World's Fair opened in Chicago but the major attraction of the

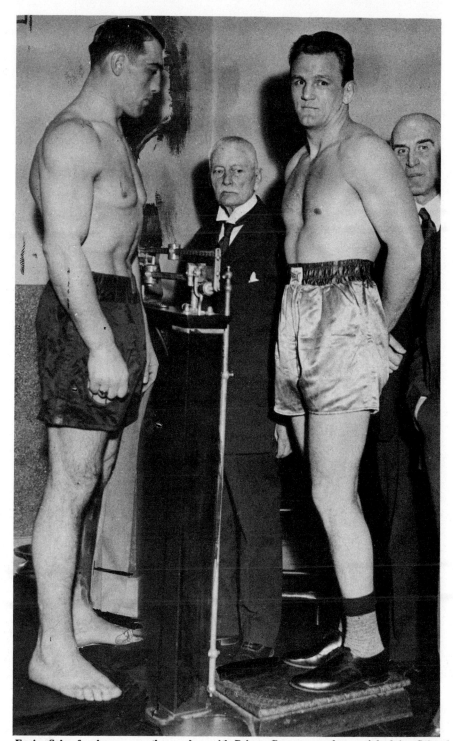

Ernie Schaaf, shown on the scales with Primo Carnera as they weighed in. Schaaf died after the bout.

fair was not the great Hall of Science but a striking blonde fan dancer named Sally Rand. . . . Another sensational kidnapping took place when William Hamm, of the famous St. Paul brewing family, was snatched. The family paid the ransom. . . . The Stahlhelm League of War Veterans was ordered to be incorporated into the Nazi Party in Germany, and its members were forbidden to belong to any other party. At the same time the Social Democratic Party was dissolved and its 121 Reichstag mandates wiped out. In the last election the party had polled seven million votes. . . In the sixth round, Primo Carnera knocked out Jack Sharkey for the world's heavyweight championship. . . . In Albany John J. O'Connell, son of the Democratic leader, was kidnapped and released after forty thousand dollars was paid. . . . Tear-gas bombs planted in the intake funnels of ventilating machines at the New York Stock

Calvin Coolidge's grave near Plymouth, Vt. Coolidge's son, who died during his term in office, is buried on the right.

Exchange made the customers weep. . . . Professor Moley, member of FDR's "brain trust," resigned as assistant secretary of state to become editor of *Newsweek*, a national magazine founded by Vincent Astor. . . . In Memphis, Tennessee, Machine Gun Kelly was captured and returned to Oklahoma City to stand trial for the kidnapping of Charles Urschel. FBI agents later dug up seventy-three thousand of the ransom money. . . . The Hitler government passed a decree making every working newspaperman a servant of the state. The Nazi Party also announced Germany had withdrawn from the League of Nations. . . . The nation was shocked when two kidnappers of Brooke L. Hart, of San Jose, California, were dragged from jail and lynched, and when Governor Rolph praised the lynching as a "lesson to every state of the union." . . .

Raymond Moley (center), with Vincent Astor (left) and Averell Harriman, who would one day become the governor of New York and would hold important Cabinet and ambassadorial posts.

George Bernard Shaw fencing with reporters on his arrival in New York in 1933.

Times Square the night Prohibition ended.

The end of Prohibition.

The "Scottsboro boys," on the way from jail to the courthouse, being escorted by troops.　As additional protection, because of the threat of lynching, machine guns were　mounted on roofs and extra troops stood by.

1930-1933: A Summing Up

A Hooverville, outside Bakersfield, Calif.

THE SPRING of 1933 was the bottom of the Depression, the pivot of the Desperate Years in the United States. A leader at last had appeared, and he had said, "We are on the way."

Even the apple-peddler, symbol of the bleakest years America had ever known, was disappearing from the streets of the big cities. Congress in the Hundred Days rushed through President Roosevelt's relief programs to take care of the nation's 15 million unemployed and the 6 million on state and municipal relief.

But while there was hope and a growing confidence in the land, it was far from over. In 1933 a survey showed that thousands of schools had closed, building construction was at a standstill, some seventy-two thousand home owners had lost their homes through foreclosure, with an estimated thousand homes a day falling into the hands of mortgage owners.

A total of 773 banks involving deposits of more than 7 million dollars, and 3,604 state banks with 2,000 millions in deposits, had closed their doors from 1930 to 1933. Yet, despite these grim statistics, 1933 was a year of hope.

133

Hoover City, New York City. This "resident" is making his tin shack "tight" for the winter of 1933.

cabs once again.

One sure sign that we were on the way to recovery was the employment again of married women teachers. In 1931 the National Education Association had reported that three-quarters of all cities had banned the employment of wives on the theory that they were taking money away from the male breadwinner. But in 1933 such restrictions started to disappear.

The three years of unemployment had taken its toll physically in America. Men and women, like unused machines, had rusted during those bitter years. When a group of unemployed stenographers was put to work on a project in 1933, more than two-thirds broke down and wept when they found it difficult to type and take dictation once again.

Hoovervilles still existed in many cities. In Youngstown, Ohio, hundreds of men huddled near the open-hearth furnaces for warmth during the winter of 1933. Uprooted families clung to the outskirts of towns and cities, living from hand to mouth. In the grim winter of 1933 the Red Cross stated it had aided one million families and J. P. Morgan abandoned his reserve to make a broadcast endorsing a block-to-block drive to ask one dollar from every employed person.

Dance marathons, stunts, and crazes like flagpole sitting, then miniature golf, then jigsaw puzzles, occupied Americans that year, but the majority just sat at home and listened to the radio. Even visiting between families had dropped off sharply, a survey showed; most people, either through pride, listlessness, or gloom, were reluctant to go out.

But it was in that spring that the country began to rise and look about, like a national Rip Van Winkle emerging from a three-year sleep. The people listened to the warm, friendly voice telling them to help him banish fear. They smiled and laughed at his quips but, even more important, they believed him.

The new temper in the country was signified by Congress's actions in rushing through all the New Deal legislation. As Will Rogers put it: "The whole country is with him [President Roosevelt]. Even if what he does is wrong they are with him. Just so he does something. If he burned down the Capitol, we would cheer and say, 'Well at least we got a fire started anyway.'"

Ads for domestic help began to appear in considerable numbers before the year was out.

Gadgets, beloved by most Americans, began to move slowly in stores, and cab drivers, who had seen their revenue drop from ten dollars a day to two, reported that people were taking

The Bohemian Corporal

cupied Von Hinden
lery at the Wilh
Reichskanzler
Nazis, to a
cations,
kanzler
Hit
In

To MOST Americans he was a ranting little man with a Charlie Chaplin mustache and a lock of hair that hung over one eye. He was in the newsreels that always appeared before the main picture. His followers were called Nazis and their goose-stepping was always good for a hoot and a laugh from the balcony. Some German-Americans were saying that Hitler would be the savior of a new Germany and were making plans to go back to the Fatherland. Even the ugly stories of what was happening to the Jews of Germany didn't interest the average American. The New Deal's alphabet of CCC, CWA, WPA, and NRA were much more important than Dorothy Thompson's 43-page book on what she thought of Hitler, or that 800-page book Hitler wrote called *Mein Kampf*.

But by 1934 many Americans were beginning to take another look at Adolf Hitler.

They learned that he was born in Austria in 1889, the son of a customs official. In his twenties he had gone to Munich, where the war swept him from the precarious position of a house painter to that of a corporal in the Bavarian army. He had fought for four years, was wounded, gassed, and came out with the Iron Cross, First Class. But in spite of his army service his request for German citizenship was denied.

His political views were anti-Marxian; he felt the future of Germany lay in that direction. It was the chance discovery of his oratorical powers that changed his conviction about the future. His contact with the German Workers Party fused his scattered and half-baked ideologies into a program. His intellectual father was Gottfried Feder, who envisioned a "new German nation, no communists, no Jews, no financial enslavement to the rest of the world."

From 1919 Hitler devoted his life to realizing Feder's dream. In thirteen years he had seen the petty German Workers Party grow into the National German Workers Socialist Party; he had seen the acquisition of a party press, the slow spread of his ideas into Bavaria and later into northern Germany.

His oratorical gifts had bewitched

Adolf Hitler at a German festival near Hameln in 1933.

first 500, then 1,000, then 25,000 Germans. An abortive *coup d'état* in 1923 almost wrecked what he had built up, and he was sent to prison. He spent most of his time there writing his autobiography, *Mein Kampf*. Dorothy Thompson told her readers in 1934 that it was "not a book, but an 800-page speech of pathetic gestures, inaccurate German, and unlimited self-satisfaction."

The failure of the coup did not halt Hitler's ambition. By 1926 his party had twelve seats in the Reichstag—Hitler's lack of citizenship prevented him from occupying one of the seats—and could poll 809,000 votes. In 1932 Hitler's party was the second strongest in Germany. He had emerged as such a power that Von Hindenburg and Bruening were forced to consult with him. His party with its uniforms, dues, pins, and buttons was described by one writer as "a sort of . . . Ku Klux Klan or some other racial racket."

By 1932 most of the experienced foreign correspondents were convinced of Hitler's aims. Miss Thompson wrote: "The moment I entered into Hitler's

room I was convinced I was meeting the future dictator of Germany. In less than fifty seconds I was sure I was not; he is a little man whose countenance is a caricature . . . a drummer boy risen too high . . ."

And another writer said: "The German people, sick to death of adversity, grab at the last straw, and that straw seems to be Hitler who imagines himself as a German Mussolini."

Hitler's strength seemed to be in attracting the "little men" of Germany, the unskilled workers, the small officials. What he offered the average German was hope, consolation, and the comforting assurance that none of their troubles were their own fault. And he gave them a villain to punish, a scapegoat to blame for their misfortunes—the Jews.

"Take the Jew out of Hitler's program and it will collapse," Miss Thompson wrote, and also pointed out that Hitler often reminded the Germans of 1918 when Clemenceau said, "There are twenty million Germans too many."

Of the man himself the alert reader of 1934 discovered that the dictator of a nation devoted to splendid sausage, cigars, beer, and babies, was a vegetarian, teetotaler, a nonsmoker and apparently celibate. As Fuehrer and Reichskanzler of Germany, Hitler oc-

1934

...burg's old Chancel-
...elmstrasse, named the
...palais, but which the
...void any monarchial impli-
...named the "Haus des Reichs-
...s." Here, devoid of any luxury,
...ruled in comparative simplicity.
...his many-roomed quarters he had
only five servants, four of them old
friends. But he liked fast cars, liked to
sit at the opera with notables. Yet he
was happy sitting in the front seat with

Chancellor Adolf Hitler with President
Paul von Hindenburg at the celebration of
the 19th anniversary of the battle of Tannenberg, won by German troops under Von
Hindenburg.

bring him to the table was Kannenberg's
version of the *Brennsuppe,* a South
German gruel, a sort of porridge made
of browned flour, butter, and caraway
seeds seasoned with a pinch of salt and
half a teaspoon of vinegar.

Hitler had no valet; in fact he never
appeared to anyone on his staff in either
dressing gown or slippers. A writer in
1934 pointed out, "Hitler's modesty
verges on the morbid."

He had a favorite costume: black
trousers and a khaki jacket cut on the
pattern of what German officers called
Litevka—the traditional lounge jacket
of the German army, without insignia.
It is perhaps significant to find in ex-
ploring those early years of Hitler that
he was fanatically clean and had a
compulsion to wash his hands frequently.

He worked irregular hours and
suffered from insomnia. He had few
guests, mainly Party friends, gauleiters
from the provinces who were served a
hearty peasant fare of soup, meat, pota-
toes, vegetables, and salads which in
German fashion were all served at the
same time. Hitler joined them only in

the dessert, usually *Schmarren* with
stewed fruit.

When he was in Munich he always
dined at the quiet little Osteria-Bavarian
Restaurant where he had eaten for
years.

Hitler's choice in women was of the
Walkuere type, and they always had to
be well dressed. It was Hitler who in
1934 vetoed Frau Goebbels' boycott
of French dresses and almost ruined
Germany's ready-made garment market.

Hitler's closest companion in 1934
was Rudolf Hess, appointed the first of
that year as his personal deputy. Hess,
as a party spokesman said after his appointment, was Hitler's "preferred companion." Hermann Goering, formerly a flight captain, was made minister
of air. As war ace he had received the
highest German decoration, and on Von
Richtofen's death had taken command
of the famous Flying Circus. Goering,
in that first year of Hitler's rule, was
the ideal of the hearty average German
and the only big Nazi popularly called
by his first name.

One Nazi who became well known
to most Americans in the early thirties
was Dr. Ernst Sedgwick Hanfstaengl,
known on both shores of the Atlantic
as "Putzi." He was an American on
his mother's side and on his father's
came from a cultivated family of art
publishers. A graduate of Harvard, he
was an early follower of Hitler. Putzi
had given the party a thousand dollars
to help finance their daily newspaper,
the *Voelkischer Beobachter,* in 1923.
In 1934 Putzi, then chief of the foreign
press department, was starting to fall
out of favor with Hitler, because he
had on several occasions criticized the
party's curtailment of cultural projects;
nevertheless, he won a libel suit against
the London *Daily Express* which had
attributed this quote to him: "Damn
those Oxford professors! I'll send some
of our swine to burn down Oxford."
Hanfstaengl satisfied the court he had
never said that.

By 1934 Hitler had demonstrated he
had no sense of loyalty or honor. Von
Hindenburg had said this on several
occasions when he discussed "the Bohemian corporal," as he liked to call
Hitler. "Thoroughly unreliable as a
politician and as a man," the aging
president of the republic had said. One
wonders what his thoughts were when
he turned over his country to the man
he said was fit only to fill the job of a
postmaster.

the chauffeur as the crowds cheered
him.

His cooking and housekeeping were
done for him by a couple named Kannenberg, who were old friends. Kannenberg, a rotund, jovial Bavarian, was
more of a court jester than a cook. His
principal chores were to play the accordion and sing the funny Bavarian
songs that Hitler was so fond of. When
Hitler made his many cross-country
tours, a special car was fitted as a
kitchen and Kannenberg packed his
accordion and his pots and took his
station in the car.

Food was something Hitler cared
little about. The one thing that would

Hitler moved rapidly to start a national awakening. The great autobahn system of roads was begun and the unemployment rolls began to shrink. After fifteen years of bumbling administrations, of humiliation and occupation, the people were willing to believe the confident new chancellor when he told them he was rebuilding the country to last a thousand years.

To most adult Germans, the uglier aspects of the National Socialist regime —the brownshirted bullies, the Jew-haters, the secret police, and the neighborhood informers—were not too great a price to pay for this new national revival.

But behind the stout doors of the Reichstag, time bombs were quietly ticking.

Hitler presided over an uneasy coalition of political and military forces. In place of the parliament was his Nazi Party, a hard core of several million. Yet despite the stiff-armed, goose-stepping millions, there were factions that were growing bigger, more dangerous. One was Gregor Strasser, a vintage Nazi who was saying that Hitler was forgetting the original purpose of the movement.

Along with Strasser and his followers there were the brownshirted Storm Troops (S.A.), a loosely knit organization of ex-soldiers, thugs, and ex-convicts, numbering about 2,500,000. This was the gang who had slugged it out with clubs, rocks and fists with Communists and other political foes. Its head was Captain Ernst Roehm, a stout homosexual who had grandiose dreams of combining his troops with all others under a ministry of defense headed by himself.

The other two factions were the Reichswehr, the professional army of 100,000 men superbly trained by the old Prussian chief of staff, General von Seeckt, and the Elite Guard (S.S.), a semi-military organization, a sort of Praetorian Guard for Hitler. Its leader was the ruthless Heinrich Himmler.

It was Roehm's group that made all the others apprehensive. The storm troopers swaggered across Germany amassing arms, establishing arsenals, and making it known they were soon to rule Germany.

In May, 1934, Hitler decided to move fast and ruthlessly to get rid of Roehm and his associates and reduce the Storm Troops to a skeleton force. Secret lists were drawn up that uneasy spring, and assignments for murder given to trusted members of the S.S. and the Gestapo (secret police).

In June Roehm, who was pressing Hitler as to what position he was to hold in the regime, went to Bavaria for a vacation. On the 29th Hitler sent him a telegram saying he would visit him at Bad Wiesse, an Alpine resort town, the following day, and asking Roehm to assemble his senior officers there for an important conference. Unknown to Roehm, orders had gone out to border police to detain and arrest all members of the S.A. who might attempt to leave the country.

Accompanied by Goebbels, Hitler left for Munich, arriving in the early hours of the morning of the 30th. From Munich his party traveled in high-powered sedans to Bad Wiesse, thirty miles to the south. Roehm, dragged out of bed, was arrested and taken to Stadelheim Prison in Munich.

Meanwhile secret police were picking up the other senior officers of the S.A. During the night men were murdered in their beds and on their doorsteps. One man with no connection with the S.A., the well-known music critic Dr. Willi Schmid, was taken from his house and shot. His body was later returned in a sealed casket. The Gestapo had made a tragic mistake; they had murdered the wrong Schmid.

A Nazi seizes a Jew on his way home and forces him to clean the streets and gutters.

Hitler and Goebbels.

From the hallowed Brown House, the birthplace of his party, Hitler established a command post with his orders clicking out over the wires, ordering men shot or thrown into prison. All that soft June day Hitler and his court sat in the Senate Hall of the Brown House, deliberating on the lives of more than a thousand men—some of whom had fought with him shoulder to shoulder to establish their party.

When he flew back to Berlin that night Hitler said, "This has been the hardest day of my life."

The following day two trusted S.S. men, Theodor Eicke and Michael Lippert, were sent to cell 474 to place a gun on the small table next to Roehm's bed.

"The Fuehrer is merciful," Eicke told Roehm. "He wants you to have a chance to use this."

When they returned ten minutes later, Roehm gave them a contemptuous look and turned away.

Twenty-three years later a police lieutenant told what happened next. Testifying at Lippert's trial in Munich in 1957, Lieutenant Colonel Walter Kopp said that Roehm, stripped to the waist, started to say something as Eicke stepped into the cell, but the S.S. officer told him to "shut up."

"Then Roehm stood at full attention and gave the S.S. officer a look of contempt. Eicke said to his companion, 'Go easy. Aim carefully!' Then two shots were fired simultaneously. Then both or one of them stepped up to the body and fired a third shot. Roehm was mumbling something. It sounded like 'My Fuehrer . . . My Fuehrer . . .' when they shot him in the head."

On the way out of the cell the S.S. men told Kopp, "Medical help prohibited."

On July 13, Hitler, reported that a "counterrevolution" had been repressed, with scores of persons executed and a number of others jailed for treason.

The fact was that 1,067 persons were killed and 1,124 jailed.

But Hitler had succeeded, with one ghastly blood letting, in reducing Roehm's Storm Troops to a feeble body of marching burghers.

In August, Von Hindenburg died. He was buried at the monument at Tannenberg, East Prussia, which had been erected as a tribute to his great victory over the invading Russians in 1914.

The path now was clear for the Thousand Years of Adolf Hitler's Third Reich.

138

Photographer for the Fuehrer

Heinrich Hoffmann, at the Palace of Justice, Nuremberg, 1945.

IN THE early 1920's when Adolf Hitler was building his Nazi Party, he included in his personal entourage of murderers, pimps, brawlers, and perverts, a slender, blond-haired, lame young photographer named Heinrich Hoffmann. Faithful as an old hunting dog, Hoffmann was for many years the only one allowed to photograph Hitler.

As a result he became one of Germany's wealthiest men. By 1935 he was worth seven million dollars, owned six estates, several studios and a valuable collection of nineteenth-century German paintings. He accompanied Hitler everywhere and many times the Fuehrer confided in him. For example, after the fall of France, when Hitler visited Napoleon's tomb at the Invalides, he told Hoffmann, "That was the greatest and finest moment of my life."

Hoffmann's estate was confiscated after the war and he was sentenced to five years. He died in 1957 at the age of 76.

Hoffmann's collection of photographs, virtually a pictorial history of the rise and fall of the Third Reich, was captured by the Allies in World War II. It includes photographs of every Nazi official from the early days up through the thirties and forties.

Hoffmann seemed to be at Hitler's side morning, noon and night, his camera constantly clicking. His lens caught the youthful Rosenberg and the soon-to-be-defeated Franz von Papen; Captain Ernst Roehm, the Nazi brawler who helped Hitler to power is shown smilingly greeting Hitler shortly before he was murdered by orders of the Fuehrer in 1934. Hess, Hitler's first secretary; Hermann Goering, many pounds lighter and much decorated; Admiral Raeder; and a youthful Paul Joseph Goebbels are all to be seen. There are hundreds of shots of the Nuremberg Congress, of countless parades, of airplane trips, Hitler with children, Hitler decorating his troops, Hitler with Von Hindenburg, and so on.

Three volumes contain a priceless history of Hitler's participation in the Spanish Civil War. They show the Condor Legion in action—an air force unit which will live in infamy for its ruthless bombing of the village of Guernica —and Hitler's infantrymen saluting the swastika in the Madrid victory parade. There is also one of Franco and a Luftwaffe general sharing the same platform draped with a Nazi flag. These are shown in the sections on the Spanish Civil War.

A Rogues' Gallery from the Hoffmann Collection

Alfred Rosenberg was the so-called intellect of the Nazi Party. Son of a shoemaker, he was born in Estonia and received a diploma in architecture from the University of Moscow. He lived through the Bolshevik Revolution in Moscow and later moved to Munich. A fierce anti-Semite, he joined the Nazis after World War I. Hitler admired his talents and appointed him editor of the Nazis' organ, Voelkischer Beobachter. Rosenberg died on the gallows at Nuremberg.

Admiral Erich Raeder. Raeder sold out to Hitler in 1933 after the Nazi head promised him and the officers' corps that the armed forces of Germany would never be forced to take part in a civil war, but would have only one mission when he became Chancellor—to rebuild Germany's army and navy. He drew a life sentence at Nuremberg.

Blomberg, Hitler, Goering, Frick, and Neurath. General Werner von Blomberg, second in command of the German Army in 1930, was an early supporter of Hitler. Three years later he was Minister of Defense in Hitler's cabinet. Later Hitler made him Field Marshal—a Field Marshal who would blindly obey every order his Fuehrer issued.

Baron Konstantin von Neurath, who was from the old school of World War I Germans, served as Hitler's first Foreign Minister. It was he who usually informed the foreign ministers of the thirties of Hitler's latest move of conquest, such as the occupation of the Rhineland. He was replaced by Von Ribbentrop.

Wilhelm Frick, who had participated in the Munich Beer Hall Putsch, was a simpleminded German civil servant who served Hitler as a spy at Munich police headquarters. Later he became the recognized head of the Nazi bloc in the Reichstag. A shy, retiring man, he kept in the background but was known in the party circles as a master of intrigue. He died on the gallows.

Hitler with Hess greets Himmler, April, 1933. Heinrich Himmler was Hitler's man of blood. In 1923 he left raising chickens and teaching elementary school to join Hitler. In 1929 he became one of the few hundred members of the Nazi SS—Schutzstaffel. The organization was somewhat of a personal bodyguard at the early rallies, but under Himmler the SS grew enormously and controlled Germany and many parts of Europe by torture and murder. Its very name froze many a human heart. Himmler committed suicide before he could be brought to trial.

Dr. Robert Ley, 1933. Ley, an alcoholic German chemist, was an early follower of Hitler, who appointed him Gauleiter of Cologne. In the spring of 1933 he signed proclamations destroying Germany's trade unions, just three weeks after the Nazis promised that they would always remain a part of Germany. He would hang himself in his cell just before the Nuremberg trials began.

Rudolf Hess, his wife, and Hitler. Hess joined the Nazis in 1930. Born and educated in Egypt, where his father owned a successful business, Hess served in the List Regiment in World War I, the same one in which Hitler served, but they did not know each other then. Like Rosenberg he was violently anti-Semitic, and caught Hitler's fancy when he wrote a prize-winning essay on what kind of man must bring Germany back as a world power. Hitler, of course, fancied himself as Hess's ideal. During World War II Hess flew on a harebrained mission to England, in an attempt to make peace, and was imprisoned. He is one of the few Nazis still in jail.

Ernst (Putzi) Hanfstaengl was a Harvard graduate whose mother was American. His family, wealthy and highly cultured, owned an art publishing firm. In 1923 Putzi gave the Nazis $1,000 and the prestige of his name at a time when the party was at a low ebb. As a reward he was made Hitler's press chief. An accomplished piano player and clown, he soon accepted the role of court jester. He later fell out of favor with Hitler and had to flee for his life. He spent World War II as a sort of unofficial adviser on Nazi Germany. Hanfstaengl is up front on the right in the seat in front of Hitler. This photograph was taken in 1933.

An early picture of Hermann Goering. Goering, second in command of the Nazi Party, was the last commander of the famed Richthofen Squadron, the Flying Circus of World War I. Restless and unable to fit into civilian life again, he became a transport pilot, then married Carin von Kantzow, the sister-in-law of Denmark's Count Eric von Rosen. When he and his bride, one of Denmark's beauties, returned to Munich in 1920, Goering heard Hitler speak and like so many converts to Nazism was hypnotized by his oratorical powers. In 1921 he joined the Party and made many large financial contributions to Hitler and the Party. He later became Hitler's air minister and economic dictator. He cheated the gallows at Nuremberg by taking poison.

Captain Ernst Roehm was one of the charter members of the German Workers Party when Hitler joined it in Munich in 1919. During those early years he helped Hitler mold the tiny group into the National Socialist Party (Nazi). A stocky, bull-necked, scar-faced ruffian, he had been a professional soldier all his life. He and many of his SA troops were murdered by Hitler's orders in the blood purge of July, 1934, after the army had warned Hitler he must break the growing power of Roehm's SA or he could no longer depend on their support. Roehm was a notorious homosexual. This picture was taken a short time before Hitler ordered him murdered.

Bormann and Hess at a Nazi rally in 1936. Martin Bormann, who once served a prison sentence for conspiracy in a political murder, was Hitler's second secretary—Hess was first. The post was called Deputy of the Fuehrer. By 1941 Bormann was Hitler's closest confidant after Goebbels. He was one of the last to leave the Berlin bunker after Hitler committed suicide. Although eyewitnesses said he was killed attempting to escape, he is believed to be still living, possibly in South America.

142

Hans Frank, a rising young Berlin attorney, joined the Nazis in 1920. Completely devoted to Hitler, he once advised a convention of Germany's leading lawyers that in Germany there was only one authority and that was Adolf Hitler. He was later appointed Governor General of Poland and there carried out Hitler's bloody orders. He died on the gallows in Nuremberg after "rediscovering God."

The hierarchy of the Nazis, Hitler, Goering, Goebbels, and Hess in 1939.

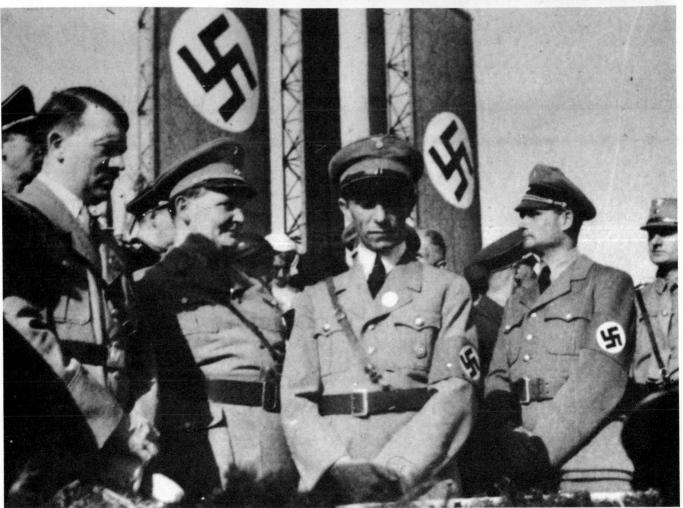

Dr. Hjalmar Horace Greeley Schacht at a Nazi rally in 1936. Dr. Schacht, the Nazi financial wizard with the unlikely middle names, in 1924 saved the early German Republic from inflation and disaster by stabilizing the country's currency. In 1931 he resigned his post as president of the Reichsbank to join Hitler. It was Schacht who brought Hitler and the German bankers and big industrialists together. Hitler later reappointed him as president of the Reichsbank. He joined the conspiracy against Hitler and was arrested.

Hitler, Von Hindenburg, and Von Papen. In his monumental Rise and Fall of the Third Reich, William L. Shirer notes that Franz von Papen probably was the key man who helped Hitler into power. He was the strangest and in a way the most ludicrous figure of the tragic-comic German Republic. Von Hindenburg, who viewed him as a protégé, made him Chancellor in 1923. But Von Papen, former General Staff officer and a military attaché who was expelled from the United States in World War I for his part in the famous Black Tom explosion, was completely outguessed and outmaneuvered by the rising Hitler after the 1932 elections. After weeks of fantastic double-crossing and intriguing by Hitler and the leaders of the other political parties, he was ousted by Von Hindenburg, who sent him his dismissal order with a picture autographed: "Ich hatt' einen Kameraden!" Von Papen was forced to serve as Hitler's Vice-chancellor, and later ruefully admitted Hitler and his gang had completely taken him over by guile, lies, double-crossing, and deals with the officers' corps and Admiral Raeder.

Eva Braun

Eva as she filled out her two-piece bathing suit.

As ALBERT SPEER, Hitler's minister for armament and war production, told British historian Trevor-Roper, Eva Braun will forever be a disappointment to the writers of history. For many years, the most important in the rise and fall of Hitler and his Third Reich, she was Hitler's mistress. But for all her closeness to the one man who changed so much of the world's history, she was no Pompadour or Lola Montez.

"The sensation of Hitler and Eva Braun is that there was no sensation," Heinrich Hoffmann said in 1950.

Hitler was very fond of her but she had little or no influence on him. She was never allowed to come to Berlin or to Nuremberg; she was confined to the Berghof on the Obersalzberg where she spent her time combing her long, dark-blond hair, riding in big, open, powerful cars along the countryside, swimming with her entourage of stocky, well-fed girls and slim, good-looking young men, and waiting for Hitler to arrive.

Field Marshal Keitel described her as slender, reticent, "and a very, very nice person. She stood very much in the background and one saw her rarely."

Eva was Heinrich Hoffmann's assistant in the photographer's studio in Munich when Hitler met her in 1929. She was soon installed in Hitler's Alpine villa. The lonely, frustrating life caused her to try suicide twice but apparently in the late thirties she adjusted to her situation and accepted the role of part-time mistress. She saw Hitler only when he wanted to see her.

"This poor girl is in love with me—what can I do? I must take care of her," Hitler once told Hoffmann.

After the fall of Berlin, American troops discovered Eva's fifteen volumes of personal photographs. Although she didn't leave behind a diary, which might have been priceless historically, she did leave a pictorial history of the Fuehrer which is fascinating.

This writer examined these volumes together with the Hoffmann volumes. The Hoffmann collection is invaluable to history, but Eva's is more personal and, in some ways, more interesting. The volumes are the size of an ordinary family photographic album and they are covered with flowered brocade.

Hitler doesn't appear until the third volume, but from then on appear fascinating candid views of one of the most powerful and most evil men of our time.

We see him both in civilian garb and in uniform. Most of the pictures were taken by Eva or one of Hoffmann's assistants. Some were of a playful, almost kittenish Hitler. We see him striking all sorts of poses, front, back, or profile. We can almost hear Eva cry, "No, no, mein Fuehrer—face this way," while the man who had so violently changed the world's history patiently obeyed her commands.

Eva, Hitler, and their dogs.

Eva and her friends, including Martin Bormann (second from left). Hoffmann, Hitler's personal photographer, is on the far right. Hoffmann introduced Eva to Hitler in 1929 when she was working as his assistant in Hoffmann's Munich photographic shop.

Hitler in evening clothes lighting candles on Christmas Eve.

The caption Eva had written for this picture was "Hitler in Teehaus." Apparently Hitler is personally supervising the table arrangements for his guests (ca. 1938).

A picture of Hitler taken by Eva in 1938.

Eva Braun, still in her apron, takes movies of Der Fuehrer and his guests in the spring of 1938. Only after the war started did Hitler abandon civilian dress for a uniform, which he swore to the Reichstag he would wear until he either won or was defeated.

Goebbels and his wife, taken by Eva Braun. Paul Joseph Goebbels was the evil genius of the Third Reich. The slight, swarthy-faced cripple first joined the party in 1923, after being hypnotized by Hitler's oratory, as were so many of the early Party recruits. Goebbels himself was an impressive orator, and after Gregor Strasser heard him at a rally and found out that he also had a poison-pen talent, he appointed him his secretary. Together with Strasser, Hitler's rival in the north, Goebbels built up a powerful Nazi Party with headquarters in Hanover. For a time Hitler, Goebbels, and Strasser broke over Strasser's demands that they join the Communists and Socialists in forcing the Republic to take over the estates of the wealthy deposed German barons. The following year Goebbels deserted Strasser and joined Hitler. He organized the Nazis' gigantic propaganda machine and was Hitler's most loyal subject. He and his wife died in the Berlin bunker with Hitler and Eva Braun, after poisoning their six small children.

The Opening Guns

ON A HOT July day, 154 Austrian Nazis burst into the Austrian Chancellery at noon and with a burst of gunfire fatally wounded Chancellor Engelbert Dollfuss. Then they held the dying Chancellor and two of his cabinet members as hostages for five hours. When they were guaranteed a safe conduct into Germany, they finally capitulated to besieging forces.

The Vienna coup was the signal for a nationwide Nazi putsch which met with some temporary success in the provinces but was ruthlessly crushed after several hours of fierce fighting. The total of deaths was placed at one hundred.

Major Emile Fey, minister of defense, told the world that night that Dollfuss had been shot in the head twice as he tried to flee. Then in an emotion-shaken voice he charged: "Hitler's Nazis are morally responsible for this cowardly assassination."

Lynch-mad mobs in Vienna were twice beaten back as the Nazis were transferred to prison, where the government, refusing the promised safe conduct, planned to hold them. Cities were placed under martial law. Curfews were established, and citizens were warned not to congregate in groups of more than three.

Chancellor Engelbert Dollfuss.

The murder shocked the world. England demanded an investigation of arms and explosives shipments from Germany into Austria. Mussolini ordered his military forces to be "ready for any eventuality" and the army was placed on a wartime footing. All army and air force units were readied to march into Austria at a moment's notice. France reiterated her earlier statement that she would safeguard Austria's independence against Nazi domination. The United States, while refusing to intervene directly, expressed the hope that intervention by France, England, and Italy would have a "stabilizing and pacifying influence."

Germany recalled its minister to Austria because he had intervened in behalf of the Nazi plotters without consulting the Foreign Office, and to show his "concern" over the Dollfuss murder, Hitler canceled an attendance at the Bayreuth Opera.

Chancellor Schuschnigg, who took Dollfuss' place, asked intervention by European powers to preserve the "integrity of my country."

Dollfuss had won the admiration of the world for his integrity and determination not to buckle under the Nazi machine, and had made many friends. If he had given way to Hitler's threats, his country would have been overrun by the Nazis.

As the uneasy days passed and quiet returned to Austria, it became known that the Nazi terrorists had missed taking over the government by ten minutes.

At eleven A.M. on that fateful Wednesday, Dollfuss had held a cabinet session. The Nazi plan had been to surprise and capture the entire Austrian government. Dressed in the uniforms of the Fourth Infantry Regiment of the Austrian Army, the Nazis pulled up in front of the Chancellery at 12:30 P.M.

An elderly army veteran was the only guard at the door. He saluted as the officers and privates swept past him. He knew that Major Fey was inside conferring with Dolfuss, and assumed these were his men.

Unknown to the Nazis, the cabinet members had departed ten minutes before. These men were able to prevent the coup from succeeding.

One hundred and fifty hostages were taken in all, from Dollfuss down to the lowliest stenographer in the Chancellery. Other Nazis meanwhile captured the radio station and announced that Dollfuss had resigned.

For three hours while the Nazis held the Chancellery, Austria was without a government. Had a host of Nazis turned out in force, Austria would have been Germany's four years before Hitler actually took it over.

The Austrian government acted with amazing slowness. It wasn't until mid-afternoon that the ministers were able to mobilize the government forces. First the radio station was recaptured. The Chancellery was surrounded, but Major Fey appeared and asked the combined police and army units not to fire. The deadlock continued until nightfall. Then the Austrian commander announced that if all hostages were not released, he would level the building with artillery fire if necessary.

The Nazis, finally realizing their coup had fizzled, surrendered.

The Nazi putsch and Dollfuss' murder was precipitated by the execution of a Socialist youth a few days before, under an Austrian law which imposed death for all terrorists. Several Nazis also had been found with explosives, but none of them were executed, and the Nazis concluded that the Dollfuss government was afraid to execute any of them. This conclusion seemed justified, for after five months of unparalleled terrorism not a single Nazi had been executed in Austria.

For weeks following Dollfuss' death American newspaper readers were treated to stories and photographs of Mussolini reviewing his "war machine," or of French troops on the march, all ready to crush Hitler if he made a move against Austria. Hitler, in the meantime, put on a great show of anger against the undisciplined Nazis who had tried the coup.

Looking back now we know why he didn't move; he wasn't ready. The tanks and Stukas were still on the drawing boards. Four years later it would be different. Schuschnigg would be forced to resign, and the Hitler war machine would move quietly into Austria without needing to fire a shot. England would sleep, France would forget her promise to protect the little country of music and waltzes, Il Duce would discover Nazi troops at his doorstep in the Brenner Pass.

Troops guarding the body of the late Chancellor Dollfuss in Vienna's Chancellery.

The Gentle Genius

A PRIME TARGET of Adolf Hitler's National Socialist Party in 1934 was Professor Albert Einstein, formulator of the theory of relativity and internationally regarded as one of the greatest scientific figures of all time. On various occasions in 1933 Hitler's brownshirts had raided the home of the gentle professor on charges that he was hiding Communists and Communist weapons. One raid got the professor and his wife out of bed during the night to wait for hours while the Nazi searchers painstakingly went from room to room, bureau to bureau, and cellar to attic.

The result: a breadknife.

Three other times in that year Einstein's home was searched and he was questioned about his "activities."

In 1933 Professor Einstein left Germany to accept an appointment as head of the mathematics department at the Institute for Advanced Study in Princeton. But before he left, the soft-spoken, gentle genius became involved in an international uproar. It was revealed that, when he applied for a visa, he had been subjected to an intensive quiz on his political views by the American Consulate in Berlin. American organizations in Berlin stoked the controversy by issuing a statement they were "shocked over the unjust statements in connection with Dr. Einstein's experiences with the American Consulate," and wired the State Department defending the actions of the consulate.

Secretary Stimson made a personal investigation and insisted that the scientist had been treated with courtesy and consideration. The secretary explained that the questioning had come about because a woman's group had complained that the professor had "Communist affiliations."

Stimson also pointed out that under the law questions as to political views had to be asked of any foreigner requesting a visa, adding that the examination of Professor Einstein had been conducted "politely and according to routine."

While the international furor contin-

Albert Einstein lecturing before the American Association for the Advancement of Science at Carnegie Tech in Pittsburgh, shortly after he came to the United States.

ued to mount, Professor Einstein kept his sense of humor. When he boarded ship at Bremerhaven he told reporters, "The trouble with hearings of that kind is that you don't realize until some time has passed that the inquisitor is trying to get under your skin. In the future I would suggest that consuls put pins in their victim's chair so they will feel stuck from the beginning and in that way save time all around."

It had been Professor Einstein's hope that he would spend most of the year in Princeton and visit Germany in the winter. But by 1934 he was *persona non grata* to the Hitler government, and he settled here permanently.

In the thirties he became a familiar figure in the college town, with his crown of long white hair, his rumpled

pants, and his pipe. Many legends and anecdotes grew up about him, such as the oft-repeated story of how he explained relativity to his secretary: "When you sit with a nice girl for two hours you think it is only one minute. But when you sit on a hot stove for a minute you think it is two hours. That's relativity."

A Princeton mother was worried one day when her daughter failed to come home from school on time. When she did appear, the angry mother demanded, "Where were you all afternoon?"

"I couldn't figure out my math, so I called on Professor Einstein on the way home," the girl said.

She held up her book to show her mother the precise, spidery writing solving an algebra problem.

Dr. and Mrs. Albert Einstein.

The End of CWA

By January, 1934, the muted criticism of the Civil Works Administration began to rise to a crescendo. President Roosevelt had asked—and got—an extension of CWA funds, but not without a fight. Many senators wanted the relief funds controlled not by the federal government but by the states. There were just as many who recoiled in horror when that suggestion was made. Senator Jimmy Byrnes of South Carolina said that turning federal funds over to the states would mean more politics in administration instead of less.

There were others who criticized the CWA, such as Henry I. Harriman, president of the Chamber of Commerce of the United States, who had this to say: "If those who are receiving the aid of the government come to regard such assistance as permanent, and if our unemployed are not restored to work in private industry, then we may well look with apprehension to the future."

Harry Hopkins by now had set up a well-organized program. The chain-smoking administrator had put together a bewildering national effort to do every conceivable kind of task, as long as there were workless men and women willing to do anything to keep from starving and to maintain their pride and self-respect.

But despite the accomplishments of the CWA, President Roosevelt was beginning to listen to his critics for the first time, particularly the Southern Democrats and his budget director, Lewis Douglas, who insisted that the budget would suffer badly if the CWA was allowed to continue.

In mid-January FDR announced that the CWA had to go. Four million would have to be dropped from the federal payroll by May. The White House was deluged with inquiries which amounted to this: "Now what? What are these four million workers to do?"

At the time there wasn't any concrete answer. The only hope was that by May the gigantic Public Works program would be sufficiently advanced to provide employment for hundreds of thousands and private employment for the others.

On February 15, the first million men

Senator James F. Byrnes with FDR.

were dropped from CWA payrolls and Hopkins announced that an additional million would be dropped every two weeks. By May 1, he said, the CWA "will be out of business."

And despite protests, Hopkins had by May 1 destroyed the excellent work-relief organization he had built out of nothing.

"That's one pork barrel busted," was Al Smith's comment.

What remained was transferred to the Emergency Work Relief of the Federal Emergency Relief Administration. The difference was that, where the CWA had offered jobs to the jobless both on and off relief, the FERA had to confine itself to those on relief rolls; the wages were substandard.

In 1934 the FERA established the Federal Surplus Relief Corporation, which bought surplus commodities from price-depressed farmers for the relief program. Pigs were the first on the list of this new agency; as the winter went on, it turned to cotton blankets and coal.

But by the summer private business was beginning to charge that FERA had put the government in competition with private industry. When the FSRC an-

nounced it would take over cattle in the drought areas so they could be slaughtered to provide canned beef and shoes for the jobless, the shoe industry protested, even refusing to rent the government the necessary machinery.

In 1934 there were also a great many "self-help" programs proposed that also roused business to protest. The programs allowed men and women without jobs to make things for barter. Congress finally authorized the FERA to allow grants for such programs.

In many states FERA is fondly recalled. Key West, with most of its citizen on relief and with local services broken down, was in a helpless state in 1934 when FERA received permission to set up a work-relief program. The Key West Volunteer Work Corps was established. The streets were cleaned of uncollected garbage, beaches were raked of debris, houses repainted, roads and highways repaired, hotels reopened, and even a government art project started.

In 1934 the FERA was holding the line of work relief as best as it could until the new and much larger program, Public Works Administration, could get fully under way.

No Cabs Today!

It was the third day of the city-wide taxi strike when more than two thousand marching, shouting taxi drivers crowded City Hall Plaza, hooting and jeering for Mayor La Guardia to come out and talk to them. But the mayor was not in his office, and after a delegation had presented their demands the strikers began to move up along the East and West Side of Manhattan.

Only a short distance from City Hall, a cab suddenly appeared. It was the spark that touched off a serious chain of riots. A mob rushed at the cab, pulled the driver from behind the wheel, and literally tore the cab to pieces. From that point the strikers divided and marched like small armies of shock troops to Times Square, to Wall Street, to other

New York taxi strikers dragging a driver from his cab.

Taxi strikers forcing an independent driver to return to his garage.

The terror and violence of the 1934 taxi strike is underscored in this scene—the cab is being hauled from the East River, with the dead driver still at his wheel.

centers, smashing cabs, brutally beating drivers, injuring riders, pedestrians, and policemen.

The undermanned police force fought them with clubs, billies, and guns, but they were no match for the screaming, maddened strikers. The Fire Department was called and both firemen and police battled the strikers. Police precincts were turned into temporary hospitals to treat not only injured drivers but pedestrians who had been run down by cabs fleeing from the mobs.

Hundreds were arrested, but much damage had been done by nightfall when the police, acting under emergency orders, rallied and broke up the mobs. By this time, however, the strikers had accomplished their purpose of driving nonunion cabs from the city's streets.

The strike was eventually settled, but middle-aged New Yorkers will never forget how the taxi drivers took over the city in one violent, bloody afternoon.

Death on the High Seas

THE BLACKENED brass bell of the popular cruise liner *Morro Castle,* pride of the Ward Line, rang out mournfully over the choppy waters off Asbury Park, New Jersey, on a September morning just before dawn. Within a matter of hours, the glistening white ship was a charred hulk worth only $33,000 as scrap.

There were 318 passengers and 240 crew members aboard when the *Morro Castle* steamed out of Havana for New York. When the dead were counted, 134 persons had been burned to death or drowned in the high seas.

The disaster is still a mystery. Official and unofficial inquiries failed to determine the cause of the holocaust.

The night before the tragedy the captain, Robert R. Wilmott, had died in his stateroom, of undetermined causes. Among the weird orders he had issued before his death were: no boat drills, no operation of the smoke-detector system, and no uncapped fire hydrants.

When the fire first broke out, Chief Officer William F. Warms was in command. At first he thought it was only a minor fire and waited for a report from his third mate. Meanwhile the liner plunged through the sea at eighteen knots. Twenty-mile-an-hour winds fanned the blaze until it was roaring through the ship. Fire-detector signals began appearing on the panel before Warms and warned him of the seriousness of the blaze. He sounded a general alarm but it was too late; the fire was out of control.

Passengers and crew had to be put off in boats, but the abandon-ship operation was disorderly and very badly managed. Crew members were later criticized for not putting more passengers in the lifeboats.

When the SOS began crackling through the airwaves, fishing boats and private craft pulled out from the Jersey coast to help in the rescue operation. There were numerous stories of bravery and cowardice. Some passengers swam

A survivor of the Morro Castle minutes after she had been dragged out of the surf on the Jersey shore.

The Morro Castle burning at sea.

miles to stumble out of the hissing surf at many points along the shore.

The ship, a torch in the windy night, finally ground ashore off Asbury Park. Although firemen poured millions of gallons into her hold and onto her red-hot plates, it was hours before they could get aboard and bring the bodies of trapped passengers to shore.

A temporary morgue was set up in Jersey City, and for days sorrowing relatives moved up and down the rows of sheeted bodies attempting to identify the charred remains of their loved ones.

Yet as a consequence of this disaster came maritime legislation that was to make the American merchant marine one of the safest on the high seas. In the course of the extensive investigation by Federal authorities, an entirely new concept of safety at sea was developed. As a result of the mistakes and deficiencies that led to the loss of the liner, such safety devices as flame-proof furniture, flame-tight bulkheading of interior spaces, compulsory regular fire patrols, steam-smothering systems, better lifeboats, suitable fire extinguishers, gas masks and emergency equipment, were established as standard equipment aboard any American passenger liner.

Jesse James, circa 1934

THE POLICE officer in charge of the Peru, Indiana, police station at night was impressed with the scholarly young man. He had identified himself as a writer for an Eastern detective magazine, preparing an article on how the constabulary of small towns and villages were protecting its citizenry from the rampaging John Dillinger gang. The two men spent a leisurely hour discussing cutoffs, roadblocks, nightly patrols, and the general emergency routine of a small-town police force.

"What about machine guns?" the writer asked. "The state police and the Federal Bureau of Investigation have been using them."

The officer nodded in a proud way. "We not only have machine guns but also bullet-proof vests," he said. "Come on and I'll show you our locker."

In the rear of the station house he opened the gun locker and pointed to three submachine guns.

The writer whistled. "Mind if I look at one? I really never handled one."

The policeman picked up one of the weapons and let the writer hold it; apparently he didn't notice that the young amateur balanced the gun and slid back the breech like an expert. He also nodded approval as he ran his hands over the heavy bullet-proof vests.

"Quite an arsenal you fellows have," the writer said as he made some notes. "You're to be congratulated."

The policeman showed him to the door. "Come back any time," he said. "We're always ready to help."

The following day the writer returned with his "co-author."

The officer found him to be a quiet, soft-spoken man in his thirties with thick brown hair and a carefully trimmed mustache. The obliging policeman was only too happy to show the second writer the machine guns and the vests. After chatting about how they would all like to get hold of Dillinger and that reward money, the two writers left, promising to send the policeman a tear sheet of their article. They also promised to come back the following day with a photographer to take pictures of the officer at his gun locker.

The two writers got in a dark-colored sedan and disappeared down the main street. Outside of town they pulled into a dark side road.

"What do you think, Johnnie?" Homer Van Meter said.

"It's a cinch," John Dillinger replied. "We'll come back tomorrow and clean the place out. Then we'll hit the Greencastle bank."

And the next day they did just that.

J. Edgar Hoover observed some years later, in telling about the great 1934 manhunt for Dillinger and his gang, that such a cool, brazen bit of playacting was typical of this modern-day outlaw. Dillinger cared little for human life, including his own, but he had iron nerve.

The Hoosier farm boy was the best known of the desperadoes who won notoriety in the thirties comparable to that of Jesse James, America's tarnished Robin Hood, in the post Civil War era.

Strangely enough the lives of the two men and their times were parallel. Both became part of American folklore before they were killed, both had a strange personality that attracted men and women who accepted and vainly tried to defend them. Although Jesse lived and robbed much longer than Dillinger, they committed their crimes at a time when the country was under the heel of Depression, when the banks they robbed were villains to their debtors and not heroes to their depositors. In the post Civil War years along the Middle Border, banks were hated and feared as were the railroads. In Dillinger's time mobs of farmers dragged bankers from behind their desks when they tried to foreclose farm mortgages.

Dillinger's brief career had all the ingredients of a Hollywood "B" picture. There were the wild chases down

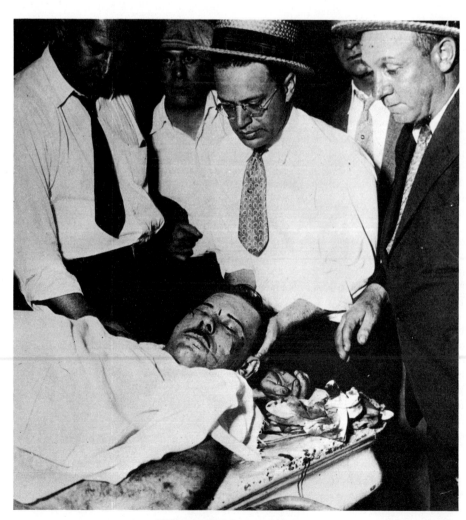

Dillinger after he was killed.

156

dark country roads, brazen bank robberies, gun duels in the squares of small towns, raids on police stations to obtain guns, political storms over his depredations, and finally, as if life had turned artist, the woman in a garish red dress who beckoned him to his death.

What was Dillinger really like? The late Basil Gallagher, former star reporter for the New York *Post* and the United Press, whom Dillinger called "that redheaded son of a bitch," had many chances to form an opinion. He had accompanied numerous Department of Justice posses on many raids in 1933 and 1934, and was the only reporter to ride with the shackled Dillinger and Van Meter across the desert in a baggage car after their capture in Tucson, Arizona.

"We played poker for hours," Gallagher told this writer. "Dillinger discussed every story I had ever written about him. He discussed bank robbery as other men would discuss their business. He said it was imperative that everything be known about a bank before it could be hit. I kept trying to probe deeper and find out why, but he would just shrug and say there really wasn't anything else he wanted to do. He was completely casual, but I had the feeling that every second, every minute, his mind was working smoothly. I could almost hear the gears mesh.

"Physically he wasn't impressive. Nobody would look twice at him in a crowd. Writers, particularly on newspapers, are apt to use the cliché—as I have often done—that a criminal's eyes are cold and hard. Actually I did get this impression. Dillinger smiled often but only with his mouth, never his eyes.

"Van Meter on the other hand was deadly. He was the best educated of the gang and while Dillinger somehow had caught the public fancy it was Van Meter who perfected the rough plans of Dillinger."

A review of Dillinger's life rightly begins in 1902, the year he was born on a small farm twenty miles northwest of Indianapolis. His mother died when he was three. His father, a respectable, hardworking farmer, moved his family to Indianapolis, where Dillinger spent most of his early years. Later the family moved to Mooresville in Morgan County, where Dillinger's career of crime began in the classic fashion.

A search of the police records on most American criminals, from early Western outlaws to Prohibition's Mad

Homer Van Meter, Dillinger's right-hand man.

Dog Coll, shows the same beginnings: a restlessness, a dislike for schooling or work, a taste for excitement, easy money, and liquor. There is also a sense of leadership and popularity. Dillinger had all these. In Mooresville he made a poolroom his hangout, and at eighteen he was well acquainted with the town speak and its bottled lightning. That year he induced another poolroom hanger-on to rob the village grocer of $555. They were caught. His friend turned state's evidence but Dillinger, pleading intoxication, received the stiff sentence of ten to twenty years in a reformatory.

"They should never have hit me with that rap," Dillinger once said. "That's what started me off."

From the Pendleton reformatory he was transferred to the Michigan City State Prison, where he met the ruthless John Hamilton and the veteran bank robber, Harry Pierpont. But Dillinger's Mooresville neighbors hadn't forgotten him. In May, 1933, they petitioned the state parole board to parole John Wilson Dillinger's son.

Dillinger was outside only a few weeks when he and two other ex-convicts went on a bank-robbing tour. When they were finished he had $29,300.

Now he had his operating fund to enter the big time. He bought several guns and tossed them over the walls of the state prison. A bribed trusty delivered them to Pierpont.

Dillinger returned to his hideout only to be grabbed by police and jailed at

Lima. On September 26, Pierpont, Hamilton, and several other convicts shot their way out of prison. Some were later killed but Pierpont and Hamilton escaped. In Chicago they recruited three other gunmen and made plans to liberate Dillinger.

In mid-October, Hamilton, Pierpont, and Russell Clark invaded the warden's office at Lima, posing as Indiana deputies assigned to return Dillinger to state prison as a parole violator. When the warden demanded their credentials they killed him. Minutes later they freed Dillinger and escaped.

The entire country was aroused by the escape. Shortly after his release from Lima, Dillinger led his gang in a raid on the Indiana police stations of Auburn and Peru (as related before) to get fresh supplies of guns and bullet-proof vests. He also recruited two more bank robbers to fill out the gang. Now they were in business.

He lost no time; on October 23, the gang robbed the Central National Bank at Greencastle, Indiana, after they had posed as the writer and photographer, and took $75,000 from its vaults.

The following month in Racine, Wis-

The Woman in Red.

J. Edgar Hoover, Director of the FBI, at his desk, November, 1935.

consin, the Dillinger gang raided the American Bank and Trust company and stole $27,000. From Racine they returned to Chicago to rob a trust company. On an underworld tip, the police surrounded a repair shop on Chicago's Broadway, but John Hamilton, accompanied by a woman, shot his way through the police lines, killing an officer.

In early January, 1934, the gang hit an East Chicago, Indiana, bank and after cleaning out the vault killed an officer. In the exchange of gunfire Hamilton was wounded.

The outlaw band and its ladies' auxiliary fled to Tucson, Arizona, where they were captured. A three-state extradition fight followed. Indiana, Ohio, and Wisconsin wanted them. It was finally resolved when the Arizona governor turned Dillinger and the others over to Indiana with the understanding that Indiana would surrender Hamilton, Russell Clark, and Charles Makley to Ohio.

Dillinger was flown to Chicago, where he was greeted by a hundred policemen armed with machine guns and revolvers. Shackled hand and foot, he viewed his reception committee.

"Believe me, fellows," he said with a wry smile, "I won't make a break."

On March 3, nine days before he was to go on trial for murder, Dillinger was admitted to the jail's exercise cor-

ridor. He leaped forward at Sam Cahoon, an elderly trusty and handyman, and thrust what Sam later said was a "real gun" into the trusty's stomach. Then Dillinger called to Ernest Blunk, a fingerprint officer. After overpowering Blunk and Warden Lew Baker, Dillinger ordered Herbert Youngblood, a murder suspect, to follow him. He took Blunk along as hostage.

Downstairs Dillinger had little difficulty cowing several other jail employees. With Youngblood he smashed the door of the jail's gun cabinet and stole two machine guns and some bullet-proof vests.

In the courtyard Dillinger waved his gun at several parked cars.

"Which is the fastest?" he demanded.

"Sheriff Holley's," Blunk said.

"We'll take that," Dillinger said.

The fugitives ejected Blunk several miles from the jail. Before he pushed Blunk from the car Dillinger waved a wooden gun at him.

"This is what I used," he was reported as saying.

That day Dillinger's "wooden gun" became another legend in American criminology. It took its place along with the famous broom-wire "noose" used by Kid Curry, the Western outlaw, in his 1902 escape from the Atlanta penitentiary, and another wooden gun used by the outlaw Harry Tracy in his

break from a Colorado prison.

After his escape Dillinger hid out in Chicago, protected by Louis Piquette, his lawyer. With him was dark-skinned Evelyn Frechette, Dillinger's half-breed sweetheart. While state and federal officials argued before grand juries as to who was to blame for Dillinger's escape, the outlaw was busy re-forming his gang, enlisting such desperadoes as Homer Van Meter, Tommy Carroll, and Lester Gillis, later known as Baby Face Nelson. But some of Dillinger's old pals weren't doing so well: Pierpont and Makley had been sentenced to the electric chair for the murder of the warden of the Lima jail.

Dillinger decided to try skin grafts to change his finger prints, but before the operations could be performed police ambushed him in St. Paul. He shot his way out and returned to his familiar Indiana hideouts, where he was joined by Van Meter.

J. Edgar Hoover later told the story of how Dillinger posed as "John Lawrence, a representative of a banking equipment house" during this period. One day he walked into a bank and was admitted to the president's office. He went into an elaborate discussion of his company's "new device" which could pump oxygen into a bank vault to prevent accidental suffocation. He was also extremely vivid in his telling of anecdotes collected by his company

158

to impress banking institutions with the horror of suffocation.

"Just think of some young secretary trapped by mistake in your vault," Dillinger said earnestly. "When you finally got that door open . . ."

The bank president mopped his brow. "I think I can get the board interested, Mr. Lawrence," he said. "How soon can you let us see this device?"

"I'll have to look over your vault," Dillinger said. "It goes by sizes and cubic feet of air."

The obliging bank official took Dillinger back to the vault and showed him how it opened and closed. Dillinger, perhaps perversely, even stood in the darkness for a few minutes as the door was closed.

He made many notes and was keenly interested in the combination type of lock and other incidentals. When he left he promised to return in a few days with his assistants.

Dillinger was good as his word. He returned with Van Meter, Nelson, and others. It took only minutes to clean out the vault.

Federal agents finally located Dillinger, Van Meter, and their girl friends in a northern Wisconsin resort. As the result of a tragic mistake, an innocent man and his two companions were wounded by federal gunfire, while the shots alerted Dillinger, Van Meter, and Nelson, who shot their way out of the trap. Nelson, later cornered, killed a federal agent and wounded two others as he machine-gunned his way past the posse.

Dillinger now was the nation's most wanted man, with everyone from Attorney General Cummings to village constables gunning for him. On June 23, the government offered $10,000 in rewards for Dillinger, dead or alive, and $5,000 for Nelson.

Dillinger and the deadly Homer Van Meter returned to Chicago, where two underworld doctors operated on their fingertips. To finance facial operations they held up a South Bend, Indiana, bank, killing an officer and wounding four bank officers and an innocent pedestrian.

Dillinger now began making independent plans to be taken to Mexico via Denver and San Francisco. The trip was to start July 23. While completing his plans, he became a frequent visitor in a rooming house at 2420 North Halstead Street, Chicago, where he saw Mrs. Anna Sage, a madam known

WANTED

JOHN HERBERT DILLINGER

On June 23, 1934, HOMER S. CUMMINGS, Attorney General of the United States, under the authority vested in him by an Act of Congress approved June 6, 1934, offered a reward of

$10,000.00

for the capture of John Herbert Dillinger or a reward of

$5,000.00

for information leading to the arrest of John Herbert Dillinger.

DESCRIPTION

Age, 32 years; Height, 5 feet 7-1/8 inches; Weight, 153 pounds; Build, medium; Hair, medium chestnut; Eyes, grey; Complexion, medium; Occupation, machinist; Marks and scars, 1/2 inch scar back left hand, scar middle upper lip, brown mole between eyebrows.

All claims to any of the aforesaid rewards and all questions and disputes that may arise as among claimants to the foregoing rewards shall be passed upon by the Attorney General and his decisions shall be final and conclusive. The right is reserved to divide and allocate portions of any of said rewards as between several claimants. No part of the aforesaid rewards shall be paid to any official or employee of the Department of Justice.

If you are in possession of any information concerning the whereabouts of John Herbert Dillinger, communicate immediately by telephone or telegraph collect to the nearest office of the Division of Investigation, United States Department of Justice, the local addresses of which are set forth on the reverse side of this notice.

JOHN EDGAR HOOVER, DIRECTOR,
DIVISION OF INVESTIGATION,
UNITED STATES DEPARTMENT OF JUSTICE,
June 25, 1934   WASHINGTON, D. C.

Dillinger reward poster.

to the Gary steel workers as "Katie from the Kostur House." At the time she got to know Dillinger, the government was taking steps to deport her to Rumania. How Dillinger met the Sage woman is not known, but it is known he took her and another woman, Polly Hamilton

Keele, former wife of a Gary policeman, to the local Biograph Theatre several times a week.

Now the bloody melodrama was drawing to a close. On the night of July 22, while Dillinger was walking to the theatre with both ladies on his arm,

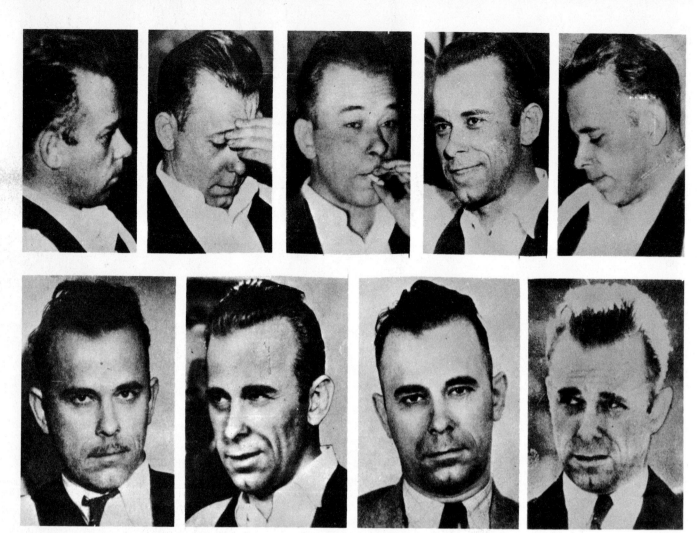

FBI photo file of Dillinger.

four police officers from East Chicago, Indiana, were contacting FBI agent Purvis with information on Dillinger's whereabouts.

It was a warm Sunday night when Dillinger and the two women walked to the theatre. Mrs. Sage, later headlined as the "Woman in Red" because of the dress she wore that night, was on one arm, Mrs. Keele on the other. Near the entrance to an alley, police and G-men moved in. As the three left the theatre, the cops acted quickly. Someone called "John!" Dillinger spun around in a crouch, went for his gun, and fell dead within seconds in a hail of bullets.

The question of just who put the finger on Dillinger was debated for years. After the shooting, FBI agent Purvis refused to say it was the Sage woman, and Mrs. Keele vigorously claimed the role. Two years later, however, in filing for a writ of habeas corpus to forestall a government move to deport her, Mrs. Sage swore in Chicago that she had "put John Dillinger on the spot."

In a sworn statement she insisted that Purvis had promised to have the government's case against her dropped if she cooperated in helping the G-men to trap the outlaw. Purvis denied this.

After Dillinger's death his gang was blown apart by the guns of the FBI, state police, and the local constabulary of small towns who fired first and asked questions after.

Homer Van Meter was now number one on the government list. On August 23, 1934, he died as his leader had, when a woman led him into a police trap.

Cold figures tell us that Dillinger cost his country almost a million dollars before he was killed. He caused, directly or indirectly, the death of twenty men, some law officers, some innocent bystanders. He caused more than twelve persons, actually not in his gang, to go to prison, many for long terms. Careers were wrecked, reputations ruined, political dreams shattered. One man, a prominent Chicago physician suspected of operating on Dillinger's fingertips, walked out of a window when the outlaw was captured. Federal and state trials, grand-jury probes, and long investigations totaled $595,000. Dillinger's loot from bank robberies was $372,500.

THE KIDNAPPER IS CAUGHT

FOR TWENTY-EIGHT months the colony of brightly colored pins on Lieutenant James J. Finn's map in New York City police headquarters had grown to a large, irregular patch covering parts of Yorkville and the upper Bronx area. Each pin represented a Lindbergh ransom bill passed in restaurants, filling stations, banks, and stores.

The theory that the kidnapper and killer of tiny Charles Augustus Lindbergh would eventually be trapped by passing the yellow-backed ransom bills had by this time almost become an obsession with Finn. By now, two years and five months after the fifty thousand dollars had been paid to the mysterious John, Finn headed a task force of over a hundred veteran detectives all dedicated to breaking what the press in United States and abroad referred to as the crime of the century.

The first note was passed only two days after the ransom had been paid. It showed up at the East River Savings Bank, at Ninety-sixth Street and Amsterdam Avenue. Treasury agents and Finn hurried there, but the tellers could not recall the persons who had passed the bill.

After that day the bills trickled into Finn's office by fives and tens. Each time Finn and his men hurried to the place where the bill had been passed only to be greeted with the disappointing news that the teller or clerk could not recall what the person looked like who had given the bill.

Finn would return to his office and carefully press another pin into his map.

Then the presidential order taking the United States off the gold standard gave impetus to the hunt. After May 1, 1933, the possession of gold notes would be illegal. On that last day a man carrying a bundle of certificates arrived at the Federal Reserve Bank. He waited patiently in line with the others and then tendered his bundle. The teller rapidly counted the bills; $2,980. Three days later bank officials checking the serial numbers were shocked to find they were all ransom bills. The name recorded was J. J. Faulkner of a West 149th Street address. As Finn suspected, the address was fictitious.

Then, on the evening of Nov. 26, 1933, a man passed a five-dollar note at the Loew's Sheridan Theatre in Greenwich Village. The cashier, Mrs. Cecilia M. Barr, recalled him because he "drew it from his watch pocket and tossed it through the window."

This time Finn got a description; five feet nine inches, high cheekbones, flat

Anna Hauptmann leaving the Bronx County Jail shortly after her husband was caught.

cheeks, a pointed chin, and a German accent. The man Dr. Condon had given the ransom to had had an accent.

By this time a pattern was emerging. The bills were creased lengthways and sideways so they could be carried in a man's watch pocket.

Finn also was sure the man drove a car and that he might be trapped through a filling station. Several had reported getting the bills. On this theory Finn concentrated his search directly on gas stations. He had a composite picture drawn by a police artist and sent out thousands of flyers asking station attendants to record the serial number of every five, ten and twenty received, and if possible who had paid it.

By mid-1934 the bills began to turn up almost weekly; the forest of pins on Finn's map now completely covered the Bronx and Yorkville.

On Saturday afternoon, September 15, 1934, a man with a German accent driving an old sedan swung into the Warner-Quinlan gas station at 2115 Lexington Avenue.

Walter Lyle, the attendant, later described the incident to a reporter. "He said he wanted five gallons of gas," Lyle said. "I noticed that he spoke with a decided German accent. Usually most people who come in at least smile and pass the time of day when you are giving them gas, but not this fellow. His face was flat and emotionless, his eyes were cold. When I hooked up the hose he gave me a five-dollar bill. I suddenly remembered the flyer asking us to watch for fives, tens, and twenties. Something told me to take down his license number. When I went in to get the change I grabbed a pencil, and when I came out I jotted down his license number—4U 13-14, New York—on the bill. Then I put the bill into the register. It went to the bank and that's how the case was finally broken."

In the Mount Morris Branch of the Corn Exchange Bank, 85 East 125th Street, William R. Strong, a teller, saw Lyle's notation and checked the bank's list of bills. With trembling hands he dialed the Treasury and got agent Thomas H. Sisk, who had been assigned to the investigation.

"We are holding a five-dollar bill, Serial Number A73976634A," Strong said. "Our records show that it is one of the Lindbergh ransom bills. Will you please confirm this?"

Sisk quickly checked and got back on the phone.

"It's one of the bills all right. Do you have any idea . . . ?"

Strong broke in excitedly, "Somebody has written a license number on the bill. Here it is."

Within minutes Sisk had phoned Lieutenant Finn and Colonel Schwarzkopf, head of the New Jersey State Police, who was directing the manhunt in that state.

The license plate was quickly checked with the New York State Motor Vehicle Records, and the name and address of Bruno Hauptmann was now in Finn's hands. The bill was also traced back to the gas station, and Lyle identified the artist's drawing of the kidnapper as a good likeness of the man who had given him the bill.

Finn and his men now began tailing Hauptmann. On September 18, just three days after the bill was given to Lyle, Finn and a carload of detectives boxed Hauptmann's car against a curb at Tremont and Park avenues in the Bronx and arrested him. As they searched him, Finn eagerly dug his fingers into Hauptmann's watch pocket. He silently held up a creased twenty-dollar gold certificate.

Hauptmann was quickly arraigned in the Bronx County Courthouse while hundreds of newsmen and newsreel photographers jammed the streets. He was held in $100,000 bail, which he did not raise, and later extradited to New Jersey to stand trial the following year.

Police and Treasury agents virtually tore Hauptmann's house and garage apart. Cleverly concealed in a hole drilled in a plank was $840, and an additional $13,750, all in ransom notes, were hidden in the garage.

Hauptmann stolidly insisted he was innocent. He told Finn that the money was given to him in January of 1934 "in a shoe box" by a friend, Isidor Fisch, who had gone back to Germany and died. Hauptmann insisted he didn't know what was in the box until months later.

"It was a nasty day. It had been raining and I went to the broom closet to get a broom. In some way I must have hit the box with the handle of the broom and I looked up and saw it was filled with money, all wet.

"I took the money into the garage to dry and even then I didn't bother to count it. I figured that Fisch was dead so it wouldn't hurt anyone if I spent some of it—so I did."

Police delving into Hauptmann's background found that he had been in the German Army in World War I and had jumped ship to get into this country. He was a carpenter and had one child, Manfred. His bewildered wife insisted to police she never knew anything about the kidnapping or the money. Police believed her.

Now that Hauptmann was in jail, Finn, his detectives, and New Jersey's attorney general David Wilentz began gathering the evidence that they hoped would someday send Bruno Hauptmann to the chair.

Bruno Richard Hauptmann.

Police searching for the Lindbergh ransom money in Hauptmann's garage.

NRA's Martyr

AMERICA'S rugged individualist of 1934 was a small, stooped Jersey City tailor who made headlines when he was sentenced to thirty days in jail and a hundred-dollar fine. His crime: he had charged 35 cents for a pressed suit instead of the 40 cents required by the NRA Tailoring Industry Code.

His case attracted international attention. In London one headline asked: "WHAT IS AMERICA UP TO?" Tailor Jacob Maged spent only three days in the Hudson County jail before he was released.

When Maged was released, he found himself a celebrity, and scores of reporters and newsreel men were waiting to interview him. That same day the Illinois Manufacturers Association hailed him as a national hero.

Maged went back to his shop on Griffith Street and held court as he sat cross-legged on his bench.

"So the NRA threw me in jail for a nickel," he said, biting off a thread. "For a nickel I wasn't a gentleman. What do they know about tailoring anyway? But I'm glad it's all over."

Then the tailor got up and motioned to a reporter, "Come over here, reporter, I want to show you how to do business without the NRA."

The reporter stepped to the door.

"Now you're coming in, you want to have a suit pressed. Say it."

"I want to have a suit pressed," the reporter obliged.

"The price is thirty-five cents," the tailor replied, "but for fifty cents I can do an extra special job. How about it?"

The reporter took the cue. "Sold!"

"You see," Maged said, "that's the way to do business. No NRA needed."

In May of 1934, however, Maged wired Hugh Johnson that the code was protecting him and that he was "heartily in favor of it." The following year, after the Supreme Court invalidated the NRA, he told newsmen, "The NRA was good for big business but bad for the little man."

The Dust Bowl

THE GRASS was dead. In the Dakotas, Nebraska, Kansas, Oklahoma, and Texas, the winds were blowing away the topsoil, millions and millions of tons. All that was left was the ugly barren clay. On the morning of November 11, 1933, the first great black cloud rose over America's Dust Bowl, darkening the sky as far east as Albany. It was the first of the blizzards that swept the Great Plains in 1933, 1934, and 1935, laying waste millions of farm and grazing acres.

In 1934, after a year's futile fight against the desolation and the black winds, refugees from America's Sahara began moving westward in ancient jalopies. So many left Oklahoma that the name Okie was applied to all the migrants. They jammed U.S. Highway 30 through the Idaho hills, 66 across New Mexico and Arizona, or the old Spanish Trail through El Paso and then westward. The cars and trucks were piled high with torn mattresses, cooking utensils, chamber pots, and bedsprings. Grimy children peered out from behind the junk and gaunt, sad-eyed women looked out of the broken windows of the truck cabs and front seats of the old cars.

It was a vast, confused migration.

Side by side with the Okies were fruit tramps from Oregon and cotton pickers from Alabama. When they reached the golden land of California, they fought each other for jobs. The market became glutted and jobs became so scarce that Hoovervilles—now an established part of the big city scene—sprang up all over California.

The permanent citizens became wary of the ragged, disheveled men and women and their dirty-faced children. "Get 'em going" they told the sheriffs, and the deputies with clubs drove the strangers out past the community's limits. The man from southeastern Colorado had suddenly become a "red," a "commie," a bomb-thrower of the worst sort. He was never considered a fellow citizen down in his luck, a man with his family who had had to flee from an avenging nature.

Human error and greed were behind the whole tragedy. In the beginning the Great Plains had been a sea of grass, first for the buffalo, then for the cattle barons. Before the end of the century the range had been badly damaged by overgrazing. Then came the sod busters, the homesteaders who tried to cultivate their 160-acre plots. The world was crying for wheat after World War I,

Dead cattle near Erich, Okla.

The Dust Bowl, Arthur Rothstein's prize-winning picture.

Herds of cattle in Oklahoma's Dust Bowl in search of a pasture they'll never reach.

164

Arthur Rothstein's famous picture of a farmer and his two children in the Dust Bowl.

and the land was torn up to supply the demand.

There never had been much rain. The annual rainfall was only 10 to 20 inches on the plains as compared with around 40 in the Mississippi Valley region. Then the years 1930 to 1933 brought drought to the plains. By 1934 a man couldn't raise enough corn to feed a baby. There hadn't been what the farmers called "a public rain." In the fall the winds started blowing. In Kansas farmers had to dig their tractors out of the black-blizzard stuff before they could plow. In Texas farmers said they were "between a rock and a hard place."

Before the year was out the displaced tenant farmers had their own legends and their own folklore. Squatting in the sun on the side of the highway, they would tell each other the story of the farmer who said to his neighbor, "I'll plow next week. I reckon the farm'll blow back from Oklahoma by then."

Or about the farmer who told the banker: "Well, we haven't lost everything. The wind blew the whole damn ranch out of state, but we ain't lost everything, banker—we still have the mortgage."

In 1934 the drought was so bad the farmers and ranchers reported the

"bush was dying"—the prickly-pear cactus containing precious moisture, which was good cattle feed.

Government census figures for 1934 and 1935 showed the displaced farmers went to the towns. But there too they met resentment; relief rolls doubled and competition for jobs was fierce. The black blizzards moved across the sky until 1936, when the first green shoots began to appear in the black wilderness. By that time rotation farming was becoming accepted, soil-protective measures were instituted, and men were returning to dig their rusted machinery out of drifts higher than a man.

JIGSAW

TIME. There was more time than people knew what to do with. There was time to sit by the living-room window and stare out at the passing cars. There was time to spend in the employment agency sitting on the hard-bottomed benches grouped like church pews, smoking the six cigarettes for five cents—three wooden matches included —waiting for the job call that would be answered by five hundred. Or there was the park, or the aimless wandering about the streets, or the balcony in the movie where one could sit hypnotized for hours.

It was out of a desperation to escape this inertia that the jigsaw puzzle was born. Before mid-1934, countless thousands of American heads were bent over innumerable tables fitting in the jagged little pieces to make the picture.

At the end of 1933, more than 2,500,000 puzzles were on the market. Before 1934 was many months old, 3,500,000 puzzles had been distributed, and many were being rented. The sales prices ranged from ten cents to several dollars for a "gigantic" job of over a thousand pieces.

At first, practically the only jigsaw puzzles were expensive ones cut from plywood. By the summer of 1934, as the craze spread, a New England distributor began the manufacture of a cheaper type of puzzle cut from heavy cardboard by punch presses. He sold hundreds of thousands before the year was over.

All over the country, not only in big-city newsstands but also in country drugstores, there were signs, "Puzzle of the Week," "The Weekly Jig," or "Circulating Library Puzzle of the Week." In large department stores "jigs," as they were called, were found all over the place—in the toy department, the adult games, the book and stationery departments. By midwinter jigsaw clubs for the purpose of exchanging puzzles were commonplace.

In 1937 the jigsaw puzzle was so

Doing a jigsaw puzzle in a Cleveland factory in the early thirties.

much a part of national life that it made an appearance before the United States Supreme Court. A Boston company was fighting for refund of $37,041 sales tax, on the grounds that the puzzle was not a "game" and could not be taxed like the ouija boards, which had been found taxable. The company's attorneys pointed out that jigsaw puzzles could be traced back as far as the American Revolution.

The high court found that jigsaw puzzles are as much a game as "solitaire."

In London a *Times* man, determined to find out why the puzzle had such an attraction for the common folk, interviewed a number of fans. One summed it up for him. "I like 'em because when I put 'em together I don't think."

A psychologist quizzed by the *Times* man had a more complex explanation: "The puzzle craze originates in man's fundamental desire to finish what he sets out to do. Why does he ever set out to finish the puzzle? Well, perhaps he realizes there are many great problems in the world and as he cannot have much of a part in solving these problems, he takes upon himself a little one and sees it through. He throws himself into the puzzle-solving and enjoys the satisfaction of accomplishment."

Highlights and Sidelights: 1934

ARCHBISHOP Leon Tourian, supreme head of the Armenian Church in America, was stabbed to death in New York City before a huge crowd. . . . FDR asked Congress to devalue the dollar and the value was established at the rate of $35 per ounce of gold instead of $20. . . . In St. Paul bank president Edward G. Bremer was kidnapped and released after two hundred thousand dollars had been paid. . . . President Roosevelt celebrated his fifty-second birthday and thanked the nation in a fireside chat. . . . A wave of violent strikes rocked the country, notably a general strike in San Francisco and a truckers' strike in Minneapolis. . . . Anti-communist demonstrations and strikes toppled French Premier Daladier's government. . . . New York City experienced the coldest day of its history when the mercury plunged to 14.3° below zero. Hospitals were busy treating frostbite, and all schools were closed. . . . The army took over flying the mail but later in the year, after ten pilots had been killed in crashes, gave it back to commercial airlines. . . . Two European kings were killed—one by an assassin, one accidentally. Albert I of Belgium plunged to his death while mountain climbing when a sharp rock snapped his rope. Yugoslavia's Alexander was cut down with pistol shots when he stepped from a warship at Marseilles. . . . Nevada, Utah, and California were rocked by quakes, but there was only one casualty—a woman frightened to death. . . . Henry Ford restored a $5-a-day minimum to 47,000 of his 70,000 workers. . . . Sam Insull, the Chicago utility magnate, was arrested aboard a chartered freighter and taken to Athens, then back to the United States, where he was later acquitted on charges of fraud. . . . In New York City the Rev. O. P. Barnhill finished his sermon with these words: "Oh, what a time it will be for you when the gatekeeper says, 'Take off your rough sandals, the journey is ended,' " then collapsed and died. . . . An international ring of spies was uncovered when two Americans, Robert Gordo and his wife, con-

Police and strikers battle in San Francisco's 1934 general strike.

fessed they were espionage agents. . . . Germany declared Albert Einstein was no longer a German citizen. . . . New York State legislated open betting at the racetracks, illegal since 1908. . . .

Max Baer knocked out Primo Carnera to win the world's heavyweight championship. . . . Texas badman Clyde Barrow and his cigar-smoking sweetheart, Bonny Parker, were killed in a

Minneapolis police battle striking truck-drivers in the crippling 1934 strike.

Insull enters Cook County Jail, Chicago.

gun duel near Acadia, Louisiana. . . . A move against "vicious" movies was started by Philadelphia's Cardinal Dougherty. The movement became the Legion of Decency. . . . Hitler and Mussolini met for the first time in Italy. . . . Honeymooners had an unexpected treat when part of the Niagara Falls, 250 feet long at the top of Horseshoe Falls, tumbled 160 feet into the gorge. . . . The S.S. *Queen Mary,* named after England's queen, sailed on her maiden voyage. She was 1,018 feet long and weighed 73,000 tons. . . . Gloria Vanderbilt, ten-year-old daughter of Mrs. Gloria Morgan Vanderbilt, was taken from the custody of her mother by Supreme Court Justice John F. Carew and made a ward of the court and her father's sister, Mrs. Harry Payne Whitney. . . . William Woodin resigned as secretary of the treasury because of poor health, and Acting Secretary Henry Morgenthau became head of the department. . . . Chrysler created a considerable stir in the automobile world when it introduced its Airflow models, designed and constructed for easier riding. . . . Ernest Hemingway and his wife Pauline, mother of his two younger sons, returned from a hunting trip in East Africa. His *Green Hills of Africa* was announced for publication in 1935. . . . Hard-boiled detective novels made their mark on the American literary scene of the thirties like the sharp bark of an automatic. This year, James M. Cain's *The Postman Always Rings Twice* was a best seller. . . . America was also reading William Saroyan's unforgettable *The Daring Young Man on the Flying Trapeze* and F. Scott Fitzgerald's *Tender Is the Night*. . . . After some walk-on parts, Henry Fonda gained success in *The Farmer Takes a Wife*. The following year Hollywood called and he anwered, to become one of the film capital's most sought-after stars. Jimmy Stewart, who had played a bit role in *Carrie Nation,* was already in Hollywood. . . . The *cause célèbre* picture starring Jean Harlow and Lionel Barrymore was finally released as *The Girl from Missouri*. It had previously

"Africa reminds me of Spain, and I would like to return," Ernest Hemingway said as he arrived in New York with his wife after hunting lions in East Africa in April, 1934.

William Saroyan, the Daring Young Man on the Flying Trapeze, in the early thirties.

1934 DeSoto Airflow.

169

Jean Harlow and Lionel Barrymore.

Burns and Allen in action.

gloried in the title *"Born to Be Kissed,"*
but in anticipation of objections from
the Production Code Administration,
the studio changed the title to *"100%
Pure."* Almost everybody objected to
that, and so it too was changed. . . .
There was no doubt Lillian Hellman
was among the giants of the theatre
after the opening night of her *The Children's Hour,* which became an American classic. . . . The Burns and Allen
team—George and Gracie—by now was
a well-established success in the radio
world.

Mussolini in a classic pose, 1934.

Mussolini's famous "Long Room" in the Palazzo Venetia in Rome. His desk, beside the fireplace, was so far from the entrance that Il Duce had full opportunity to study his guests as they approached. The long walk often caused visitors to be ill at ease.

"The Trial of the Century"

THE TRIAL of Bruno Richard Hauptmann opened on the first day of January, 1935, and the instant Judge Thomas W. Trenchard's gavel slammed down on his worn desk, the eyes of the civilized world turned to the rural village of Flemington, New Jersey, and its century-old courthouse, where Hauptmann was charged with the kidnap-murder of tiny Charles Augustus Lindbergh, son of the first man of the skies.

The trial lasted until February 15. There were more than 380 exhibits and approximately 1,500,000 words of testimony. At the time of the kidnapping, there had been no law about summoning the FBI into a kidnapping case after twenty-four hours had passed. Hauptmann was tried for causing the baby's death while in the commission of a felony; that is, breaking into the nursery and stealing something of value—not the boy, but the nightclothes in which he slept.

Such evil, as cited in the indictment, "offended the peace of this state, the government and dignity of the same."

There were many preliminary witnesses who testified primarily to lay the groundwork of the State's case, but the star witness for the prosecution was Colonel Lindbergh. To millions of newspaper readers and radio listeners, Lindbergh was no longer the Lone Eagle, but a tight-faced, bereaved father describing how he had done everything possible to recover his infant son. The highlight of his testimony came when he told how Dr. John Condon paid the $50,000 ransom. Lindbergh had been only a few feet from Condon when the money was passed to the kidnapper.

He told a hushed courtroom that he had heard the shadowy figure in the wind-tossed night call out to Condon, "Over here, doctor."

Attorney General David Wilentz asked Lindbergh if he had heard that voice since.

Lindbergh nodded. "I have."

"Whose voice was that?"

Lindbergh said without hesitation,

1935

Colonel Lindbergh arrives to testify against Hauptmann.

172

A study of Bruno Richard Hauptmann.

"It was the voice of Bruno Hauptmann."

Another unforgettable witness was old Amandus Hockmuth, a gnarled farmer of eighty-seven, long a resident of the back country of Hopewell. As with many old men, his principal occupation was watching the long and lonely road that stretched past his farmhouse, hoping that something would happen—anything—to break the monotony of the dragging days. Something did happen, he said, at about noon on March 1, 1932, ten hours before the discovery of the kidnapping.

"I saw a car coming around the corner, pretty good speed—and I expected it to turn over," he said. "And when it got to be about twenty-five feet away from me the driver looked out at me like this—" the old man looked startled, then scowled. "The driver looked like he had seen a ghost."

"And that man you saw, is he in this courtroom?" Wilentz asked.

The old man slowly peered about the courtroom. "Yes, alongside that trooper there."

"Point him out," Wilentz snapped.

The old man with trembling movements rose from his chair and, head thrust forward like a hound on the scent, picked his way through the forest of chairs and desks until he paused in front of Hauptmann. Then slowly, dramatically, he touched him.

"Right here," he called out.

Hauptmann snarled in German, "The old man is crazy!"

But it was obvious the drama was not lost on the jury.

Hauptmann finally took the stand, and the Western Union telegraph keys clattered all day delivering his testimony to the remote points of the globe.

"I saved a lot of money," he said, and went into a detailed explanation of how he had dabbled with small accounts in Wall Street. He also repeated on the stand the story he had told police of how Isidor Fisch had given him the money police had found in his garage.

"He threw a party when he left for Germany; it was at his request we held it in our house. We invited a couple of

friends, and about nine o'clock Fisch came out and got a little bundle in his hand. My wife was in the baby's room. We went into the kitchen and he said, 'I leave it, don't mind, keep care of it and put it in a tight place.' I didn't ask what it was; I put it in the broom closet on the upper shelf."

When he had finished his direct testimony Wilentz launched a savage cross-examination, at one point pounding with fury as he shouted, "You lied to police, didn't you? Didn't you lie?

. . . They're all lies."

Hauptmann shouted back angrily, "No . . . no . . . you stop that!"

Fingerprints played no part, yet were forever cropping up because, for all the evidence against the defendant (physical evidence at that) not one fingerprint was discovered to accuse him. The State's explanation was, of course, that the kidnapper had worn gloves.

Several witnesses testified about a plank or board that had disappeared from Hauptmann's attic, laying the groundwork for Koehler, the wood wizard, to give his testimony about the ladder.

The floor of the Hauptmann attic. A piece of the flooring was used in building the kidnap ladder.

Max Rauch, who owned the house in which Hauptmann lived, testified that in October, 1931, the attic floor was complete. Two weeks after Hauptmann's arrest, Rauch went into the attic and discovered that a strip of board was missing.

This was the board that Hauptmann was alleged to have used in making the ladder.

Detective Lewis J. Bornmann told of going into Hauptmann's attic and discovering that part of one of the floorboards had been removed. He also found a small pile of sawdust, indicating the spot where the board had been sawed.

On Oct. 9 he accompanied Arthur Koehler, the wood expert, to the attic.

Q: What did you do?
A: We checked the nail holes in the beams with nail holes in what we know as Rail 16 in the ladder.
Q: Where are the nail holes in Rail 16?
A: Rail 16—you notice there are two here and one here [indicating].
Q: Referring to the bottom of the ladder?
A: Referring to the bottom of the ladder. There is another one here coming toward the top and another one here coming almost to the top.
Q: You had this railing and you checked it with the flooring. Is that correct?
A: That is correct.
Q: I show you a photograph with Rail 16 on the floor, is that correct?
A: Yes, sir. It is.
Q: Now show the jury where those nail holes of Rail 16 check with the joist.
A: There is one of the nail holes right here and the other one is down here—you see the shadow of it—and down here are the other two.
Q: They are the same nail holes that you have just shown the jury in Rail 16, is that correct?
A: They are.
Q: Now, did you check the nails?
A: Yes, sir.
Q: In the holes through Rail 16 to the holes that were in the joists?
A: We placed four cut nails in this Rail 16 and placed it upon the beams. Those nails fitted perfectly into the holes that were still in the beams here.
Q: What was the slant of those nails?
A: They were on a slight angle, sort of toed in.
Q: Necessary to pound the nails in, or could you push them in with your finger?
A: We pushed them in with our fingers.
Q: Did you make any comparison of Rail 16 with the board that was still attached to the floor?
A: Yes, sir, we did.
Q: What do you say as to the grain in Rail 16 and the grain that was still attached to the floor?
A: It appeared to match perfectly.
Q: Did Mr. Koehler match them?
A: Yes, sir, he did.

The stage was then set for Arthur

Courtroom scene with Hauptmann conferring with one of his attorneys, Egbert Rosecrans. The reporters who covered the trial are directly behind them. Prosecutor Wilentz is seen (top center). At the right, second from bottom, is Damon Runyon, writing out his story in longhand.

Koehler, the wood expert of the U.S. Forest Service Laboratory at Madison, Wisconsin, who appeared that afternoon. It was his testimony—and the ladder—that really sent Hauptmann to the electric chair.

Nobody saw the ladder built. Nobody saw it used. But the story of its journey from a South Carolina mill to the Bronx lumberyard, to a floor in Hauptmann's attic to the ladder dis-

The courtroom where Hauptmann was tried and convicted. At left, with his hand to his face, is Edward A. Mahar, presently city editor of the New York Journal-American. Next to him is James Kilgallen, father of the well-known columnist and TV personality, Dorothy Kilgallen.

carded outside the Lindbergh home in Hopewell, was an amazing tale of scientific detection.

Koehler told his story with a cool, calm, calculated manner, beginning with the homemade ladder police had found fifty feet from the house.

Koehler told how for eighteen months he had canvassed the mills of the East until he traced the wood to a ten-dollar purchase the carpenter had made in the Bronx—some of it to replace a floorboard in the attic of his house at 1279 East 222nd Street.

Koehler explained his microscopic examination of machine-plane marks on the surface of famous Rail 16—the one he matched with lumber stripped from the attic floor.

He showed that "someone" had sawed the attic board into almost equal lengths—and that in grain, distortion caused by knots, texture, and rings there was proof that "Rail 16" was once part of the attic board.

He pointed to four nail holes in the rail and matched them, to a minute fraction of an inch, against four nail holes found in a joist in the Hauptmann attic. He demonstrated how nails driven through the rail and into the joist "fitted perfectly, though one of them had been driven in slantingly."

"The ladder rail and the attic board were originally one piece," Koehler testified.

"In examining this ladder rail," he said, "I noticed that both edges had been planed with a hand plane. The plane was not in very good condition and left little ridges. . . .

"The ridges are of different size, and when I plane a piece of wood with that plane (taken from Hauptmann's tool chest), it makes similar ridges, of the same size and the same distance apart as those found on the ladder rail."

Then he gave an amazing demonstration.

"I learned to do this with coins when I was a boy," he said, and placed a piece of paper over the edge of the rail and rubbed it with heavy crayon.

The ridges made by the defective plane showed in bold relief.

Koehler then affixed a piece of wood to the bench where Judge Thomas W. Trenchard presided, clamped it tightly, marked it with a blue pencil to

Mrs. Anna S. Hauptmann at the trial of her husband.

show the depth he would shave it and went to work with Hauptmann's plane. Discarding the shaving, he took more paper, placed it on the scraped surface and applied the crayon.

The markings on the two papers, one from the wood he had planed, the other from the ladder, were identical.

But Koehler was not finished. He returned to a discussion of machine-plane marks on the rail and told how the work was done by eight knives in revolving "cutter heads" and how one was not set properly and had left a ridge—visible only under a microscope.

"This lumber," he testified, "passed through the planer at 93/100ths of an inch for every revolution of the top and bottom cutter heads, and 86/100ths of an inch per revolution of the side heads. This meant there were eight knives in the top and bottom cutter heads and six knives in the side heads.

"Now from an investigation of planers used in this section of the country on Carolina pine, I found that comparatively few planers have eight knives in the top and bottom heads and six in the side heads.

"The fact is, I made a thorough canvass of all planing mills from New York to Alabama. There are 1,598 all together and I found only twenty-five firms that had such a planer. Two of these I could rule out because they did not dress this kind of lumber.

"I got samples from the other twenty-three firms and I found that only one of those firms made revolution marks of the same spacing as on the ladder rail. All the others made wider or narrower revolution marks."

That company was in McCormick, South Carolina, and out of forty-six shipments during the period in question, Koehler had traced one with the distinguishing plane marks to the National Lumber and Millwork Company in the Bronx. Hauptmann had bought ten dollars worth of it in December, 1931.

The hunt was over.

The jury began deliberating at 11:23 A.M., February 13. The verdict was announced at 10:44 that night. The routine of automatic appeals took months. Then at the last minute Governor Harold G. Hoffman gave Hauptmann a two-day stay of execution. But after the flurry of headlines was over, the stolid, impassive German carpenter finally walked into the death house of the New Jersey State Prison at Trenton, on the night of April 3, 1936, and was electrocuted.

The horror, the false hopes, the heartbreaks, the hoaxes are now only faded clippings or excerpts in anthologies. But the memory of Charles Augustus Lindbergh, age twenty months, is perpetuated in the law that bears his name—the Lindbergh kidnapping law.

The famous kidnap ladder.

$800 of the ransom money was found stuffed in a hole in this plank in Hauptmann's garage.

The KINGFISH

HUEY PIERCE LONG once said that when fascism came to the United States it would be called by some other name, probably democracy. Huey was an expert on fascism, and he felt that the United States would have to become a controlled state. When that happened, he wanted the controller to be Huey Long.

A psychological enigma and a political phenomenon, Huey Long rose from a cotton patch to national prominence as the dictatorial boss of Louisiana. He attained the highest degree of state control ever recorded under America's democratic form of government. He conceived and did things that none but he had thought were possible. His followers called him a "genius," "the one friend the poor has," and the "man who champions the little people's rights."

But his enemies, who were legion, dubbed him "demagogue," "madman," and "destroyer of constitutional government." The latter, of course, were right.

Long liked to call himself "Kingfish." He had once used this term sarcastically to describe a political opponent, but when he saw it was popular, he kept it for himself, and continued to live up to it. As a matter of fact, from the time he left the family farm in Winn Parish until a subservient legislature passed laws transferring control of the state's every activity to his political machine, he was a law unto himself.

Long was born on August 30, 1893, on a 320-acre farm which became part of the town of Winnfield, Louisiana, when the building of a railroad brought growth to the town and transformed the fields into city lots. He was the seventh child in a family of nine. He attended Shreveport High School, but did not finish the course. His college work was confined to three months in the law department of the University of Oklahoma and about seven months of intensive cramming in the law school of Tulane University. But he passed a special examina-

Huey Long.

tion for admission to the bar and was admitted to practice in May, 1915, when just short of twenty-two.

When he was nineteen years old, he had been arrested at Shreveport, accused of being involved in a shooting scrape. An alibi cleared him; Miss Rose McConnell testified that he had escorted her to a theatre that evening and produced the ticket stubs as proof. The next year they were married. They became the parents of two sons and a daughter.

After winning admission to the bar, Long hung out his shingle in Winnfield and launched himself into politics. In 1918, at twenty-five, he was elected state railroad commissioner for

the north Louisiana district, and moved to Shreveport. It was soon afterward that he began his long fight with the Standard Oil Company.

In his autobiography he explained that as a Winnfield attorney he had acquired stock in several independent oil companies, either as fees for legal work or by purchase from clients. In Shreveport he built up a $40,000 income and was "in a fair way to becoming a millionaire" when the big companies controlling the pipelines refused to take oil from independent wells. "My shares became worth less than forty cents over night," he said.

Long manipulated a finding favorable to the independents through the

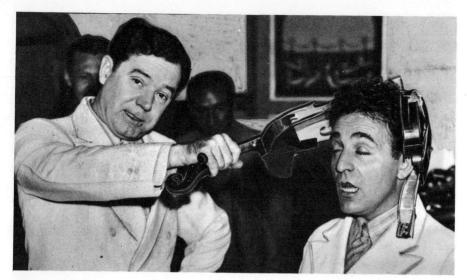

The "Kingfish" on the stage of a Broadway theatre breaking a fiddle over the head of a bandleader.

Public Service Commission, and later the legislature declared the pipelines public carriers.

At thirty, Long ran for governor and lost, but four years later he ran again and won. Immediately, he went after his political foes, clearing them out of various state offices, and arousing bitter enmities. In March, 1929, when he called a special session of the legislature to enact a tax of five cents a barrel on crude oil, the storm broke.

The Louisiana house of representatives presented articles of impeachment containing nineteen charges. Among them were accusations that he had attempted to bribe legislators, used the appointive power to influence the judiciary, and flouted the constitutional limitations on the governorship, that he had told a bodyguard to kill an opposition legislator, and that he had participated in a scandalous "studio party" in New Orleans.

Long defeated the impeachment proceedings in the senate. A two-thirds vote was necessary to convict, and he got fifteen senators, one more than one third, to sign a statement that they would not vote for impeachment because the articles were faultily drawn. All fifteen were rewarded by political preferment.

While in the statehouse Long further consolidated his political power, and in 1930, in a close fight, he won election to a seat in the U.S. Senate, defeating the veteran Joseph E. Ransdell.

Ordinarily Long would have taken his seat in the Senate on March 4,

1931, but he had fallen out with the lieutenant governor, Dr. Paul Cyr, and decided to hold on to the governorship until he could be assured that no political foe would succeed him. Dr. Cyr finally went before a notary and took the oath as governor, then filed an ouster suit against Long. The latter, declaring that Cyr by his action had vacated the office of lieutenant governor, got A. O. King, president pro tempore of the state senate, to assume that post, and then went to court and personally argued the case against the ouster suit to a victory.

His next move was to engineer O.

K. Allen through the gubernatorial primary of January, 1932; the whole Long slate for state offices and a majority of his nominees for the legislature also won in the primary. Since this was tantamount to election, Long could finally entrain for Washington, leaving the state in the hands of his machine. Meanwhile, he had formed a law partnership in New Orleans and purchased a home on Audubon Boulevard.

The Senate custom that new members listen and learn meant nothing to red-haired Huey. He declaimed about his "share-the-wealth" project and denounced his party's leader, Senator Joseph T. Robinson of Arkansas, for "compromising" with the Republicans. In one of his early speeches he became so personal in his comments upon fellow senators that he was forced to stop.

In February, 1932, Long went back to New Orleans, had himself named Democratic national committeeman, and supervised selection of a delegation to the party's national convention in Chicago. Before that body met he came out in favor of Roosevelt's candidacy for the presidential nomination, and when his delegation's credentials were challenged, he won a majority vote in the convention, which was interpreted as the first test of Roosevelt's strength. After the convention, he campaigned in Arkansas for Mrs. Hattie Caraway, who was running for the Senate seat of her late husband; she

Senator Long, after speaking before the Senate for 15 hours and 15 minutes on June 12-13, 1935, in favor of the NRA.

became the first woman to win election to that body. Then he canvassed Louisiana for his close political ally, John Overton, and helped him win Louisiana's other Senatorial seat, and also took his sound trucks and literature-distributing forces to the Dakotas, to stump for Roosevelt.

Thereafter he shuttled between Washington and Baton Rouge, defending his state organization against attacks and reinforcing it until his personal power was virtually absolute. In Washington, he kept himself in the limelight by bitter attacks upon the administration and with his campaign to restrict big incomes and "spread the wealth" by making every person in the United States free of debt and giving each individual five thousand dollars. (In Louisiana, a debt moratorium law had been passed by the legislature.)

Although Long's opponents dubbed his pet measures "claptrap" or worse, and sought to discredit him by pitiless exposure of personal scandals, he went blithely on his way. He had undisputed talents as a shrewd lawyer, always rewarded his adherents, and waged incessant warfare against his foes, but chiefly he relied upon a rare persuasiveness as a speaker. He knew just when to say "ain't," when to quote Scripture, and when to speak logically and clearly. His eloquence was a talent that had long stood him in good stead. Even during his brief high-school career he had been outstanding as a debater, and his ready tongue had been just about his greatest asset on his very first job—"on the road" as a traveling salesman.

In the 1930 election in which he had won his Senate seat, Long had had submitted to the voters bond issues of $68,000,000 for roads and $5,000,000 for Louisiana's new thirty-three-story capitol, which were approved. His expenditures of 79 million dollars in the year 1931 finally produced a state treasury crisis, and in 1932 an extensive program of fresh taxation was put through. This started a revolt that reached a climax in January, 1935, when the Square Deal Association, organized by anti-Long people, assembled in Baton Rouge to demand that Governor Allen summon the legislature in special remedial session. Senator Long hurried home. Many of the Square Dealers were armed, and the militia and state police were called out. One citizen was wounded in a clash

A reconstruction of the assassination of Huey Long.

and extensive bloodshed was narrowly averted.

Long now opened a court inquiry into a conspiracy which he said his enemies had formed to kill him. The hearing was conducted inside a ring of machine guns and bayonets, and Long claimed afterward that he had proved his contention.

The end came for Huey Long later that same year when a prominent physician, Dr. Carl Austin Weiss, stepped from behind a marble column in the skyscraper capitol at Baton Rouge to fire one, perhaps two, bullets into Long's stomach. The Kingfish had the

strength to walk down the steps of the capitol, muttering, "Why did he do it? Why did anyone want to shoot me?"

Three days later he died in a hospital room. He was buried in a spectacular grave on the landscaped grounds of the capitol he built, overlooking the miles of ribbon-like highways, the silver bridges, mammoth Louisiana State University, and the swank Greek-revival governor's mansion of the state he once controlled.

A book based on Long's life, *All the King's Men,* won the Pulitzer Prize, and the movie based on it in 1949 took an Oscar.

RIOT

POVERTY, unemployment, idleness, racial discrimination, and insufficient policing had made Harlem, the Negro-population section of New York City, a ticking time-bomb. It exploded with a terrifying roar on the afternoon of March 18, 1935. Before the last echo died away, eleven men and women had been shot, a boy was dead, one hundred and thirty-five men, women, and children were in hospitals, hundreds more had been injured, and eighty-nine men were under arrest. Damage was estimated at almost half a million dollars.

The rioting began in the afternoon, when the manager of a five-and-ten-cent store caught a small boy stealing a toy knife from a counter. He repri-

manded the boy, who ran away. But within minutes rumors were spreading that the boy had been beaten to death in the basement of the store. A crowd began to gather, and when by chance a black funeral car came to a stop nearby, a roar of anger went up. A brick flew and the store's large plate-glass window fell into splinters. This was the spark; the fuse sputtered and the bomb exploded.

The mob, more than a thousand men and women, reduced the store to kindling wood within minutes; the manager fortunately ran out the back door and escaped with his life. From the store the mob moved down West 125th Street, beating whites and blacks alike. Rifles and revolvers were fired down on the rioters from the rooftops. Garbage cans, bottles, and bricks torn from chimneys showered into the streets. The mob ran down subway entrances and flung whites from platforms onto the tracks. One man nar-

rowly missed being ground to death under the wheels of a train, by pressing himself under the platform.

By this time, riot squads had arrived and were battling the frenzied mob. But word was sent back to Police Commissioner Valentine, "We can't control them, they're too many."

Every available policeman in New York City was sent to Harlem by taxi, patrol car, and patrol wagon. Some were beaten into unconsciousness with their own clubs and had their uniforms torn from their bodies.

The mob started fires in several buildings and openly looted wrecked stores. White men returning home from work were set upon and beaten and robbed. Drivers of cars were dragged from their vehicles and the autos wrecked with baseball bats stolen from sporting-goods stores.

By nightfall Harlem was a battlefield. This writer, with two other newsmen, spent a terrifying hour after

The handbill given out by the Communist Party to incite the Harlem race riot of 1935.

An example of the rioters' looting and damage.

the three became separated from the police detail they had accompanied to the scene. They were running for their lives from a howling mob marching under torches made of tarred brooms, when a radio car appeared and picked them up. They roared away in a shower of bricks and clubs.

All night the streets were filled with shouting, cursing men and women, the splintering of glass, the screeching sirens of emergency trucks, radio cars, and fire trucks, and the sharp reports of shots.

Every policeman was a target. A truckload of paving bricks was overturned and the bricks used as weapons. Several officers received skull-fractures. Ambulances from hospitals outside the city were summoned for emergency use; the casualty lists at hospitals might have come from a city under attack. The rioting was given impetus when thousands of leaflets, probably prepared by Communists, floated down from rooftops. Each leaflet denounced the "Cossack cops" and the "whites

who killed a Negro boy for stealing a ten-cent knife."

As the night went on, police reported to Commissioner Valentine that whereas the injuries at first were from bats and clubs and bricks, more gunshot casualties were now being received at the hospitals. Several times patrolmen were forced to shoot into a mob to save the life of a man, black or white.

Police officers, both patrolmen and detectives in unmarked cars, were ruthless as they charged the mob with clubs and billies. But their ruthlessness finally brought the rioting under control, and by dawn of the next day Police Commissioner Valentine reported to Mayor La Guardia that the area was quiet.

The city and the nation were shocked. Many prominent New Yorkers demanded immediate action, and La Guardia ordered every city agency into the investigation even as a committee of prominent Harlem residents began its own probe.

Communists were blamed but it

appeared that, although they had taken advantage of the rioting, they had not started it. It was, as one committee member charged, the result of bad housing, poverty, and an unfeeling city that had allowed Harlem to become one vast slum, the largest in America, where vice of every kind was bred, helped in many ways by whites who profited from it.

"Where Harlem begins, license begins," he said bitterly.

The situation was summed up by a Catholic priest who said: "The colored people of Harlem do not want communism or riots or mobs. But when you realize the financial state of these people, you can understand they must do something. They are desperate, they have their backs to the wall. In my own church, fifteen hundred parishioners are on relief. When a man sees his family starving, his shoes filled with cardboard, his babies crying for milk, he is ready to use his fists, his brain, his everything to fight back."

The Chicken that Killed an Eagle

No one could recall when it had happened before, not even the oldest court attendant: the United States Supreme Court had a hearty laugh. Every one of the nine justices, usually so solemn and staid, was shaking with laughter, and the sound echoed through the beautiful but cold-looking courtroom.

The cause of their laughter was a young and earnest attorney, Joseph Heller, who was excitedly describing the art of killing chickens. Heller was representing the A. L. A. Schechter Live Poultry Company of Brooklyn, which had been convicted and fined for violating the NRA code. The case had finally reached the highest court in the land, which had to decide whether the NRA had authority to fix wages and hours of labor. On this case would rest the fate of the National Industrial Recovery Act.

But the scene that afternoon was not of the character usually associated with that august tribunal. After Donald R. Richberg, as special assistant to the attorney general, had completed the government's presentation, attorney Heller attempted to demonstrate that the NRA's code provisions, under which his clients had been convicted, had no authority over a business operated entirely within one state and therefore outside the jurisdiction of the federal government.

The Schechters had been convicted for failure to observe the "straight killing" provision of the Live Poultry Code, and when the court asked Heller to explain the meaning of "straight killing," Heller had gone into the long, detailed, and at times excited description that sent the justices into gales of laughter.

One after another the members of the court took the cue and prodded him with questions until it was finally clear to the court that "you have got to put your hand into the coop and take out whichever chicken comes to you first. You then hand the chicken to the rabbi, who slaughters it."

"And it was for that that your client was convicted?" asked Justice McReynolds.

"Yes, and fined five thousand dollars and given three months in jail," Heller retorted.

Heller also pointed out that if a customer wanted to buy half a crate of chickens under the NRA code, he had to divide the crate itself and take one half. Justice Sutherland then created another uproar when he asked what would happen if all the chickens were huddled at one end of the crate.

Mr. Heller admitted that was a "puzzler" and the laughter continued.

But if the high court found the art of killing chickens entertaining, they did not feel the same about the question of the NRA's authority. In a unanimous decision the justices upheld Heller's arguments and scuttled the NRA in May, 1935.

It was a wild day in the Schechter home on Brighton Beach Avenue in Brooklyn. Reporters crowded the living room of the modest house to interview the victors. But Joseph Schechter, head of the company, pointed out that he and his three brothers had no reason for jubilation—the legal battle had cost twenty thousand dollars.

"We're down to our last nickel," he said. "If I had known it would cost that much, we would have gone to jail."

The death of the NRA's blue eagle seemed to haunt the Schechters for some time. In 1936 Joseph Schechter declared the brothers were "broke" and had lost even their house to a bank.

"We beat the government and everyone cheered," he said. "They wrote us letters and offered to help in every way. All we got was thirty dollars. One guy sent ten dollars, and that was the most. But we're a long way from being destitute.

"The Schechter brothers are going to start a new chicken business. We'll get back on top. Anyway, we'll always be known as the four Schechter brothers whose chicken killed the NRA's blue eagle. Maybe some day we'll even be in a book. . . ."

(Seated) Jacob Heller, assistant to his brother Joseph Heller, attorney who fought the NRA. (Standing) Alex, Aaron, and Joseph Schechter.

The DUTCHMAN

THE POWER wielded by the gangsters, racketeers, and criminal syndicates who, with the aid of crooked politicians, controlled our larger cities, was beginning to arouse widespread public indignation.

Special Prosecutor Thomas E. Dewey, with his mustache and tight-lipped smile, was appointed by New York State's Governor Lehman to break the hold organized rackets had on New York City. His picture was soon familiar to most newspaper readers. His spectacular roundup of bail bondsmen and loan sharks, executed with military precision, had touched off his special grand jury investigation. It was Dewey who inspired the new term, "racket buster." The image of the young crusader had caught the public fancy, replacing Hollywood's "Little Caesar."

One of the central figures in this melodrama of the thirties was Arthur (Dutch Schultz) Flegenheimer. He was far from the popular conception of the sleek, dark-haired gangster; Dutch was too plebeian. Usually dressed in an unkempt gray suit, he looked like an unsuccessful salesman.

Thomas E. Dewey.

Dutch Schultz and Dixie Davis.

Yet Dutch was always mindful of his appearance. In Syracuse, when he was on trial for income-tax evasion, he was told by an admirer that a man of his position should dress better. He gave the man a bland look. "Such display is vulgar," he growled. "Personally, I think only queers wear silk shirts." He was more explicit with reporters: "Now take silk shirts—I never bought one in my life. A guy's a sucker to spend fifteen or twenty dollars on a shirt. Hell, a guy can get a good one for two bucks!"

Schultz always looked shabby compared to his fellow conspirators: Abe (Bo) Weinberg; Bo's brother, George, who was to become Dewey's first witness; and Dixie Davis, the mouthpiece of the underworld, who would become a state's witness so he could live out the rest of his life with his showgirl sweetheart, Hope Dare.

Money was the one god in the Dutchman's life. Dixie Davis once said, "You can insult Arthur's girl [he was always formal when talking about his boss], spit in his face, push him around—and he'll laugh. But don't steal a dollar from his acounts. If you do you're dead."

Schultz was born in the Bronx on August 6, 1902, the son of Herman Flegenheimer, a saloon-keeper and livery-stable owner. His mother was Mrs.

Emma Neu Flegenheimer, a hard-working housewife who tried to teach her son to go straight. Schultz, in his formative years, was a constant truant and juvenile delinquent. When he was fourteen, his father deserted the family. His mother took in washing, and Dutch sold newspapers for a year. During this time he became acquainted with the old Bergen Avenue gang, a band of young toughs who operated at Third Avenue and 149th Street. He also tried his hand as a roofer and a printer's devil; he later liked to remind reporters he had "worked in your racket once."

As a member of the Bergen Avenue gang, Schultz was in and out of jails in his youth. He adopted the nickname Dutch after a young fighter who was known not for his skill in boxing but for his raw courage.

After Schultz had opened a few speakeasies, he graduated from the retail end of Prohibition and was soon running beer in from the breweries of Frankie Dunn in New Jersey. By 1931 he had several beer drops in the Bronx and was fast becoming someone to reckon with.

In the same year, the menacing figure of Vincent (Mad Dog) Coll entered Schultz's life, but this threat was finally ended when "The Mick," as Schultz called him, was rubbed out in a Manhattan phone booth.

Dutch Schultz thanking his attorney after his Syracuse trial.

Mrs. Arthur Flegenheimer, widow of Dutch Schultz.

Schultz then branched out into the lucrative policy racket. This operation required the protection of politicians, so Schultz's companions now included prominent Tammany Hall figures. Labor unions and crooked fights were next on his list of enterprises. He became more brutal as his power increased. For instance, Jules Martin, his henchman who went into the taxi-cab business at his orders, was brutally killed in an upstate hotel room.

When Schultz was indicted by the government for income-tax fraud, he hired a well-known public relations outfit "to create a good press among the citizens." The agency's front men paved the way for the Dutchman's trial by making the tax people the villains. "The Dutchman's trouble might be yours or mine" was the common argument. The first jury disagreed. The second, at Malone, New York, succumbed to Schultz's propaganda; they found him not guilty.

Schultz returned to New York City,

but the police made it impossible for him to stay. "Get that bum out of the city," La Guardia thundered, and Police Commissioner Valentine obeyed. Schultz was finally arrested as a tax evader in New Jersey. At that time it became known that Tom Dewey had dug deep into the Dutchman's empire and had come up with many dark secrets.

While awaiting trial, the sullen Dutchman made his headquarters in the Palace Chop House on Newark's Broad Street. On a fall evening in 1935 he was going over some financial reports with his henchmen, "Lulu" Rosencranz, Abe Landau, and Otto (Aba Daba) Berman. Schultz had gone to the men's room when a lone gunman walked in. He was Charlie (The Bug) Workman, a cold-eyed trigger man now in New Jersey State's Prison, who had been hired to kill the Dutchman by Murder, Inc., the powerful national crime syndicate headed by Lepke Buchalter. The mob thought the Dutchman's plan to

kill Dewey would touch off a national furor, and when the Dutchman ignored their orders to forget the wild scheme, the syndicate voted he had to die.

The Bug was a methodical, cool-nerved killer. Although his companion bolted, he completed his assignment with dispatch.

The Dutchman had just come out of the men's room when Workman began spraying the bar with bullets. Rosencranz, Landau, and Berman died in their seats. At the same time, several miles away, syndicate gunmen walked into a Times Square barbershop and shot Schultz's lieutenant, Martie Krompier, and another henchman, Samuel Gold. Both men survived the bullets, but of the group in the Newark chop house only the Dutchman was still alive after Workman fled.

Essex County Prosecutor Wachenfeld stated later that the bullet that proved fatal to Schultz came from Rosencranz's gun, but no explanation of this mysterious circumstance has ever been made.

His liver torn by .45 caliber bullets, Schultz was carried into the Newark City Hospital. Photographers took a memorable picture of the dying gangster as he peered at the bullet holes in his body and mumbled, "Please fix me up . . . please help me."

Although five hundred cubic centimeters of blood were given to him in a series of transfusions, Schultz died the next night.

Transcript of Dutch Schultz's Last Words

A FASCINATING document in the history of the American underworld is the record of statements made by Dutch Schultz as he lay dying in the Newark City Hospital. At his bedside from late Thursday afternoon until he died the following day at 8:40 P.M. was a police stenographer, F. J. Lang, who took down everything Schultz said. The mobster was delirious most of the time but lucid at intervals. Here is the official transcript of all Schultz said, from Lang's shorthand notebook, still in the possession of the Newark Police Department:

George, don't make no full moves. What have you done with him? Oh, mama, mama, mama. Oh stop it, stop it; oh, oh, oh. Sure, sure, mama.

Schultz at this time was irrational and running a fever of 106 degrees. Sergeant Luke Conlon and other detectives from Newark police headquarters and from the prosecutor's office were at his bedside. One of the officers had a newspaper. Schultz noticed it and said, "Has it been in any other papers?"

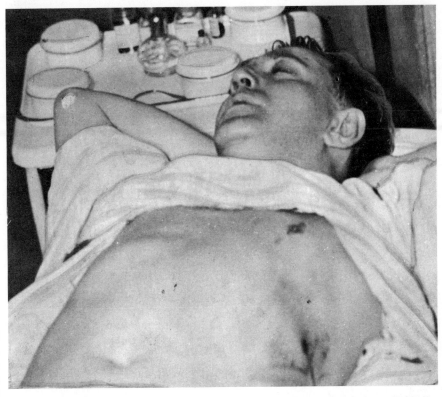

Dutch Schultz in the corridor of the Newark Hospital, minutes after being admitted.

Now listen, Phil, fun is fun. Ah please, papa. What happened to the sixteen? Oh, oh, he done it. Please.

John, please oh, did you buy the hotel? You promised a million—sure. Get out, I wished I knew.

Please make it quick, fast and furious. Please. Fast and furious. Please help me get out; I am getting my wind back, thank God. Please, please, oh, please. You will have to please tell him, you got no case.

You get ahead with the dot-dash system—didn't I speak that time last night. Whose number is that in your pocket book, Phil 13780.

Who was it? Oh—please, please.

Reserve decision. Police, police, Henry and Frankie.

Oh, oh, dog biscuits and when he is happy he doesn't get snappy —please, please to do this. Then Henry, Henry, Frankie you didn't meet him, you didn't even meet me. The glove will fit what I say oh, Kayiyi, Kayiyi. Sure who cares when you are through? How do you know this?

How do you know this? Well, then—oh, Cocoa know—thinks he is a grandpa again. He is jumping around. No Hobo and Poboe I think it means the same thing.

When he was questioned by Sergeant Conlon, the following exchange took place:

Q: Who shot you?
A: The boss himself.
Q: He did?
A: Yes, I don't know.
Q: What did he shoot you for?
A: I showed him boss: do you hear him meet me? An appointment. Appeal stuck. All right, mother.
Q: Was it the boss shot you?
A: Who shot me? No one.
Q: We will help you.
A: Will you get me up? Okay. I won't be such a big creep. Oh, mama, I can't go through with it, please. Oh—and then he clips me; come on. Cut that out, we don't owe a nickel; hold it; instead, hold it against him; I am a pretty good pretzler—Winifred—Department of Justice. I even got it from the department. Sir, please stop it. Say listen the—last night.
Q: Don't holler.
A: I don't want to holler.
Q: What did they shoot you for?
A: I don't know, sir, honestly I don't. I don't even know who was with me, honestly. I went to the toilet. I was in the toilet and when I reached the—the boy came at me.
Q: The big fellow gave it to you?
A: Yes, he gave it to me.
Q: Do you know who this big fellow was?
A: No.

If we wanted to break the ring no, please—I get a month. They did it. Come on. ——— [a name not clear] cut me off and says you are not to be the beneficiary of this will. Is that right? I will be checked and doublechecked and please pull for me. Will you pull? How many good ones and how many bad ones? Please I had nothing with him he was a cowboy in one of the seven days a week fight. No business, no hangout, no friends, nothing; just what you pick up and what you need.

I don't know who shot me. Don't put anyone near this check; you might have—please do it for me. Let me get up, heh? In the olden days they waited and they waited. Please give me shot. It is from the factory. Sure, that is a bad—well, oh good ahead that happens for trying. I don't want harmony. I want harmony. Oh, mama, mama! Who give it to him. Who give it to him. Let me in the district—fire—factory that he was nowhere near. It smoldered.

No, no. There are only ten of us there are ten million fighting somewhere of you, so get your onions up and we will throw up the truce flag. Oh, please let me up. Please shift me. Police are here. Communistic—strike—baloney—honestly this is a habit I get; sometimes I give it and sometimes I don't. Oh, I am all in. That settles it. Are you sure? Please let me get in and eat. Let him harness himself to you and then bother you.

Please don't ask me to go there. I don't want to. I still don't want him in the path. It is no use to stage a riot. The sidewalk was in trouble and the bears were in trouble and I broke it up. Please put me in that room. Please keep him in control. My gilt-edge stuff and those dirty rats have tuned in. Please, mother, don't tear, don't rip; that is something that shouldn't be spoken about. Please get me up, my friends. Please, look out, the shooting is a bit wild, and that kind of shooting saved a man's life.

No payrolls. No walls. No coupons. That would be entirely out. Pardon me, I forgot I am plaintiff and not defendant. Look out. Look out for him. Please. He owed me money; he owes everyone money. Why can't he just pull out and give me control?

Please, mother, you pick me up now. Please, you know me.

No. Don't you scare me. My friends and I think I do a better job. Police are looking for you all over. Be instrumental in letting us know. They are Englishmen and they are a type and I don't know who is best, they or us. Oh, sir, get the doll a rofting. You can

play jacks and girls do that with a soft ball and do tricks with it. It takes all events into consideration. No. No. And it is no. It is confused and it says no. A boy has never wept nor dashed a thousand kim. Did you hear me?

Q: Who shot you?
A: I don't know.
Q: The doctor wants you to lie quiet.
A: That is what I want to do.
Q: How many shots were fired?
A: I don't know.
Q: How many?
A: Two thousand. Come on, get some money in that treasury. We need it. Come on, please get it. I can't tell you to. That is not what you have in the book. Oh, please warden. What am I going to do for money? Please put me up on my feet at once. You are a hard-boiled man. Did you hear me? I would hear it, the Circuit Court would hear it, and the Supreme Court might hear it. If that ain't the pay-off. Please crack down on the Chinaman's friends and Hitler's commander. I am sore and I am going up and I am going to give you honey if I can. Mother is the best bet and don't let Satan draw you too fast.
Q: What did the big fellow shoot you for?
A: Him? John? Over a million, five million dollars.
Q: You want to get well, don't you?
A: Yes.
Q: Then lie quiet.
A: Yes, I will lie quiet.
Q: John shot you and we will take care of John.
A: That is what caused the trouble. Look out. Please get me up. If you do this, you can go on and jump right here in the lake. I know who they are. They are French people. All right. Look out, look out. Ph, my memory is gone. A work relief. Police. Who gets it? I don't know and I don't want to know, but look out. It can be traced. He changed for the worse. Please look out; my fortunes have changed and come back and went back since that. It was desperate. I am wobbly. You ain't got nothing on him but we got it on his helper.
Q: Control yourself.
A: But I am dying.

Q: No, you are not.
A: Come on, mama. All right, dear, you have to get it.

At this point, Schultz's wife, Frances, was brought to his bedside. She said, "This is Frances," and Schultz began to talk again.

Then pull me out. I am half-crazy. They won't let me get up. They dyed my shoes. Open those shoes. Give me something. I am so sick. Give me some water, the only thing that I want. Open this up and break it so I can touch you. Dannie, please get me in the car.

At this point Mrs. Schultz left the room. Sergeant Conlon questioned Schultz again.

Q: Who shot you?
A: I don't know. I didn't even get a look. I don't know who can have done it. Anybody. Kindly take my shoes off. [He was told that they were off.] No, there's a handcuff on them. The Baron says these things.

I know what I am doing here with my collection of papers. It isn't worth a nickel to two guys like you or me, but to a collector it is worth a fortune. It is priceless. I am going to turn it over to . . . Turn your back to me, please, Henry. I am so sick now. The police are getting many complaints. Look out. I want that G-note. Look out for Jimmy Valentine for he is an old pal of mine. Come on, come on, Jim. Okay, okay, I am all through. Can't do another thing.

Look out, mama, look out for her. You can't beat him. Police, mama, Helen, mother, please take me out. I will settle the indictment. Come on, open the soap duckets. The chimney sweeps. Take to the sword. Shut up, you got a big mouth! Please help me up, Henry. Max, come over here. French-Canadian bean soup. I want to pay. Let them leave me alone.

Schultz sank into unconsciousness then. It was 6:40 P.M. He died two hours later, without saying anything else.

The Babe Came Home

THE SULTAN of Swat went home to Boston in the fall of 1935.

Babe Ruth, greatest ballplayer of all time, had been released by the New York Yankees and had immediately signed a three-year contract as vice-president and assistant manager of the Boston Braves. Thus he returned to the city where he had first made himself known as the man who could hit a baseball farther than any man who ever lived —the longest home run on record. In the winter of 1919-1920, Ruth had come to the New York Yankees in the richest deal of baseball history up to that time. The Yankees gave $139,000 to Harry Frazee, then owner of the Boston Red Sox, for the big fellow who later became the all-time home-run king.

Colonel Jacob Ruppert had made it plain that he would not "accept one cent" for the assignment of Ruth's contract if Babe could get a manager's job. For a time that fall, it seemed as if Ruth's chances of getting such a post had faded forever when the Washingtons sold Joe Cronin for a price exceeding even that which the Yankees had paid for Ruth. It had taken one of the greatest player deals in baseball history to get Babe out of Boston, and now it took another to get him back there. With Cronin chosen as the player-manager of the Red Sox, there had been a slim possibility that Ruth might be kept in the American League in Washington. With that in mind Ed Barrow, business manager of the Yankees, called Clark Griffith, owner of the Senators, and said: "Well, Clark, now that you sold Cronin I've got your new manager for you."

"Who is he?" asked Griffith.

"Babe Ruth," replied Barrow.

"No chance, Ed," said Griffith. "He's much too high-powered for me down here in this small city."

Meanwhile, ever since the Babe had announced in the World Series that he was through with baseball unless he could land a manager's post, the Braves had been trying to get him.

The American League did not want to let the greatest gate attraction the game had ever known get out of circulation. Colonel Ruppert had said he was anxious that the Babe stay in their own loop, but in a historic conference with

Joe McCarthy and the Babe.

Jacob Ruppert and Babe Ruth.

Ruth at the Ruppert Brewery, he made it clear he would not stand in the Babe's way if no offers developed in the American League. Detroit said flatly it didn't want Ruth. St. Louis was out of the question for financial reasons, and when Cleveland had its chance it signified its satisfaction with Walter Johnson by signing him to a new contract. And as for the A's, there never would be another boss as long as Connie Mack lived. Finally, Ruth made his deal with Boston, where he had wanted to go in the first place.

The Ruthian Record

During his twenty-one years in the American League, Babe Ruth pounded out over 700 homers. He reached his all-time high in 1927, when he clouted 60 circuit blows.

Following is his lifetime record:

LEAGUE HOMERS

Year	With	
1914	Red Sox	0
1915	Red Sox	4
1916	Red Sox	3
1917	Red Sox	2
1918	Red Sox	11
1919	Red Sox	29
1920	Yankees	54
1921	Yankees	59
*1922	Yankees	35
1923	Yankees	41
1924	Yankees	46
**1925	Yankees	25
1926	Yankees	47
1927	Yankees	60
1928	Yankees	54
1929	Yankees	46
1930	Yankees	49
1931	Yankees	46
1932	Yankees	41
1933	Yankees	34
1934	Yankees	22
1935	Braves	6
Total		714

* Out until May 20; suspended for barnstorming after 1921 World Series.
** Out until June with illness after collapsing during training trip.

WORLD SERIES HOMERS

Year	Against	
1915	Phillies	0
1916	Dodgers	0
1918	Cubs	0
1921	Giants	1
1922	Giants	0
1923	Giants	3
1926	Cardinals	4
1927	Pirates	2
1928	Cardinals	3
1932	Cubs	2
Total in ten series		15

The DEATH of the NRA

WHEN THE United States Supreme Court announced its bombshell decision that the NRA was unconstitutional, with the plain implication that much other New Deal legislation was suspect, an almost complete legislative paralysis, administrative inertia, and official confusion settled over Washington. It became a city of hurried conferences and doubt as government leaders sought a way out.

President Roosevelt, the White House announced to a wild press conference, had ordered a full study of the devastating decision, and would make no plans for further New Deal programs until the results were known. When the smoke had cleared, these facts were plain:

All code-enforcement under the NRA was suspended.

Organized labor under William Green of the AFL and John L. Lewis of the United Mine Workers was threatening a series of nationwide strikes if management "chiseled" wages and hours as a result of the court's decision.

All labor elections and disputes under Section 7A of the NRA were held in abeyance on orders of Francis Biddle, head of the Labor Relations Board.

Legislative leaders in both houses, on the verge of pushing through the controversial AAA (Agricultural Adjustment Administration) bill, called it back for modification to conform with the court's decision.

All New Deal legislation—including the Wagner Act, the Social Security Program, unemployment insurance, and the thirty-hour work bill—was delayed until the bills could be studied in the light of the Supreme Court ruling.

The bewildered new liquor industry had to revert to its pre-Prohibition status, with no restrictions as to manufacturing or marketing. Only the tax features were left. Codes for distillers and breweries as well as manufacturing restrictions went by the boards.

The Supreme Court decision also decreed the end of highly centralized federal government. The language used by the court in setting these limits, was

A janitor scraping the familiar Blue Eagle emblem from a door in the Commerce Department after the Supreme Court had killed the NRA.

FDR addressing a joint session of Congress. Vice President Garner and Speaker Byrns are in the rear, with the President's secretary, Marvin McIntyre (left).

held to be the most significant in its effects on future New Deal legislation. The court said:

"It is not the providence of the court to consider the economic advantage of such a centralized government. It is sufficient to say that the federal Constitution does not provide for it."

The decision also signaled the start of FDR's unprecedented move to change the high court, to "pack" it with justices who might be more favorable to his programs. The following year would see the stubborn squire of Hyde Park and the bearded patriarch of the high court, Charles Evans Hughes, face each other for the final battle.

From the Supreme Court Decision

"EXTRAORDINARY conditions may call for extraordinary remedies. But extraordinary conditions do not create or enlarge constitutional power."

"The codes of fair competition which the statute attempts to authorize are codes of laws."

"The discretion of the President in approving or prescribing codes, and thus enacting laws for the government of trade and industry throughout the country, is virtually unfettered. We think that the code-making authority thus conferred is an unconstitutional delegation of legislative power."

"In determining how far the Federal Government may go in controlling intrastate transactions upon the ground that they 'affect' interstate commerce, there is a necessary and well-established distinction between direct and indirect effects. Otherwise there would be virtually no limit to the Federal power and for all practical purposes we would have a completely centralized government."

"We are of the opinion that the attempt through the provisions of the code to fix the hours and wages of employees of defendants in their intrastate business was not a valid exercise of Federal power."

Highlights and Sidelights: 1935

THE FIFTEEN-YEAR-OLD "ideal marriage" of Mary Pickford and Douglas Fairbanks dissolved in a trial lasting only three minutes in a Los Angeles courtoom. "America's Sweetheart" told the court Fairbanks had lost interest in her in 1930. The dashing Doug was in St. Moritz with Lady Ashley, who had been divorced in a suit which named Fairbanks as corespondent. . . . The Ethiopian government announced that Italian troops had invaded its country at several points. Heavy casualties were reported at Addis Ababa, where fierce Danakil Desert tribesmen had hurled themselves at Italian troops moving from Eritrea. In Rome, Premier Mussolini announced national mobilization of 20,000,000 soldiers and warned that "acts of war will be met by acts of war." In Geneva, the League of Nations said it might ask France to send an airplane to "determine the facts of the reported invasion." In Washington, Secretary of State Cordell Hull said the United States would adopt a policy of strict neutrality. . . . In the Saar Territory, a plebiscite on the future of that region revealed that 476,000 voted to return to Germany. . . . Moscow's first subway was opened, and a few days later the jubilation changed to sorrow when the Kremlin announced that the *Maxim Gorky,* the world's largest land plane, had crashed, killing all 48 aboard. . . . The new $6,000,000 liner *Normandie* arrived in New York on her maiden voyage. She had sailed 2,971 sea-miles in four days, three hours, and thirteen minutes. . . . A Communist mob tore a swastika from the bow of the steamship *Bremen.* . . . At Nuremberg, the Nazi Party gathering ended with a show of military strength — 100,000 men, heavy tanks, artillery, and 100 planes joined to destroy a sham town. . . . President Roosevelt signed the Neutrality Act, which required all American arms-makers to register with the government. . . . Persia became Iran. . . . Badman Alvin Karpis and Harry Campbell shot their way out of a trap in Atlantic City. . . . The $4,000,000 U.S. dirigible *Macon* sank in the Pacific off Point Sur, California, with 83 men and officers lost . . . . Father Coughlin,

Father Coughlin leaving Madison Square Garden with a high-echelon police escort.

the controversial hate-mongering "radio priest," in a scathing speech denounced FDR before a huge crowd in New York's Madison Square Garden. . . . The Florida State Supreme Court ruled "there is no greater cruelty inflicted on man than that which is inflicted by a contentious, unreasonable, and nagging wife." . . . Baby Doe, "Silver Dollar" Tabor's widow, was found frozen to death in a one-room shack near the fabulous Matchless

The Mussolini salute.

President Roosevelt greets Rear Admiral Richard E. Byrd after Byrd's Antarctic expedition.

Professor Robert H. Goddard examines one of his rockets at his desert laboratory in Roswell, N. M. His rockets were the forerunners of the German V-2's used to bomb Britain in World War II. Goddard was continuously rebuffed when he tried to interest government officials in rockets. He died, in obscurity, in 1945.

Mine. . . . Detective William King, the Philo Vance of the New York City Police Department, solved the six-year-old mystery of what had happened to Grace Budd. He proved that she had been murdered by a handyman. The murderer himself had provided the crucial clues, by writing letters to the Budd family. . . . Rear Admiral Richard Byrd arrived home from his Antarctic expedition and was greeted by President Roosevelt. . . . Eliot Ness, the G-man who crushed Al Capone, was appointed safety director of the city of Cleveland. . . . Professor Robert H. Goddard, rocket genius, tried in vain to get government support for his rocket program. If he had been successful, the U.S. might have been ten years ahead in the rocket race. . . . Eddie Cantor fired the starting gun for the six-day bike race at Madison Square Garden. . . . Joe Louis gave Primo Carnera a terrific beating in their fight at Yankee Stadium and disposed of him in six rounds. . . . The Detroit Tigers won the American League pennant, helped enormously by their home-run slugger, Hank Greenberg of the Bronx. Though Greenberg's injury in the second game of the World Series

kept him out of action for the last four games, Detroit won the series 4 games to 2. . . . Outstanding in radio were Major Bowes (Amateur Hour), Dick Powell and Frances Langford (Hollywood Hotel), and Harry Von Zell. . . . 1935 was a banner year for writers. The best-seller lists were headed by Anne Morrow Lindbergh's *North to the Orient,* John O'Hara's *Butterfield 8,* Vincent Sheean's *Personal History,* S. S. Van Dine's *The Garden Murder Case,* James Branch Cabell's *Smith: A Sylvan*

Interlude, Ellen Glasgow's *Vein of Iron,* Louis Paul's *The Pumpkin Coach,* and Max Miller's *The Great Trek.* Thomas Wolfe published *Of Time and the River,* sequel to his *Look Homeward, Angel.* England's Alfred Hitchcock exploded on the American screen with his adaptation of John Buchan's *39 Steps.* Who can forget the woman's scream blending with the shriek of the locomotive whistle? Gershwin's *Porgy and Bess* began its fabulous career, and his immortal music was whistled from coast

191

to coast. Earlier, he had written the scores of *Girl Crazy* and *Of Thee I Sing,* the first musical to win a Pulitzer prize. Jerome Kern is another composer who will not soon be forgotten; two of his greatest songs were very much a part of those Desperate Years: "All the Things You Are," from *Very Warm for May* (1939) and "Smoke Gets in Your Eyes," from *Roberta* (1933). Rodgers and Hart's long and successful collaboration was at its peak, but *On Your Toes, Babes in Arms, I Married an Angel,* and *The Boys from Syracuse* were still to come. By now there was a new age of comedians: The Marx Brothers, Stoopnagle and Budd, Laurel and Hardy, Ed Wynn, Frank Morgan, Jimmy Durante, and Bob Hope. The incomparable W. C. Fields, the big bumbling irascible rascal with the bulbous nose, had also been discovered. There wasn't much plot to his pictures but this child-hating, animal-despising character made millions of Americans forget for a few hours the insecure job, the daily battle to survive.

Novelist Thomas Wolfe in Berlin in 1935.

Eliot Ness, who crushed Al Capone. The picture was taken in December, 1935, following his appointment as Cleveland's safety director.

Jimmy Durante.

The six-day bicycle race was one of the favorite sports of the early thirties. Eddie Cantor starts them off, including the famous racer Georgetti (second from left).

Major Bowes, master of ceremonies of the famous Amateur Hour.

Harry Von Zell.

W. C. Fields and his trusty cane.

Joe Louis and Primo Carnera weighing in.

Ed Wynn.

Gabby Hartnett, Cub catcher, tags out Tiger slugger Hank Greenberg in the second game of the 1935 World Series. Detroit won the series, 4 games to 2.

Will Rogers, one of America's popular humorists in the 1920's and 1930's, and one of the great American humorists of all time, died in an airplane accident in Alaska on August 15, 1935. His companion, pilot and fellow victim was Wiley Post, the famed one-eyed airman. They had been in Fairbanks, where they consulted Joe Crosson, the veteran Arctic pilot. He shook his head as he studied the weather reports that had just come in.

"I don't think you ought to go, Will," he said. "There's going to be fog up at Barrow before you can get there."

Wiley Post looked up. "I think we ought to go anyway. What do you say, Will?"

Will Rogers grinned his famous grin. "Sure, why not? There's a lot of lakes we can land on."

A few minutes later the small new red plane with its 500-horsepower motor lifted gracefully into the gray sky.

The famous pair were on their way to Point Barrow, five hundred miles away, northernmost white settlement in America. The hop was all part of the happy-go-lucky aerial tour of Alaska they were taking as a prelude to a trip to Siberia and then on to Moscow.

Fifty miles out of Fairbanks they encountered thick fog. Post set the plane down on Harding Lake, then resumed the journey. Apparently unaware of his bearings, he set his pontooned plane down on a shallow river fifteen miles west of Point Barrow, just ten minutes' flying time from their destination.

Will Rogers waded ashore and chatted with the Eskimos, who ran down to the shore, while Post tinkered with the plane's engine.

"Okay, Will," Post shouted, and Rogers

Will Rogers.

waved good-bye to the natives and climbed back in. The prop spun and the red plane slowly lifted. Suddenly it backfired. Post quickly banked to the right. Then the ship plummeted, nose-first, out of control, into the edge of the stream, where the water was only two feet deep.

The Eskimos ran to the water's edge and shouted; when there was no answer they became alarmed. One volunteered to go to Barrow for help. For three hours he ran over the rough tundra, encircling small lakes and wading shallow streams. Finally, his chest heaving like bellows, he stumbled into the office of Sergeant Stanley R. Morgan, of the U.S. Signal Corps. Morgan rushed to the scene in a whaleboat and recovered both bodies.

Dick Powell and Frances Langford.

194

Preview of Armageddon

General Franco accompanied by Luftwaffe General Kinderlane making an address to his supporters.

ON JULY 17, 1936, a revolt against Madrid's Republican Government began in Morocco and spread to Spain. As the hours passed, most of the army, the air force, and half of the navy joined it. The following day Madrid reorganized the government and José Giral became premier. An Insurgent force in Madrid was defeated by a Loyalist army, and Insurgent groups captured the cities of Cadiz, Granada on the south, and a large area without ports in the north. Seven days after the outbreak of hostilities Insurgent chiefs set up their own government and began aerial bombardment of Madrid.

Generalissimo Francisco Franco was proclaimed head of the Nationalist (Insurgent) Government on October 1, and the siege of Madrid began twenty days later.

Spain was now in the grip of a long and bloody Civil War, and swords sheathed reluctantly in Europe were now held half-drawn. In a matter of months Spain became the proving ground for the battlefields of World War II. The Soviets took the side of the Loyalists, and Italy and Germany sided with Franco.

For the first time in military history aircraft would emerge as an impressive arm of war, cities would be subjected to the terror of all-out bombing, artillery would prove effective as an antiaircraft defense, but the foot soldier, as always, would emerge as the most important force in military victory.

The remarkable success of the anti-aircraft guns on both sides set Europe feverishly building quantities of them. European nations saw that areas behind the fighting front could not be protected from raiding planes without such guns. Great Britain bought the entire anti-aircraft gun output of the Borors Swedish factory for three years. These

1936

acquisitions helped in the great air battles over London not many years in the future.

The effective employment of anti-aircraft guns in Spain impressed the United States too, which at the time had only 42 three-inch aircraft guns and American-built robot fire-directors—barely enough to defend a shipyard. With the military nudging Congress, a program was reluctantly started to provide funds to begin antiaircraft defenses.

Even more importantly, the Spanish Civil War proved the effectiveness of aircraft in battle. When hostilities broke out, the original Spanish air force consisted of 440 obsolete aircraft. The majority of these remained in the possession of forces loyal to the government. German and Italian planes shifted the superiority to the Franco forces, but Russia helped change it back to the government forces.

The early German and Italian planes were German Junkers and three-engine commercial transports modified to

195

carry bombs. The Russian fighters which temporarily changed the balance of power were similar to the Boeing P-12 and P-26. They quickly gained leadership in the air battles over Madrid. Then Germany and Italy agreed to provide an aircraft equal to the Russian craft. Toward the end of the war Franco had an airfleet of over 600 planes, mostly two-engine planes, as compared to the government's 400.

The comparatively large air forces on both sides in this battleground settled for all time the question of whether single fighters could attack modern bombers successfully. Before the air battles of the Spanish Civil War pilots had insisted that single-fighters could never penetrate large formations of bombers with their heavy armaments of four to six machine guns per bomber. The fighter pilots in Spain settled that question; they showed that the fighter pilot, not hunting singly as in World War I, but in packs like hunting eagles, could roar down out of the sun and pick off bomber after bomber. It wasn't easy but they proved for military history that it could be done.

The proving ground in Spain also destroyed the Hollywood notion of chivalry of the skies. Gone was the airborne knight who would graciously wave to the parachuting pilot he had just downed. In Spain both sides shot pilots as they dangled from their parachutes. This butchery brought another first: the delayed opening of a parachute, which gave the pilot a chance of falling fast enough to avoid being a target as he swayed helplessly under a balloon of silk. This was the forerunner of today's free fall.

To sum up, Spain was the perfect proving ground for all phases of World War II. It showed the Axis observers that the way to take a town or a city was first to soften it up with a heavy artillery barrage, then a sweep by heavy bombers, followed by tanks, and then the infantry advance. It was the coordinated employment of all his weapons in this manner that enabled Franco to take 200 miles of the Spanish north coast that was held firmly by the entrenched government troops. He used 35,000 men in these combined operations as against the government's 70,-000. The perfect teamwork of artillery, aircraft, tank, and infantry divisions made up for the disparity in numbers.

German plane of the Condor Legion on an actual bombing run over Madrid.

Members of an antiaircraft unit of the Condor Legion under attack by Republican planes in a position before Madrid.

General Franco making an address shortly after he announced the establishment of the rebel government in 1936.

Andalusian horsemen in their wide sombreros, who participated in the capture of Malaga, resting and allowing their horses to drink.

197

The battle for Mount Aragon. The attack in the winter of 1936. Only one of the men is fortunate enough to have a helmet.

Col. Duc de Seville commanding in the front lines during the attack on Malaga.

A soldier on guard at Guadalajara looks up at approaching planes.

The Man Who Was Better Off Dead

ROWS OF books, from geometry to medieval poets, two singing canaries, a large filing case, a huge glass-top desk, and various toilet articles. This was the home in 1936 of Dickie Loeb, who with Nathan Leopold had been sentenced to life imprisonment in Illinois's Joliet Prison eleven years earlier, for the brutal murder of little Bobby Franks, a crime that shocked all America in its maddest days.

From this expansive cell Loeb strutted about the prison buying favors, special passes for himself and a clique of followers. Although the law had insisted that he and his co-murderer, Leopold, must be separated for life, they met many times for poker parties while the bribed guards turned their backs. They never ate with the other prisoners but with the officers of the prison. They had special visitors, special food, and even passes that allowed them to go outside the prison wall for flowers for Leopold's garden.

As a mark of distinction they wore white flannels instead of the usual prison garb. They drank bootleg whiskey made from stolen sugar, and could buy narcotics at "a dollar a jolt." If they wanted to make an outside telephone call they were welcome to use the phone in the prison storeroom. To insure their status, Dickie gave a deputy warden a new convertible as a Christmas present.

From the outside, Joliet was a forbidding but perfect example of an American prison. Whenever the state's investigators appeared the guards were smart, the prisoners perfectly disciplined. But inside, Joliet was a hellhole, an incredible prison ruled by gangs and cliques of those who boasted they held power in high places—as did Leopold and Loeb.

One day Loeb's eye was caught by Jimmy Day, a slender and good-looking larcenist who had just been sent to Joliet for seven years. Day, slightly backward, was impressed when Loeb began paying attention to him, offering him cigarettes, food, and a chance to enter his "Statesville Correspondence School."

"The other pupils have to pay, but it won't cost you a cent," Loeb told the young thief.

Day soon learned why Loeb sought

Richard Loeb enters prison.

him out. One day when they were alone in the library Loeb told him about his fondness for him and said Day should be "broad-minded and be nice to me."

Day pushed him aside and walked out. From that day on, he later testified, "I never had a peaceful day . . . he was always after me. I became desperate, I had to get him off my back. I was looking for the right day . . ."

That day came in January, 1936. He described it:

This morning after breakfast I asked Loeb if I could talk to him. Loeb was eating breakfast in his cell with Leopold. He said, "Surely." After dinner he came to my cell and said he was on his way to take a bath and I could see him in the bathroom.

I went to the bathroom and waited. Loeb came in in five minutes and locked the door. He said, "What is on your mind? Get it off quickly. I'm warning you it won't do any good as far as my attitude toward you is concerned."

He started taking off all his clothes. I was leaning against the wash basin. His back was to me and he bundled the clothes . . . in a towel.

He got between me and the door and I noticed he had a razor in his hand. He had taken it out of the bundle. He said, "Keep your mouth shut. Get your clothes off."

I knew the door was locked. Loeb said: "Get your clothes off before I start in on you." I started undressing. I got off all my clothes and left them in the shower. I decided to pretend I had given in so I could watch my chance to do something. He followed me in the shower. He took two steps and stepped over the sill of the shower. I kicked him in the groin. He grabbed for his groin with his free hand and slashed at my face with the razor as he fell. He missed me by inches.

I hit him on the neck with my fist. The hand in which he had the razor hit the sill and the razor fell. He grabbed for it as I jumped over his body, and as he turned around at me I caught him by the wrist and throat and we fell to the floor together. He dropped the razor again.

I grabbed the razor and jumped over him. He got up and swung his fist at me. It caught me on the left side of the face. I slashed at him. Blood flew in my face as he locked his arms around me. I remembered

slashing at him as I fell back across the sill and felt the sharp sting across my left kidney.

I dropped the razor. Loeb fell on top of me and he got the razor and caught me with one hand by the throat. Something told me I would die there unless by superhuman efforts I could get out from under him.

Somehow I threw him off. He swung at me, laughing and saying I could fight when I had to.

I got up with the razor in my hand. I slashed at him and he backed under the shower and

Richard Loeb (left) listens to Nathan Leopold during their trial.

turned on the hot water. I stepped in after him. Steam was in my eyes. I kept slashing. After what seemed like several minutes of fighting under the shower, he sank into a sitting position and in a funny way used two fingers of his right hand to push in some of the flesh of the abdomen, which was cut open.

I turned to leave the shower. He started to get up. His eyes were big and staring. He lunged at me with everything he had. His hands were clenched like claws. I slashed at him some more and kept on slashing until he fell, mumbling.

I turned off the hot water. Turned on some cold. I stepped under the shower to wash off the blood. My whole body was red. I left the shower and wiped the water out of my hair and eyes. I heard laughter or a groan. Loeb stood straight up. He lunged at me and knocked me down. His body slipped over me and fell by the door.

He got up and fumbled with the key. He ran out to the dining room tunnel. I did not see him after that.

Loeb was dead.

His death resurrected the terrible stories of the Bobby Franks trial and led the state to make a closer investigation of the murder. How did Loeb (or Day) get the razor? How did he get his personal washroom key? And how were Loeb and Leopold together when the sentencing judge had emphasized they were to be separated for life?

The governor appointed a committee, including Warden Roy Best of Colorado State Prison and Lewis E. Lawes, warden of Sing Sing. After a preliminary investigation Warden Best described Joliet as a "Fifth Avenue club." Joliet's warden later testified that he had inherited the conditions, which were so bad gangs built more than a hundred shacks in the prison yards and formed extortion rings which forced weaker prisoners to turn over their food packages and their money and made them steal from the commissary. One prisoner, nicknamed the "Midget" because of his size, actually ran a stock operation from his cell.

While the scandal continued to grow, the mortal remains of Loeb, reared in all the comforts of great wealth, only to spend a third of his life in prison, were turned into ashes in a Chicago crematory.

Clarence Darrow, whose dramatic plea had saved the lives of Loeb and Leopold and who is still held as one of the greatest lawyers in the history of criminal trials, tersely wrote Loeb's epitaph:

"He is better off dead . . . for him death is an easier sentence . . ."

CHARLIE LUCKY

Charles (Lucky) Luciano once called his birthplace, Lercara Friddi, near Palermo, Sicily, "the deadest joint in the world." He was born there on November 11, 1896, the son of a miner in the nearby sulphur fields. When he was nine his parents migrated to the United States. He went to Public School 19 on New York's Lower East Side until he was fourteen, then got a job as a shipping clerk.

But work and Luciano never mixed. Until the day he died he always maintained that a man who worked for a living was "a crumb." Actually, Luciano worked only a few months. He quit when he discovered that a nice profit could be acquired from pushing heroin to the shaking wrecks of his own East Side neighborhood. He was nineteen when he was arrested with several kilos of heroin and sent to prison.

When Luciano came out he was determined never to be caught again. For a time he hung on the fringes of Manhattan's underworld and caught the

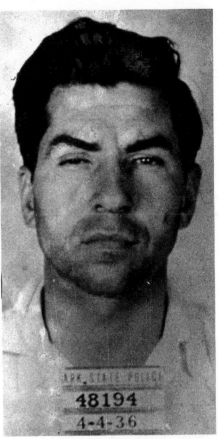

A 1936 rogues' gallery photo of Charlie (Lucky) Luciano following his arrest in Hot Springs, Ark.

eye of Guiseppe (Joe the Boss) Masseria, who headed the so-called Mafia.

It was when he was carrying a gun for Masseria that Luciano won the nickname that was to make him one of the best-known underworld figures of this generation. A rival mob took him for a ride, beat, tortured, and slashed him with knives. He was dumped on a lonely road in Staten Island and left for dead. Luciano startled the underworld by turning up in a few days, scarred but very much alive. He was promptly dubbed "Lucky" Luciano.

In 1931 Masseria was gunned down in a Coney Island restaurant as he swilled spaghetti and wine. Just before the gunmen entered, Lucky found it convenient to go to the men's room. When he came out he was undisputed boss of Masseria's rackets.

In the day when Hollywood gangster films were the rage Charlie Lucky looked the part of a movie mobster, He moved about the city in fast, sleek cars and was always surrounded by an entourage of hulking, beetle-browed hoods. He favored silk underwear and custom-made shirts and lived like a dictator in plush quarters.

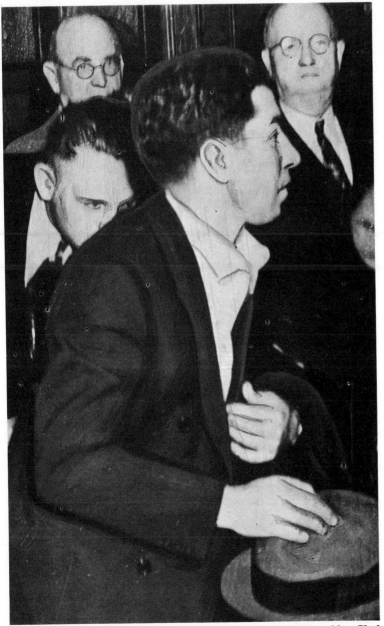

Lucky Luciano in Little Rock, where he fought extradition to New York.

Thomas E. Dewey and his racket-busting staff at an early press conference in his Woolworth Building headquarters. The four behind the desk are (seated) William B. Her- lands and Dewey; (standing) Charles D. Breitel and Milton Schilback.

In the thirties he became a director of the national crime cartel and boss of the loan shark and industrial rackets. He both bought and forced his way into the national slot machine industry and became a partner of the notorious Louis (Lepke) Buchalter, in Murder, Inc. When Al Capone was sent to jail on a charge of income tax evasion, Lucky fell heir to some of his rackets.

In 1932 Lucky saw the handwriting on the wall for the Prohibition rackets, so he looked for new fields to conquer. He first opened a chop suey restaurant in midtown with a small-time hood named Harry Spinach. Included in this venture was his current girl friend, a tarnished tart by the name of Cokey Flo, whose birth certificate read Flor- ence Brown. She had received her un-

derworld tag because of her addiction to heroin.

Before long two other notorious madams were included in Lucky's en- tourage, Jennie the Factory and Gas- house Lil. With the three women Luciano organized prostitution in New York City. Each house had to pay "bondsmen" tribute of fifteen dollars a week whether they were raided or not. The madam of each house had to turn over half the gross. And each working girl had to give a percentage of her earnings to the syndicate.

In 1936 Lucky was running a $12,-000,000 business, when Tom Dewey, a tight-lipped, cold-eyed young prose- cutor, appeared. Lucky had never heard of the youthful prosecutor from Owosso, Michigan, until Dewey was appointed

special prosecutor in 1935 by Governor Herbert H. Lehman.

Dewey established headquarters in the Woolworth Building and maintained an unusually tight security about his investigations. One morning New Yorkers awoke to the headlines that sweeping arrests of bail bondsmen and prostitutes had taken place. While the New Yorkers, used to sporadic raids and halfhearted crusades, yawned, Dewey and his assistants were carefully screening the prisoners. He was looking for a weak witness, one who could lead him to the top man—"the Boss."

Luciano's indictment as the organizer of New York's prostitution racket was not long in coming. "The most dan- gerous if not the most important racket- eer in the United States," Dewey called

Lucky. And in 1936, after a blistering trial, Justice Philip J. McCook sentenced Luciano to a thirty- to fifty-year term.

After ten years—during which period such big-time mobsters as Frank Costello visited him in his cell—Luciano's sentence was reduced to the time he had served, on condition he return to his native Italy. Ironically, the commutation was ordered by the man who had sent him to prison—Thomas E. Dewey, who meanwhile had been elected governor. Dewey said he acted because of Luciano's efforts on behalf of this country in World War II.

As Lucky was ever to boast, "I won the war singlehanded."

The paroling of Luciano was to haunt Dewey, whose political foes attempted to make capital of it year after year. But Dewey was able to show that the State Parole Board had recommended such action. Luciano left the United States on a Liberty ship, February 10, 1946.

"I'm sorry Italy is getting this bum back," Mayor La Guardia commented.

Shortly after he was returned to Sicily, Luciano turned up in Cuba. In that pre-Castro era the United States frowned on having its former number-one gangster within ninety miles of Florida. Dictator Batista took the hint and sent Lucky back to Italy.

In the fall of 1957, when the now-famous Apalachin underworld meeting took place at the mountaintop mansion of Joe Barbera, government agencies charged it had been called on orders of Charlie Lucky.

"Somebody's smoking the pipe," was Lucky's comment.

Lucky was unhappy in Italy. He was periodically being picked up and soon got tired of visiting Italian race tracks.

"The action at these joints is no good," he told a reporter. "I need New York, that's where the real action is."

When he was expelled to Naples, he complained, "They don't speak my language here." Once, in a sidewalk café there, a reporter caught Lucky in a talkative mood and asked him if he had his life to live over again, whether he would live it as a "crumb"—using the former racketeer's own term for men who work for a living—or would live "normally" and have a wife and kids and a small bank account.

This was his answer:

"I'd do the same thing all over again, only I'd do it legal. I learned too late that you need just as good a brain to make a crooked million as you need to make an honest million. These days you apply for a license to steal from the public."

He sipped at his thick, dark coffee.

"If I had my time again I'd make damn' sure I got that license."

And how did he feel about a man who had to work?

"A crumb—strictly a crumb," Lucky snarled.

In January, 1961, Charlie Lucky Luciano dropped dead of a heart attack. He never got his chance to apply for his license.

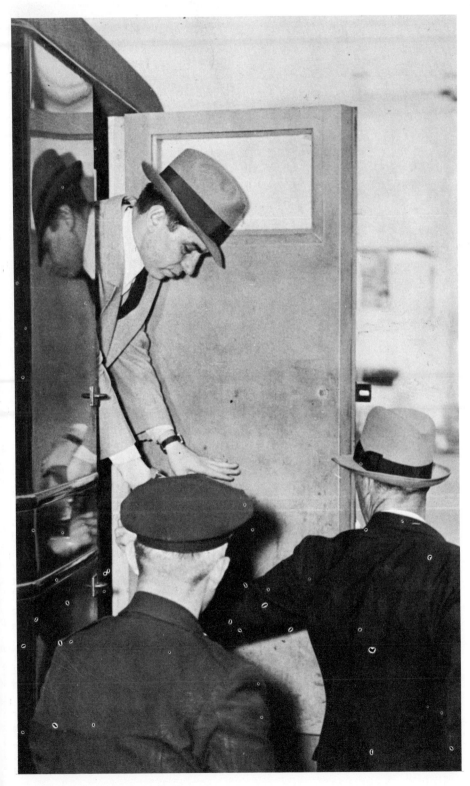

Lucky Luciano entering New York City's Supreme Court to be arraigned as vice lord of the city.

203

The Brown Bomber Fizzles

On that June night in 1936, when the last count was finished, there was little doubt that the Joe Louis-Max Schmeling bout would go down as one of the great upsets of boxing history. There was Louis, the 22-year-old Negro pugilistic sensation from Detroit, heralded by some fistic experts as the greatest fighter in history, flat on the canvas, face downward, resting on one elbow as he was counted out. Carried to his own corner, he shook his head in a bewildered manner, scarcely realizing that

Joe Louis and Jack Blackburn, who helped bring Joe to fame in the ring.

the most meteoric career in ring history had just been exploded by a whistling right from the beetle-browed 33-year-old German veteran of many ring battles.

Before the first bell rang the odds were ten to one in favor of Louis, and sports writers at the ringside were referring to Schmeling as "the condemned man."

Later, experts agreed that when Schmeling dropped Louis with a right-hand punch to the chin in the fourth round, though Louis was up before the referee could start counting, that had

been the deciding blow of the fight. From then on Joe seemed to fade as he took a drum-fire of right-hand punches to the chin. Finally, in the twelfth, after they had been fighting two minutes and twenty-nine seconds, the German contender nailed Louis under the chin with a savage uppercut. Joe's legs started to buckle and Schmeling went after him with both hands. Then another right, and Louis went down, to the amazed roars of the 39,875 spectators in Yankee Stadium who had paid $547,-000 to see him cut the German fighter to ribbons.

So completely had the tradition of Louis' invincibility been established that it had cut deeply into a gate that was expected to go over a million dollars.

The following day there were the usual excuses of how tight bandages, etc., had "hurt the champ." But Arthur McGovern, famous boxing expert, writing in the *N.Y. World-Telegram,* put his finger on the reason for Louis' knockout:

"The fight was not, in my opinion, Louis against Schmeling but rather confidence versus overconfidence."

Three weeks after the bout, a Chicago detective employed by some "colored interests" made an affidavit to a Chicago newspaper that Louis had been doped just before he entered the ring. The highlight of the affidavit was an interview with Louis' sister, who declared that Joe had been given a hypodermic injection in the left arm the day of the fight.

The sensational charges were forwarded to the New York Boxing Commission, which investigated and found them without foundation.

A few hours after the story appeared the late Bill Farnsworth, then sports editor of the *N.Y. Journal,* located Joe Louis in Chicago.

"What about this story that you were doped, Joe?" Farnsworth asked.

"Sure I was doped, Bill," came the clear voice of Louis over the phone.

There was a pause. Farnsworth frantically slid a sheet of copy paper in his typewriter, sure that he had a national scoop. Then:

"As I said, Bill, I was doped," Louis went on with a laugh, "but the dope wasn't in a hypo—it was in Schmeling's right hand."

Miss Nellie Bly: Circa 1936

The world was steadily shrinking in 1936, but it was a slender young newspaper reporter who really demonstrated how close Times Square was to Hong Kong, when she became the first woman to fly around the world.

In the fall of that year, Dorothy Kilgallen, then a reporter for the New York Journal, was given one of the most unusual assignments any reporter had ever received from a city editor. She was told to join New York Times reporter Leo Kieran and H. R. Elkins of the New York World-Telegram, who were about to begin a globe-circling race. Dorothy, equipped with a small suitcase and her journalist-father's portable typewriter, took off on the dirigible Hindenburg.

The world race caught the imagination of the public both here and in Europe, and the progress of the young girl-reporter and her two rivals was broadcast and printed from Indochina to London. The race once took on a grim note when a Siamese pilot lost his way flying Dorothy from Bangkok to Hong Kong. His tiny two-seated plane ran into the tail end of a Manila typhoon, and the bouncing little plane seemed about to crash in a rice field. But it stayed up and at last reached Hong Kong.

Miss Kilgallen finally arrived in New York on October 26, 1936, after circling the globe in 24 days, 12 hours, and 51 minutes. H. R. Elkins came in first, Dorothy was second, and the Times man loped in third.

EAGLE IN EXILE

IF COLONEL Charles A. Lindbergh had any thoughts on the execution of Bruno Hauptmann, the man who had stolen and murdered his son, he kept them to himself—not in the lonely white house in the Sourland Mountains of New Jersey where the great tragedy of his life had taken place, but in a rambling, timbered house called "Long Barn," hidden away in Knole Park near Sevenoaks in Kent.

It was here, to the feudal family seat of the fourth Baron Sackville, that the Lindberghs had fled—as Lindbergh said in an official statement—to "escape from the atmosphere of observation and publicity that has made our lives intolerable in the United States."

Lindbergh, his wife, and his tiny son Jon had slipped aboard the American steamship *Importer* and docked in Liverpool at about the time the *N. Y. Times* was announcing in a history-making exclusive news story how Lindbergh had left his native land.

Lindbergh found the British press no less persistent than the American. When he refused to submit to interviews he was told bluntly by British newsmen, "The war is on." From then on, his suite in the Adelphi Hotel was besieged by an army of reporters who followed him all over England just as he had been pursued in his native land. Although he did give out a brief statement, Lindbergh still refused to be interviewed.

By 1936 a special *N.Y. Times* correspondent was reporting that Lindbergh was a regular country squire and very much a part of the rural countryside. His name had been mentioned only four times by the London *Times* since his arrival in England: when he went to Germany to receive the "pin of honor" of the German Aero Club from Air Minister Goering, when he attended the International Congress of Experimental Cytology in Copenhagen, Denmark, and presented his "robot heart" to the Biological Institute of the Carlsberg Foundation, and twice when he was overdue after visits to Ireland and Italy.

Lindbergh's decision to leave his country raised a storm in Congress, where a demand grew that something be done about the steady rise in crime. It was pointed out that in the first nine

months of 1936 there was a murder for each 50,000 of the American population, a record seven times as bad as England's, and for the same period there had been 150,000 burglaries or an average of about one for each thousand population, a record thirteen times as bad as England's.

By 1936 Congress was enacting stricter laws and demanding more rigid enforcement of the existing ones. In

New York Mayor La Guardia started an all-out war on crime, and in Chicago and other large cities the police were joining forces with the FBI to curb the crime and the violence which was sweeping the nation.

It seemed that the final chapters in the tragic Lindbergh story—the execution of Hauptmann and the voluntary exile of the man who was an American idol—had touched the American conscience and awakened the citizenry and lawmakers to face the fact that much of their country was in the hands of racketeers and criminals.

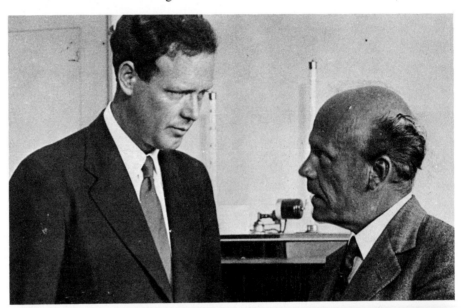

Colonel Charles E. Lindbergh in Copenhagen with Professor Albert Fischer, who aided him in demonstrating the artificial heart, which he worked on in conjunction with the famous physiologist Dr. Alexis Carrel.

Colonel Lindbergh and Colonel Smith, an American military attaché, as Lindbergh arrived in Berlin in 1936.

The Woman I Love

THE WORLD had been shaken by such events as Mussolini's invasion of Ethiopia, the increase in bloody Soviet purges, the grinding Civil War in Spain, and the growing menace of Hitler's Nazism. This was a time of grimness and fear. But 1936 will be remembered also for an amazing episode of love and romance.

That year worldwide attention was focused on Edward VIII, the handsome bachelor King of England, and an attractive Baltimore divorcée named Wallis Warfield Simpson. They had met early in 1931 at an English house party. Moving in the same set, they had seen each other in the passing years and their attachment had deepened into love. After he became King, her name was frequently on the royal guest list and gossip spread rapidly.

Edward had served only eleven months following the death of his father, George V, when he decided to marry Mrs. Simpson. Weeks before the public was finally told, Conservative Prime Minister Stanley Baldwin privately sought—obliquely, then bluntly—to dissuade the King. Behind Baldwin, although not acting directly in the coming crisis, was the Archbishop of Canterbury, primate of all England. The King sought the sympathy of his mother, Queen Mary. She gave him that, but when he suggested that he abdicate for marriage she was horrified.

At Edward's request the papers, conservative and sensational, had either suppressed or played down the news of the Simpson divorce case. But finally it exploded into international headlines.

Edward had one ally, Winston Churchill, who espoused his King's cause in private, then openly. When they first learned the news of the "Simpson affair," large segments of the British population rallied in personal affection for their young King. There was talk of a "King's Party," but it came to nothing because Edward refused to bring his cause down to the level of factionalism.

For weeks there was turmoil in the Empire, chiefly because the news of the growing crisis had been kept from the public, and wild rumors were circulating.

The Star
THE LONDONER'S EVENING PAPER

LATE NIGHT

No. 15,139.   ONE PENNY.   THURSDAY, DECEMBER 10, 1936.   RADIO: Page Ten.   WEATHER: Page Three.

THE SPEAKER IN COMMONS ANNOUNCES

ABDICATION

KING EDWARD VIII

MR. BALDWIN.

THE DUKE OF YORK THE NEW KING

KING EDWARD'S MESSAGE:—"I RENOUNCE THE THRONE FOR MYSELF AND FOR MY DESCENDANTS"

FINAL AND IRREVOCABLE

RENUNCIATION DOCUMENT WITNESSED BY HIS THREE BROTHERS

THE KING'S MESSAGE TO PARLIAMENT, ANNOUNCING HIS ABDICATION, WAS READ BY THE SPEAKER (CAPT. FITZROY) IN A CROWDED HOUSE OF COMMONS THIS AFTERNOON.
THE SPEAKER ALSO ANNOUNCED THE ACCESSION TO THE THRONE OF THE DUKE OF YORK.

The message had been handed to the Speaker by Mr. Baldwin. It said:—

After long and anxious consideration I have determined to renounce the throne, to which I succeeded on the death of my father, and I am now communicating this my final and irrevocable decision.

Realising, as I do, the gravity of this step I can only hope that I shall have the understanding of my peoples in the decision I have taken, and the reasons which have led me to take it.

Further delay would but be most injurious to the peoples whom I have tried

the stability of the Throne and Empire and the happiness of my peoples.

I, EDWARD THE EIGHTH OF GREAT BRITAIN IRELAND AND THE BRITISH DOMINIONS BEYOND THE SEAS, KING EMPEROR OF INDIA DO HEREBY DECLARE MY IRREVOCABLE DETERMINATION TO RENOUNCE THE THRONE FOR MYSELF AND FOR MY DESCENDANTS AND MY DESIRE THAT EFFECT SHOULD BE GIVEN TO THIS INSTRUMENT OF ABDICATION

FROM PLANE TO No. 10

Mrs. Simpson's Lawyer Returns

THERE was unusual activity to-day at the Villa Lou Viei, Cannes, where Mrs. Simpson is staying.

Mr. Herman Rogers (Mrs. Simpson's host) said to-day that there was not the remotest possibility of the King going to Lou Viei either now or in the future.

He added, says Reuter, that the King would not go to the Riviera, and Mrs. Simpson's intention was to stay on at the villa indefinitely.

No one else was expected at the villa.

Mr. Goddard (Mrs. Simpson's solicitor), Mr. S. Barron, and Dr. Kirkwood, came accompanied them when they went to Cannes, on Sunday, flew to Gatwick from Bourget Aerodrome. They came from Croydon. Always anxious

MR. BALDWIN
Recounts Story With The King

Prime Minister, in moving that King's message be considered, said he must tell what he had to tell plainly, with no attempt to dress it up or adorn it.

When he and the King said "Goodbye" on Tuesday night at Fort Belvedere they both felt and said to each other that their friendship far from being impaired by discussions of the last weeks, bound them more closely together than ever and would last for life.

Mr. Baldwin referred to the many letters he received expressing perturbation and uneasiness at what was appearing in the American Press.

BB

He knew also there was in the near future a divorce case coming on. He felt it essential to see the King and warn him of the difficult situation that might arise.

Advisers of Crown can be of no service to his Master unless he tell him at all times the truth as he sees it, whether that truth be welcome or not.

ALWAYS TRUTH
An adviser of the Crown could be of

PEERS IN A QUEUE AT THE HOUSE

King Edward VIII and Mrs. Wallis Warfield Simpson on a vacation cruise at Rab, Yugoslavia.

Marriage to a commoner was not unknown in British history, but marriage to a divorced person could not be recognized by the Church of England, of which the monarch is titular head. And marriage without that sanction would precipitate a constitutional crisis. It was on these grounds that the battle was quietly but savagely fought behind the doors of 10 Downing Street. The King and Churchill on one side, the Church and the Conservative party on the other. There were the trappings of a great Elizabethan royal drama: swift midnight journeys between London and country houses, where meetings were held between the King and trusted emissaries; secret meetings in the palace; couriers scurrying across the Channel.

Both sides refused to budge; there could be no compromise. The result was inevitable. Early in December, with his brothers, the Dukes of York and Gloucester, as witnesses, Edward signed his "Instrument of Abdication" and became the first King in modern English history to abdicate. A few hours later he went on the B.B.C. with his now-famous message to his people, explaining that he "found it impossible to carry the heavy burden [as King] without the help and support of the woman I love."

The Duke of York became King as George VI.

Mrs. Simpson had left England by this time. Edward did not see her again until her divorce became final. Several months later, they were quietly married in France.

BIG CITY IN THE MID-THIRTIES

An A & P window (1936).

Milk wagon at Grove Street (1936).

During the years 1935-38 Berenice Abbott, noted photographer, working in the Federal Art Project, made a remarkable series of photographs of the life and the scenes of New York City. Although the photographs are all of one city, together they represent an invaluable document, a view of an American city, long since changed, and of a way of life that has passed.

Many of the historic structures no longer exist, many of the subjects pictured have vanished. And as for the prices—they belong to the Desperate Years.

The Brevoort Hotel, Fifth Avenue and Eighth Street (1935).

Provincetown Playhouse on MacDougal Street, where O'Neill's plays were produced (1936).

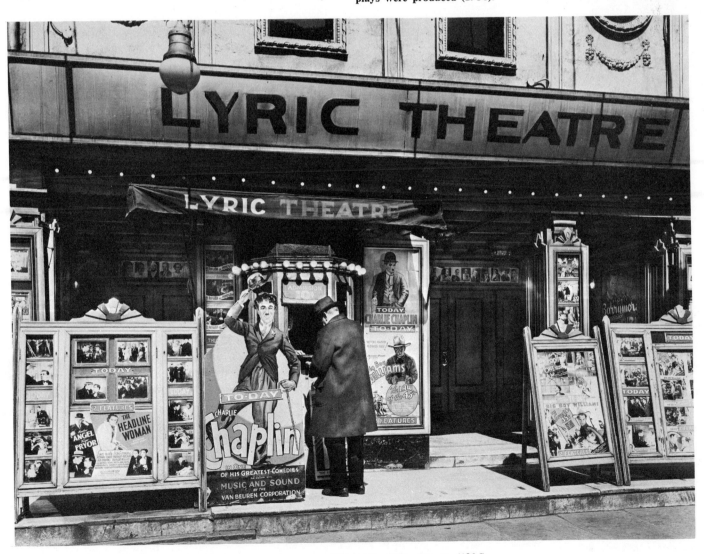

The famous Lyric Theatre, located on Third Avenue between 12th and 13th Streets (1936).

The Murray Hill Hotel (1935).

Third Avenue car barns, Third Avenue and 65th Street (1936). There's a great big apartment house on the site now.

El Station, Sixth and Ninth Avenue lines, 72nd Street and Columbus Avenue (1936).

210

Getting ready for a fiesta, Oak and New Chambers Streets (1935).

Billy's Bar, First Avenue and 56th Street (1936). It looked much the same in 1962, but was one of the very few old-time bars left.

211

A hot-dog wagon (1936).

Home Sweet Home on Pier 5, East River (1938).

A small snuff shop on New York City's Division Street (1938).

212

VOX POPULI: The 1936 Presidential Election

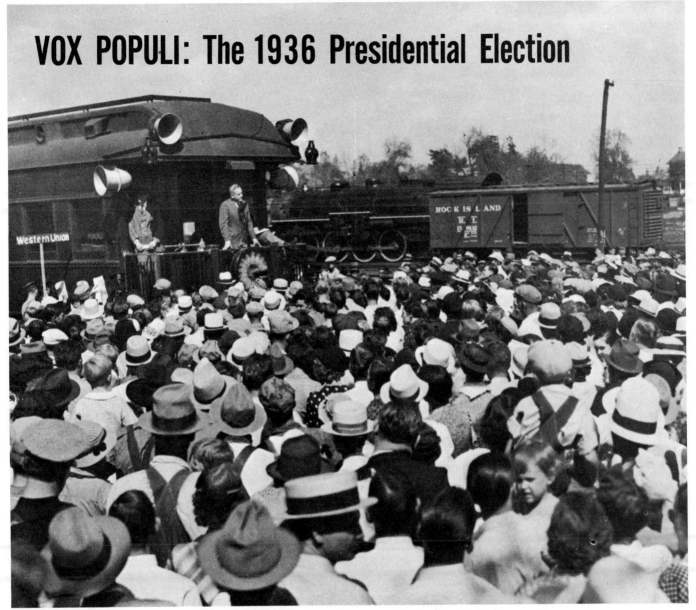

Governor Alfred M. Landon during a whistle-stop campaign en route to Des Moines.

EVERY American politician has a secret dream in which he faces an election which virtually is no contest—because of his own immense popularity with the voters, his opponent doesn't have a chance. For FDR, as early as the fall of 1935, this was not a dream; it was a reality.

"We are going to win easily next year," he told his Cabinet in November of 1935, "but we are going to make it a crusade."

By now Roosevelt knew how the New Deal had captured the hearts and the imagination of the American people.

Since the grim days of 1933 unemployment had dropped by four million. Under the Roosevelt administration four million jobs had been created by federal agencies, which were paying out more than five billion dollars. Payrolls and stock prices had both doubled. Industrial production had leaped skyward, and the income of the nation's farmers was near the seven billion mark.

Old people were now looking forward to their pensions. The National Youth Administration was helping thousands of high school and college students finish their education. Bank depositors would no longer lose their deposits, and everyone, it seemed, was working on the WPA, from the actor to the xylophone player.

The United States was on the march, and in the minds of the voters Roosevelt had accomplished it all almost singlehandedly.

It was easy to see why FDR was making the 1936 election a crusade, building his campaign on the new hopes and new dreams wrought by his administration's alphabetical agencies.

But always the practical politician, early that year FDR paved the way for November by soothing businessmen with a lavish White House luncheon, by talking about a spending cut, and by laying plans for seeking out votes from the vast storehouse of the many religious, civic, and business groups in the nation. To accomplish the latter he organized the Good Neighbor League, which would prove to be a wonderful vote-tapping scheme in the fall.

213

The Democratic Convention was held in Philadelphia, but it was FDR in the White House who dominated it. He drafted the platform, which mostly underscored the good works of the New Deal, and approved the major speeches and all major moves. For five days Jim Farley kept the convention moving in high gear, making sure that the airwaves and nation's press were chock-full of Democratic propaganda. On Saturday night FDR gave his acceptance speech in one of the most dramatic scenes in America's political history. Franklin Field was black with humanity. The crowd, sitting or standing in the light rain that had begun to fall, was restless with impatience. As FDR's sleek, black car nosed into the field, the rain stopped and clouds scooted overhead under a freshening wind.

A mighty wave of sound greeted Roosevelt when the heavy curtains parted. As he flashed that electrifying grin and waved his hand the billows of ecstatic cheering rolled out.

When finally he was allowed to speak, FDR lashed out at a class of new villains, "economic royalists." He also warned America of the growing dictatorships across the sea, and ended with his historic, "This generation has a rendezvous with destiny."

After Philadelphia, FDR did little campaigning—so little, in fact, that Farley and the Democratic leaders be-

FDR arrives at Franklin Field to deliver his 1936 acceptance speech.

came worried. Lewis and the other CIO officials put up a million dollars for the campaign and started beating the drums in industrial areas, while Farley's machine began churning at top speed in every state in the union.

The Republicans meanwhile had selected Alf M. Landon, the governor of Kansas, who made an impressive showing at the Convention by winning over Senator Borah by a wide majority on the first ballot. Farley refused to

Senator Borah.

Mr. and Mrs. Alfred Landon at home in Topeka after the GOP convention in 1936

had selected Landon as its candidate for President.

view Landon lightly; again and again he pointed out to party leaders that the smiling, tanned Kansan was no hard-shell reactionary. In fact, he had made several strong points about liberalizing the GOP's 1936 platform. Farley was also aware of the dangerous potential of Al Smith's Jeffersonian Democrats, who were leaving the Democratic Party in the election. And although the forces of Father Coughlin, Francis E. Townsend, or Gerald L. K. Smith (who had jumped into the breech in Louisiana after Huey Long's assassination) couldn't constitute a major threat singlehandedly, as a combination they might make trouble. Later, they all backed the Union Party, with William Lemke as their candidate.

But FDR refused to become concerned. He went fishing, joked with reporters, and to all outward appearances still considered the election no contest.

He told Raymond Moley, "There's one issue in this campaign. It's myself, and people must be either for me or against me."

When the election was nearing the finish wire, Lemke, the Union Party's candidate, was fading fast, and Landon,

Al Smith, who "took a walk" in 1936. Here he is arriving in Washington to make the principal address at the Liberty League dinner.

Congressman William Lemke.

Gerald L. K. Smith studies a picture of the late Huey Long.

who constantly hammered away at the New Deal, seemed to be making little impression on the voting public.

In October, with his superb sense of political timing, FDR became the campaigning politician. A ten-day tour of the northeast brought out the largest crowds in the history of American politics. On city streets and country roads, millions lined the way to wave at and cheer this man they loved so much. In Boston, 150,000 people mobbed the President's entourage, and in New York City, millions choked the streets for the thirty miles of his route.

The climax came before a wildly cheering crowd in Madison Square Garden when FDR again attacked his new villains, the economic royalists. "They are unanimous in their hate for me—and I welcome their hatred," he said, and was hailed with an ear-splitting roar.

Finally it was all over. FDR was swept back into office by a tidal wave of votes, carrying every state except Maine and Vermont. He won over Landon 27,476,673 to 16,679,583, the largest popular plurality in history. As Farley had predicted, the electoral vote was 523 to 8. In addition, he filled Congress with more Democrats. It was now 334 Democrats to 89 Republicans.

With one loud, clear, unprecedented voice, the American people proved they were for FDR.

President Roosevelt meets the press at Campobello in the summer of 1936. Jimmy Roosevelt is at the extreme right.

Dr. Francis E. Townsend confers with Father Coughlin at a 1936 convention of the Townsendites.

A composite picture of FDR and Alf Landon campaigning over the radio in the 1936 election.

216

OUR PRESIDENT

FDR speaking before a crowd in Worcester. (Left) Mrs. Roosevelt, (third from left) Davis I. Walsh, and (right) Senator Marcus Coolidge.

Jesse Owens, four-medal winner of the Olympics, coming up Broadway during a ticker-tape shower.

FDR's FEDERAL job-insurance plan went into effect. A one-percent tax on payrolls was enacted to raise the initial funds for an unemployment insurance fund, which would be put into effect in 1938. It would then (the following year) be supplemented by an additional tax for social security or old-age pensions, with both employers and employees contributing.... The New Deal suffered another defeat at the hands of the United States Supreme Court when, by a vote of 6 to 3, it upset the Agricultural Adjustment Act on the ground that it was an invasion of rights of the states to regulate their local activities. ... At Decatur, Alabama, Haywood Patterson, first of the "Scottsboro Boys," was sentenced to 75 years for attacking a white girl aboard a freight train five years before. ... At Fred-

FDR gets a rousing welcome in Buenos Aires. In the front seat is Gus Gennerich, the President's personal bodyguard, who died shortly after this picture was taken.

ericksburg, Virginia, baseball's immortal Walter Johnson threw a coin across the Rappahannock River, a distance of 286 feet 6 inches, on the birthday of George Washington, who, legend had it, had done the same thing when he was a young man. . . . In Japan several thousand troops mutinied, including the entire Tokyo garrison. The Minister of Finance was murdered, and by order of the Emperor martial law was declared throughout the land until the ringleaders were arrested and shot. . . . Floods raged through the East, especially in New Jersey, where highways were under water and washouts wrecked several trains. Damage of $500,000,000 was reported and 200 were dead. . . . The Dionne quintuplets received $250,000 for a two-year movie contract. . . . A crowd police estimated at 200,000 (including FDR) attended the opening of New York's $64,000,000 Triborough Bridge, a WPA project. . . . Great Britain announced that she was placing an embargo on Spain and Brazil and recalled her consuls, and Germany sent a vigorous protest to Madrid for the anti-Nazi broadcasts coming from a Russian station there. . . . Aviation history was made when the Deutsche Lufthansa flying boat *Zephyr* flew from Germany to Long Island in 22 hours. It was the beginning of an aerial survey by the company, which announced it planned to institute "regular transatlantic air service." . . . Waterfront activity in West Coast ports ground to a standstill when 39,000 maritime workers went on strike, soon to be joined by those in Gulf and East Coast ports. . . . FDR was given a tremendous welcome when he arrived in Buenos Aires for the Pan-American Peace Conference. . . . Germany reoccupied the Rhineland, thereby breaking the Locarno Pact and

Ted Weems, (left) and Perry Como, Elmo Tanner, Parker Gibbs, Country Washburn, and Red Ingle.

killing the Treaty of Versailles. . . . William Faulkner's *Absalom, Absalom!* won critical acclaim but was not a best seller. The impact of the Depression obviously had an effect on the writings of another giant of the era, John Dos Passos. In the twenties he was concentrating on the individual, but now in the mid-thirties his major theme was the effect of commercialism on social values. He used unique technical devices such as the "newsreel," "camera eye" or "biographies" to broaden the scope of his novels. The third volume of his trilogy *U.S.A., The Big Money,* was published this year. But everything in the book world was overshadowed by the

publication of Margaret Mitchell's all-time best seller *Gone With the Wind.* (It won the 1937 Pulitzer prize.) This huge, sweeping novel of Scarlett O'Hara's South during the Civil War would continue to sell in the millions long after the author's tragic death in a traffic accident. . . . Ted Weems' orchestra, with its young vocalist Perry Como, was one of the most popular of the year. . . . On Broadway, pretty Margaret Sullavan, having survived several flops, went on to stardom in *Stage Door.* . . . Jesse Owens, winner of four gold medals, was the oustanding star of the U.S. team that achieved great success in the Olympics at Berlin.

Pierce-Arrow, Model 8 Travel-lodge, a trailer.

The famous 1937 Cord Phaeton sedan boasted "a cloth top that could be lowered and when raised provided a complete closed auto." Still sought by collectors, it was built on a 125-inch wheel base and had a 125 H.P. Lycoming V-8 engine.

Margaret Mitchell and her editor, Harold Latham (who "discovered" her), receive the news that her Gone with the Wind had won the Pulitzer Prize.

President Roosevelt with Park Commissioner Robert Moses at the dedication of the $64,000,000 Triborough Bridge.

German troops rumble through the streets of Cologne in 1936 as Hitler sounded the death knell of the Versailles Treaty.

The Redwood Murder

THE STAGE for murder was set in the early evening of February 6, 1937. In their home on Laurelton Parkway in Teaneck, New Jersey, gray-haired Victoria Redwood was waiting for a telephone call from her husband Norman, a husky sandhog who only a few months before had been elected business manager for the Compressed Air, Subway and Tunnel Workers, Local 102.

Finally at 6:10 P.M. the phone rang. It was Redwood, telling his wife he would be home within the hour.

Mrs. Redwood had started dinner, when suddenly a series of sounds like

Sam Rosoff (right) and Norman Redwood (left).

Mrs. Norman Redwood.

large boards being clapped together split the suburban quiet. She hurried out and found her husband sprawled on the front seat of his car. He had been shot to death.

The murder created a sensation. It was another dramatic demonstration of the corruption and criminal influence in labor. Redwood, it developed, had intended to ignore an injunction brought against him in Supreme Court by Sam Rosoff, a pudgy, colorful contractor who had once hauled a million dollars in cash before the New York City Board of Estimate to bid on an ash removal contract.

Rosoff, one of the wealthiest and most powerful contractors in the country, was located in Atlantic City. He immediately posted a $5,000 reward for the arrest of the killers, and hurried

back to New York—out of the jurisdiction of New Jersey.

Bergen County Prosecutor John J. Breslin, Jr., took over the case and demanded that Rosoff be extradited to New Jersey. Detectives served the contractor with a subpoena and he was placed under technical arrest.

Rosoff vigorously denied he had anything to do with Redwood's murder, as did Joe Fay, the so-called czar of the metropolitan building trades. Labor officials, mobsters, pretty show girls, all trooped into the uptown precinct where the New Jersey authorities had established a command post. Detectives were sent across the country on clues that fizzled. The only tangible clues were the two murder weapons; one was found near the scene, the other dragged up by detectives after their famed chief, Harry Lockwood, had surmised that the killers would probably throw the remaining gun in the Hackensack River as they sped away.

Using clam rakes, the detectives spent many weary days in rowboats, and Lockwood's hunch finally paid off —the gun was found. The serial numbers had been filed off the weapon, but two New Jersey amateur criminologists, who had invented a secret acid process to raise obliterated marks on metal, brought out the numbers.

Detectives doggedly checked thousands of gun records. The weapon was at last traced to a New York gun dealer, Moe (Luger Moe) Saraga, known to the police as the gunsmith for the Dutch Schultz mob. Moe was located in Europe and arrested by Breslin as a material witness. After many grillings,

Saraga finally admitted that he had sold the gun to a man known as "Little Davey." He was shown countless rogues gallery pictures, but as time passed, his memory became progressively worse. "Little Davey" was never located.

The second gun was traced to a gun dealer in Pittsburgh, but the specific records dealing with this one gun had been lost in the Pittsburgh floods of that year.

The murder brought to light the tangled jurisdictional fights among labor unions which were delaying projects and costing the taxpayers millions. Testimony before the Labor Relations Board also revealed shady deals between unions and contractors, and that union charters were sold across the counter for as much as $40,000.

On February 28, 1937, Prosecutor Breslin issued a sensational statement in which he insisted that his investigation had forced him to the conclusion that Rosoff and Fay had plotted the killing. Breslin disclosed that Redwood and Fay had become bitter enemies after Fay accused Redwood of "fooling around with the fellows from the C.I.O.," and Redwood refused to deny the accusation.

Rosoff, Breslin said, had threatened Redwood at a stormy meeting, saying that he had "two guns and if I don't use them I will get the men who will use them."

In New York, Rosoff angrily continued to deny he had anything to do with the murder. He later stormed the Supreme Court and had the subpoena dismissed and his technical arrest lifted.

The winter dragged on. There were grand jury investigations, hurried trips to many states, angry recriminations between Breslin and New York's Police Commissioner Lewis J. Valentine, but the murder was never solved.

1937

The first group photograph of the Supreme Court in 1937 after FDR's appointment of Hugo L. Black (back row, extreme right). (First row, left to right) Justices George Sutherland, James Clark McReynolds, Chief Justice Charles Evans Hughes, Justices Louis D. Brandeis and Pierce Butler. (Back row) Justices Benjamin N. Cardozo, Harlan Fiske Stone, Owen J. Roberts.

The Nine Old Men

Senator Carter Glass of Virginia.

THE MESSAGE President Roosevelt sent to Congress that afternoon of February 5, 1937 seemed terribly dull and prosaic. Page after page went on at great length about the delays in federal courts. The title would have delighted any stodgy researcher in the history of law; it was "Reorganization of the Judicial Branch of the Government."

But to the alert congressman who dared to wade through the pages of eye-wearing type, one item listed under proposals and recommendations was enough to lift him clear out of his chair: FDR was proposing that Congress give him power to appoint an additional justice for each member of the United States Supreme Court who was over seventy years old, up to a maximum of six. There were then six justices over seventy out of the nine in the court and even a freshman in Congress would have realized what FDR was up to. By nightfall, as word of the proposal swept Capitol Hill like a prairie fire in the wind, the pamphlet had a new name. It's the one that remains in the history books—FDR's court-packing plan.

It was no secret that the President was incensed over the court's conservative decisions. Today, the grounds seem strange indeed. For example, in reviewing a case involving a New York State law fixing a ten-hour maximum working day for bakers, the court found in the due-process clause of the Fourteenth Amendment—providing that no state take a man's life, liberty, or property without due process of law-a protection called "liberty of contract." The court's ruling meant the baker must be allowed to work twelve hours a day even though the state had decided it was unfair and injurious to his health.

The New Deal lawmakers and liberals of the thirties had watched with dismay as year after year the high court chopped down fine economic and social experiments—always on the ground that they were unconstitutional. With 12,-800,000 still unemployed, resentment against the "nine old men" had increased after each ruling.

Senator Hugo L. Black of Alabama put it: "They [the justices] are amending the Constitution according to their economic predilections."

Thomas H. Eliot, one of the principal drafters of the social security legislation, has written that he was "unceasingly conscious of the threatening shadow cast by the Constitution and the justices—or both."

In the beginning, it appeared that perhaps FDR's plan might be approved. His popularity was at an all-time high, as evidenced by his overwhelming victory at the polls. And resentment was growing against the Supreme Court. Even Congress was planning bills to force the aging justices to retire, to permit Congress to override judicial decisions, to pass a constitutional amendment making explicit the government's power over the economy, to require a 7 to 2 majority in decisions of unconstitutionality. Many of the court's decisions overturning New Deal social legislation had been 6 to 3 or 5 to 4.

There was strong opposition, however. Senator Carter Glass of Virginia was an outspoken foe of the plan. There were others, even among the New Deal's inner families, who regarded FDR's plan as the end of an independent judiciary. FDR's method of cloaking his real policy—the court as against his social legislation—with his public statements on the aging justices who needed a hand, also didn't help the fight.

In the spring of 1937, the court overruled its former decision against minimum wages and upheld the Wagner Labor Relations Act and the Social Security Law. Then FDR's argument that vacancies had to be created was dealt a blow by the retirement of Justice Van Devanter. One can only guess at the sardonic delight felt by the President as he appointed Senator Black to the vacancy—Black who had been the strongest supporter of the court-packing plan.

But fate unexpectedly intervened; Senate Majority Leader Joseph T. Robinson of Arkansas, who had been feverishly working behind the Senate scenes in an attempt to save face for the President by having a compromise bill passed, died of a heart attack.

On July 22, FDR was given a humiliating defeat when Congress completely buried his bill. It was the first real legislative defeat Roosevelt had experienced and it tarnished the legend that he was a political invincible who could get any domestic reform measure through Congress.

Looking back over the files of the major newspapers and searching out forgotten memoirs, one is struck by the heat and bitterness surrounding the court-packing issue and the decisions of the high court.

The court in those years was sternly taking the administration to task for attempting to interfere in areas of American life which the Constitution had declared were immune from legislative regulation. Today, high court decisions reflect not only how it has changed but how America and the times have changed.

It has been suggested that today's more liberal high court was directly connected with FDR's court-packing plan. Historians point out this theory is doubtful.

Had FDR held back his plan, the court would have changed through inevitable retirements. Roosevelt would have filled the vacancies with men who approved of his liberal social and economic legislation. Furthermore, they would have represented a new generation. They would not have been men like those who Senator Black insisted were basing their decisions on their own economic predilections.

Robert Jackson, who helped Roosevelt mold the plan, writing in his later years, pointed out that as long as the country lasts there will be arguments over the power of the Supreme Court. Yet, despite these criticisms, the people of the United States will always insist that the power of the court be sustained because "the people [seem] . . . to feel that the Supreme Court, whatever its defects, is still the most detached, dispassionate, and trustworthy custodian that our system affords for the translation of the abstract into concrete constitutional commands."

Death of the Air Giant

The Hindenburg over Manhattan in 1937.

The 803-foot zeppelin *Hindenburg* rose slowly. The airship, carrying 97 passengers, slid over the huge hangars and began her journey across the ocean to her mooring mast at the U.S. Naval Air Station in Lakehurst, New Jersey.

It was an uneventful journey. Passengers who expected to find themselves pitching and tossing were amazed to discover how smooth the giant ship rode through the skies. They slept on mattresses of air cushions under sheets of balloon cloth, sat in aluminum chairs that a child could lift with a finger, even played on a piano that was aluminum. And everything was collapsible.

The passenger quarters were located about one-third of the distance aft of the nose and a third of the depth up from the keel. They were arranged in a square area enclosed within the shell, extending the width of the ship and consisting of two decks. Deck A was

the main deck; on the port side it was the freight department. Two 50-horse-power diesel electric motors provided auxiliary power for cooking, lighting, refrigeration, and radio.

From B Deck a passenger could step into the duralumin bowels of the zeppelin. A narrow catwalk covered with rubber sheeting ran through the center of the ship from nose to rump. Everyone who walked this plank wore sneakers. As Captain Ernst Lehmann pointed out, "one doesn't fool around with hydrogen." In fact, all the motors of the airship were diesel. They used only crude oil fuel, which wouldn't ignite even if you put a match to it. Everything — men and machines — respected the explosive hydrogen which was used to inflate the giant dirigible instead of the safer helium because of its greater lifting power; the resulting economy made the ship more profitable.

W. B. Courtney, writing in *Collier's,* pointed out the innumerable safeguards that the Germans took in conveying passengers across the ocean at $400 for a one-way trip. He ended his article: "After watching their methods, it is the firm conviction of this reporter that only a stroke of war or an unfathomable act of God will ever mar this German dirigible passenger-safety record."

This trip, the first of the 1937 season, the *Hindenburg* found herself battling storms. However, before she reached the ocean, she sailed majestically over the large cities of the world and as always men, women, and children of all nationalities watched her cast her huge shadow over streets and buildings.

As the zeppelin approached Lakehurst at 4:20, weather reports that heavy winds and a thunderstorm were approaching forced Captain Lehmann to delay the mooring. Instead, he cruised

224

up and down the New Jersey coast until sundown. The delay provided a treat for thousands of New Yorkers. Traffic was halted in some sections of the city while motorists paused to watch the customary air show the *Hindenburg*'s captain liked to put on. Newspaper photographers and amateurs snapped countless pictures from the Empire State Building and Rockefeller Center as planes escorted the big ship to Staten Island; steamships and harbor craft set up a deafening din by horn and whistle.

As she sailed down the New Jersey coast, home-going school children looked up and waved and farmers leaned on their plows and marveled.

At 7:20 that evening she finally dipped down to her mooring mast at Lakehurst. Passengers could be seen laughing and gaily waving from the windows of the observation deck.

Suddenly there was a bomblike blast, then flames spurted from the rear and spread like an inferno forward along the great silvery bag. A second later the ship buckled in the center, the nose shot upward and then collapsed to the sandy field, belching flames and thick black smoke. Two hundred sailors ran for their lives as the flaming fabric fell about them. Men and women staggered from behind the sheet of flame, their clothing burned away, their skin peeling from their bodies.

One of the first to emerge was Captain Lehmann. As he staggered toward rescuers he kept crying, "I can't understand it! I can't understand it!"

There were 61 survivors. Their accounts of the tragedy emphasized the speed with which the *Hindenburg* was destroyed. Officials of the zeppelin company later offered two possible causes. The rainy weather could have produced a spark of electricity when the landing ropes were dropped, and such a spark could have touched off the highly explosive hydrogen gas. A second theory suggested that a spark had flown from one of the engines when they were throttled down for the landing. The *Hindenburg* had been valving hydrogen preparatory to her landing and some of the gas might have pocketed under the tail surfaces and detonated when the spark flew back.

Dirigible engineers later discounted a theory that the ship had been struck by lightning. They pointed out that as the ship passed through a sharp electrical storm earlier that day, a charge of static electricity could have been stored in the metal of her frame. When her wet mooring ropes were thrown overboard and touched the ground, the charge could have been released, supplying the spark that touched off the blast.

But no matter what the theory, the *Hindenburg* was now a mass of black, twisted steel and there was little future for the zeppelin.

Associated Press photographer Murray Becker's famous picture of the end of the Hindenburg.

A Hindenburg passenger, his clothing in shreds, is helped to safety.

FLINT: the Dynamite City

EVERYONE in Flint, Michigan, which next to Detroit was the automobile capital of America, was lined up on one side or the other—on the side of the strikers or on the side of General Motors. The strike that now, in the last days of 1936, had the city under the bristling rifles and machine guns of 1,200 troops was described by one correspondent as a "hunk of dynamite ready to go off at any moment."

Already troops of the 126th Infantry Division were forming a cordon approximately two miles wide about the Chevrolet (General Motors subsidiary) motor assembly plant, held by the newest and most effective technique yet devised by a union for paralyzing an industry—a sitdown strike. The men on the job simply sat down, occupying the

(Left to right) John L. Lewis, Governor Murphy, and Walter P. Chrysler, who signed the 1937 agreement with the UAW.

space in the plant, but doing no work and preventing others from working. Governor Frank Murphy had ordered the troops into the strike-torn city after rioting broke out in the Chevrolet plant.

For several hours strikers and nonstrikers milled about in the sprawling plant. Then pitched battles erupted between strikers, nonstrikers, police, and sheriff's men. The rioting started when the day shift bunched together at the gate to prevent the night shift from entering. Outside the gate a small army of union men armed with clubs formed a wedge to help those inside. Plant police, outnumbered three to one, tried to rush the human phalanx and break it up with tear gas. Men rolled on the

Walter Reuther in 1937.

William S. Knudsen signs for General Motors. Governor Murphy is on the left and Federal Conciliator James F. Dewey is on the right. Behind Murphy is Lee Pressman, CIO attorney. Behind Knudsen is Donaldson Brown of General Motors.

Ford Workers

UNIONISM NOT FORDISM

Now is the time to Organize!
The Wagner Bill is behind you!
Now get behind yourselves!

General Motors Workers, Chrysler Workers, Briggs Workers have won higher wages and better working conditions. 300,000 automobile workers are marching forward under the banner of the United Automobile Workers Union.

JOIN NOW IN THE MARCH AND WIN:

Higher Wages and Better Working Conditions
Stop Speed-up by Union Supervision
6 Hour Day, 8 Dollars Minimum Pay
Job Security thru Seniority Rights
End the Ford Service System
Union Recognition

Organize and be Recognized - JOIN NOW!

Union Headquarters for Ford Workers: } **Michigan Avenue at Addison**
Vernor Highway West, and Lawndale

Sign up at Union Headquarters for Ford Workers or at any office of the United Automobile Workers

1324 Clay at Russell	8944 Jos. Campau at Playfair
2441 Milwaukee at Chene	11440 Charlevoix at Gladwin
11725 Oakland at Tuxedo	1343 East Ferry at Russell
4044 Leuschner at Dwyer	3814—35th Street at Michigan
11640 East Jefferson	2730 Maybury Grand at Michigan
10904 Mack at Lemay	4715 Hastings Street
77 Victor at John R.	Room 509 Hofmann Bldg.

Distributed by
United Automobile Workers of America

License No. 4

Printed by Goodwill Printing Co.
33

CIO leaflet distributed during the strike.

ground in the swirling fumes of the gas bombs. Rocks and chunks of metal flew. Clubs wielded by both sides smashed faces and heads. While the battle raged, women hurled rocks and metal parts through the plant windows as they shouted encouragement to the fighting union men.

This was not the first riot Flint had seen. A few weeks before, other clashes had taken place at Fisher Plant 4. Here five hundred men and women led by Walter Reuther, the union's organizer, appeared before the plant. Windows were broken as the six thousand workers left the factory. Suddenly the plant police, armed with tear gas and clubs, ran from the building and attempted to push the union men outside the gate. The union men picked up two-by-fours, metal strips, and racks and attacked the police, who fired tear gas in retaliation and jumped at the union men, clubs swinging. The tide of fighting moved in and out the gates amid the billowing, choking gas, subsiding only when union organizers operating from sound trucks ordered the men to retreat.

As the strike paralyzed the city and spread to Detroit and elsewhere, involving Ford and other plants, a so-called "vigilante" committee was formed to "keep the peace." Armed men, it was reported, were "escorting" union organizers out of the city.

"They were told what would happen to them if they came back," a vigilante member said.

Standing head and shoulders above the strikers and the company was beetle-browed Governor Frank Murphy, who, as the weeks passed, slowly brought both sides together. But the so-called Flint Alliance, admittedly nonunion, brought the negotiations to a grinding halt when they demanded of Murphy that he guarantee protection for all General Motors workers going to and coming from work. The incensed governor, in a biting interview, told the group that this could well mean the militia would be patrolling the streets of Flint. He said he had heard reports that mobs were to be let loose on the streets "for the purpose of involving the militia."

"You must remember that the men on strike are as sincere and as earnest as you," he told the group, "and that they are acting from an outraged sense of justice, as they see it."

Murphy finally negotiated a peace, signed in February, that lasted until April of the following year, when General Motors shut down its plants after UAWA pickets sought to compel workers to pay union dues by allowing only workers who had paid-up dues books to enter.

Out of the violence, bloodshed, and bitterness, two giants emerged who would make their mark on the Desperate Years in which they lived: Walter Reuther, who would become head of one of the most powerful unions in the world, and Governor Frank Murphy, who would end his days as a justice of the United States Supreme Court.

227

The WPA in Action

THE FIRST few years of the New Deal saw more social legislation passed than at any other time in our nation's history. Among the measures adopted were the National Labor Relations Act, the Social Security Act, and the Public Utility Law. But ranking above them all was the Works Progress Administration, the most liberal relief-work program ever undertaken by any government.

The WPA, later the Works Projects Administration, first of all raised the morale of millions of Americans at a time when they had reached the lowest ebb of their lives. In place of direct city or state relief there was honest work and a paycheck. Monthly wages averaged between fifty and sixty dollars, and the work week was forty hours.

From the summer of 1935 to its end in 1942, the WPA spent ten billion dollars and employed almost eight million men and women, who in turn supported family groups numbering thirty million Americans.

In the beginning, the WPA took over unfinished state or civic projects which had been shelved by the Depression. Today thousands of libraries, schools, hospitals, bridges, highways, roads, courthouses, and other public structures stand as lasting memorials to the WPA and its workers. Besides public works, the WPA also taught women how to sew, how to weave baskets, teach school, catalogue local and national historical documents for future scholars, take care of nursery-age children, and conduct naturalization classes to instruct immigrants in the fundamentals of Americanism.

The Federal Music Project, employing more than ten thousand musicians, performed, as Deems Taylor put it, "more American music than all our other symphony orchestras combined." And researchers collected American folklore melodies, from the haunting ballads of the Kentucky mountains to the bouncing songs of the old Missouri. These were preserved on tape and wax and now are in the Library of Congress.

The Federal Theatre Project, with an annual budget of seven million dollars,

Grand Coulee Dam, where 16 additional gaps had to be made to allow for the Columbia River's spring flood.

employed more than twelve thousand actors, actresses, and entertainers across the nation. Their efforts encompassed the entire entertainment world. A small circus group might enthrall a crowd of children in Central Park on a Saturday morning, while on a sage-covered hill in the Far West a marionette show was bringing squeals of delight from the combined families of local sheep-herders.

It was the New Deal at its finest hour.

State fish hatchery at Gray, Maine.

Eau Claire River Dam, Wisconsin.

Mt. Hood Timberline Lodge, Ore., built by the WPA.

The Ramsey (N.J.) Municipal Building before it was rebuilt.

The Ramsey Municipal Building after it was rebuilt by the WPA.

A WPA mural in Enid, Okla.

Richard Wright, well-known American Negro novelist, once a WPA laborer, received a 1939 Guggenheim Foundation grant.

A trainee in the WPA household project in North Carolina.

Jesse J. Cornplanter of the Seneca tribe working on ancient tribal masks at a WPA project on the Tonawanda Reservation in New York.

Children in the WPA children's theater in Duluth.

South Dakota basketry class.

A one-armed WPA worker in southern Illinois.

A Federal Theater Project Christmas program presented on the steps of the New York Public Library, Fifth Avenue.

The WPA Strikebound

FROM SHORTLY after its beginning in the summer of 1935 until the start of World War II, the WPA was constantly harassed by strikes inspired by Communist and left-wing groups. Almost at its inception, the WPA was infiltrated by the Communist-dominated Workers' Alliance, which once boasted that it had more than a half-million members. The figure was highly exaggerated, as Congressional investigations later proved.

The usual Marxist program was put into high gear; cells were set up in as many projects as possible, and a vigorous effort made to recruit all the card-carrying members they possibly could.

The Workers' Alliance promoted hunger strikes, picketing, and demonstrating before state legislatures, and put the finishing touches on the technique of sitdown strikes, which began to spread from state to state. In the larger cities from New York to the West

WPA workers protesting job dismissals in Washington. More than 3,000 marched on the White House.

The casts of two WPA musical shows, How Long, Brethren? and Candide, stage a strike in 1937 to protest WPA wage cuts.

232

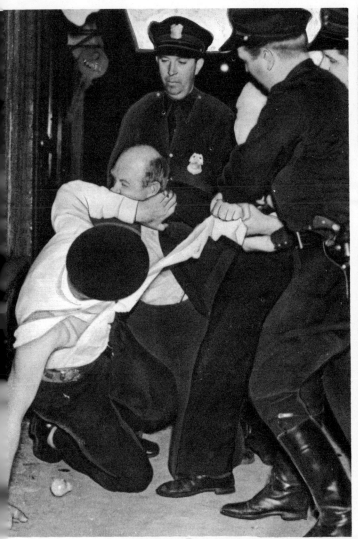

Minneapolis policemen fight WPA rioters. One man was killed and scores were hurt (1939).

WPA pickets in New York protesting job cuts in 1937.

Coast, WPA workers, sponsored mostly by left-wing groups, camped in their offices, refusing to move. Food was hoisted to them by rope. In some instances, to attract the most in public attention, women handcuffed themselves to their desks.

At the high point of the WPA labor unrest in the late thirties, New York City's WPA projects were frequently tied up by strikes resulting in riots. On many occasions mounted police were forced to back their horses in on the screeching, placard-wielding pickets. The next day, of course, they were denounced by the left-wing groups as "Cossacks."

"I wonder if the Cossacks ever received as many busted heads, black eyes, cuts and bruises, and torn uniforms as my men have," Police Commissioner Mulrooney observed after one wild Fourth Avenue riot.

A WPA protest meeting in New York's Columbus Circle.

Highlights and Sidelights: 1937

UNDER THE Mexican flag in Tampico, Mexico, Leon Trotsky—"a man without a country," as he described himself—asked that a court of world opinion decide the issues between him and Joseph Stalin. The medium would be a non-partisan international body. Trotsky, appearing to the reporters more like a contemplative scholar than a man whose

Leon Trotsky

words once shook the world, predicted an early war in Europe. . . . The rebels in Spain greeted New Year's Day by shelling Madrid. . . . Joe Louis won the heavyweight championship of the world by knocking out Jim Braddock in the eighth round, June 22. . . . On May 12, England celebrated the coronation of King George VI and Queen Elizabeth. . . . Explorer-photographer Martin Johnson lost his life in an airplane crash near Burbank, California. . . . John Fiorenza, who strangled Nancy Titterton in her Beekman Place apartment, died in the electric chair in Sing Sing. . . . Bass choral singer Joseph Sterzine, stabbed accidentally in the hand by singer Lawrence Tibbett during a dress rehearsal of *Caponsacchi,* died in the hospital. An autopsy showed he had suffered a heart attack. . . . In March, John L. Lewis of the CIO and Myron Taylor, board chairman of U.S. Steel, announced that agreement had been reached for the recognition of the

James J. Braddock, "the Cinderella Man," and Joe Louis strike a pose before their 1937 bout.

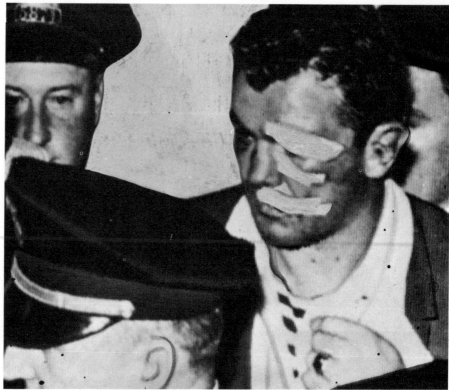

Braddock, showing his battle scars, leaves Madison Square Garden.

234

The royal coach turning out of Buckingham Palace enroute to Westminster Abbey, May 12, 1937, for the coronation of King George and Queen Elizabeth.

War Admiral winning the 1937 Preakness at Pimlico. Jockey Charles Kurtsinger is up; owner, Samuel D. Riddle. War Admiral was pushed hard in that memorable race by the fast-stepping Pompoon.

United Mine Workers. . . . Howard Hughes established a transcontinental flight record. . . . At a meeting of the American Jewish Congress, Mayor La Guardia told a packed audience he wished he had a "chamber of horrors" at the coming World's Fair where he could put a figure of that brown-shirted fanatic who was now "menacing the peace of the world." A few days later, Secretary of State Cordell Hull sent the German Embassy a note of regret for the Little Flower's words. . . . An explosion of escaping natural gas killed nearly 300 pupils and teachers in the New London, Texas, school minutes before dismissal. . . . In Kansas City the first union action against Ford was taken by workers who seized the plant overnight. But Henry Ford told them bluntly, "I'll never recognize any union." . . . Thousands of college students put on a massive "peace strike" across the nation from New York to California. Highlight of the "strike" was their reciting the American version of the Oxford oath: "I refuse to support the government of the United States in any

George Gershwin, composer of Porgy and Bess, An American in Paris, Rhapsody in Blue, and many other works for the concert as well as the musical comedy stage, died July 11, 1937.

Carl Hubbell, Giant pitcher, scoring in the second inning of the fourth World Series game in 1937.

Amelia Earhart, the world's No.1 aviatrix, who vanished mysteriously on a flight with her copilot, Frederick Noonan.

Luise Rainer and Clifford Odets.

Howard Hughes, motion picture producer and famous flyer, receiving the Harmon International Trophy from President Roosevelt in 1938. (Left to right) Hughes; FDR; Colonel Charles W. Kenwood, president of the American section of the Ligue Internationale des Aviateurs; W. Burke Harmon, nephew of the donor of the trophy; and Charles F. Horner, president of the National Aeronautic Association.

236

A sitdown strike in the Ford plant in Kansas City, staged by 1,400 members of the UAW.

Supreme Court Justice Hugo L. Black pictured as he reported to the people about his Klan membership.

The little U. S. gunboat *Panay* went down after being bombed by Japanese planes.

Klan cross burning near York, Pa.

war it may conduct." . . . Donald Budge, great tennis master, was voted the country's No. 1 athlete of the year. He had helped the U.S. recapture the Davis Cup, was national singles champ, and had won three titles at Wimbledon. . . . . War Admiral won the Kentucky Derby, the Preakness and Belmont Stakes. . . . . The N.Y. Yankees defeated the N.Y. Giants in the World Series. . . . In China, Japan's troops marched into Peiping. Japan's blockade of the east China coast was now 2,700 miles long. . . . In December, the U.S. gunboat *Panay* was bombed and machine-gunned by Japanese planes and sank in the Yangtze River. The attack occurred only minutes after refugees from Japanese shellfire in Nanking had boarded the boat for safety. The incident, which created a great international furor, was explained by the Japanese as "a mistake." . . . Amelia Earhart, the world's No. 1 aviatrix, and her copilot-navigator Frederick Noonan, disappeared mysteriously on their hop from Australia to Howland Island, the most dangerous leg of their round-the-world flight. The search for them went on for months, but no trace of the flyers or their plane has ever been found. . . . Notable books of the year were John P. Marquand's *The Late George Apley,* which won the Pulitzer prize (1938), and John Steinbeck's *Of Mice and Men.* . . . Outstanding on Broadway were Clifford Odets' *Golden Boy* and the musical *I'd Rather Be Right* by George S. Kaufman and Moss Hart, with music and lyrics by Richard Rodgers and Lorenz Hart. . . . Premier Mussolini, in a bullet-proof car, arrived in Munich, to be greeted by Adolf Hitler. Later, both dictators reviewed large troop maneuvers. . . . The *Pittsburgh* (Pennsylvania) *Gazette,* in an exclusive story, revealed that former Senator Black, now on the Supreme Court, had been and still was a member of the Ku Klux Klan. Black later denied the charge and said he had resigned from the Klan "some time ago." . . . The rejuvenated Klan reached as far north as Pennsylvania, where a state convention was held at York. . . . In New York, fun-loving American Legionnaires attending their nineteenth annual convention paralyzed traffic in Times Square and made life frantic for almost any female who walked down the street.

Lanky Donald Budge, the hero of the American recapture of the Davis cup in 1937.

A Chinese peasant boy leads his aged, blind mother to safety from the native section of Shanghai, shelled and bombed by Japanese land guns and planes.

The VIENNA COUP

THE FIRST shadows of war were starting to edge over the world that spring. Europe's smallest dictator had challenged the biggest. Chancellor Schuschnigg, master of tiny Austria, had thrown down the gauntlet to Chancellor Adolf Hitler, leader of the most powerful state on the Continent. For the first time in the history of dictatorships, one dictator was ready to use the despised political instrument of democracy—the vote, the ballot, the voice of the people—to defeat another.

In early March, while the world powers waited, watched, and fumbled in international diplomacy before the shouting, spellbinding Hitler, Schuschnigg proclaimed a plebiscite for the Austrian people. England and France were openly jubilant. Rome, the correspondents heard, was secretly delighted. Austria flamed with excitement and all Europe—except Berlin—applauded the audacious summons of the Austrian Chancellor, calling his people to the polls to determine in the best democratic fashion whether they preferred to be independent or be united with the Nazi German Reich.

For that was the real sense of the plebiscite, despite the clever wording. The question which was put to the people of Austria was: "Are you in favor of a free, independent, Christian, social, and united Austria for peace and work and equal rights for all those pledged to the people of the Fatherland?"

The fiery little Chancellor knew that to this question every Austrian except the Nazis would answer "yes." The significant word was "independent." Nobody wishing *anschluss,* meaning union with Germany, could vote "yes." All Catholics would do so on account of the word "Christian," and all workers, even the Socialists, would do so because of the words "equal rights."

With these expectations, Schuschnigg knew that he had victory in his grasp. Another important factor, as diplomats pointed out, was that the voting age was twenty-four, which automatically barred half the Nazi followers, called "blood young" in both Germany and Austria.

Schuschnigg's proclamation crashed like a thunderbolt among the Nazis in

Chancellor von Schuschnigg wearing an army uniform for the first time, while attending memorial services for Austrian troops, in May, 1936, shortly after he stripped Prince von Starhemberg of all authority. Vice-Chancellor von Baaenfels is behind Schuschnigg.

both Germany and Austria. So sudden and unexpected was the announcement that even Hitler's man Friday in the Austrian government, Interior Minister Arthur Seyss-Inquart, did not know about it.

This was the first time since 1934, when the Nazis murdered Chancellor Engelbert Dollfuss, that the people of Austria had had a chance to express themselves. After the Dollfuss murder, the country had sat on the edge of the sword of civil war, and until Schuschnigg's proclamation no one had dared dream of the possibility of any free election at any time. The Chancellor had ruled with the iron fist of dictatorship over a country that was roughly estimated to be 40 per cent Nazi, 40 per cent Socialist, and 20 per cent pro-Government.

Schuschnigg and Hitler had met at Berchtesgaden, and after that stormy meeting the Austrian chancellor had hastened to make friends with the Socialists. Now he had staked his last card on this proclamation. But he was well

1938

aware that even if he won he would gain only a breathing space, perhaps a few months. In the long run, nothing would stop the Nazi's take-over of Austria except a third world power. What Schuschnigg was attempting to do that long, long dead spring of 1938 was appeal to the conscience of Europe, when the time came for it to witness the shotgun wedding of the two German peoples, which was the fanatical desire of the Austrian-born fuehrer of the Third Reich.

While the world waited for that fateful Sunday, England warned Germany that any move in Austria would be regarded as a "hostile act." This information was relayed to German Minister Joachim von Ribbentrop, the former champagne salesman, by England's foreign secretary, Viscount Halifax. Von Ribbentrop hastened to Berlin with the note, which Hitler ignored. In England there were wild demonstrations against the Germans; crowds had hooted and jeered at the dapper Von Ribbentrop as he hurried into the Foreign Office for his hasty farewell. Lord Halifax refused to accept a note from Germany in which the Third Reich demanded that English newspapers refrain from their anti-German remarks.

Even as the world powers were hand-

Hitler in Hofburg Square, Vienna, shouting that Austria and Germany "are one—once and forever indivisible."

ing out notes and making pious statements, Hitler acted. On March 12, in a nationwide manifesto, Der Fuehrer announced that his troops had moved into Austria and rescued the state from "brutal oppression." Hitler himself appeared in Linz, proclaiming, "My mission is now fulfilled."

An ultimatum was given the chancellor: to resign or to expect immediate bombardment of Austrian frontier towns by the German air force. If he did not resign and abandon his plebiscite, the authorities would not guarantee his safety or that of his wife and children.

Sadly Schuschnigg resigned, and Austria collapsed under what can only be viewed as almost unbelievably gangster-like threats.

No Caesar was ever accorded the welcome Hitler received the day he arrived in Linz. Children showered his car with flowers as the crowd roared, "Heil Deutschland," and four hundred army bombers roared overhead. Before and after his car came his general staff and the rumbling tanks. From the balcony of the Linz city hall Hitler announced to the world that a plebiscite on the question of merging Austria and Germany would be held under the Nazi rule.

In an interview two days later with Ward Price of the London *Daily Mail,* Hitler said he had been forced to intervene after Schuschnigg's proclamation, which had "betrayed" him. "What harm have we done to any foreign power?" he asked. "French and British protests over my action have no more sense than if Germany protested about relations between England and Eire."

The plebiscite itself was typical of the Third Reich in the thirties. All na-

tional votes taken under the Nazi rule were opened with the announcement that there was no practical reason for them. In the words of Propaganda Minister Goebbels, they were held only to "show the doubting world."

A Third Reich vote had nothing to do with settling an issue. As in the case of Austria, it was taken after the issue had been settled. According to Goebbels, any referendum in Germany was simply a "spiritual exercise." The Nazis saw their plebiscites as demonstrations of national solidarity in which a wholly united people took the opportunity to show a hostile world how much they loved and supported Hitler.

From this viewpoint, naturally the campaign before any plebiscite was more imoprtant than the vote itself. The Nazis, always superb in putting on a dramatic show, had Hitler in Innsbruck, Linz, Graz, and Salzburg. The final rally in Vienna the night before the vote, April 10, was an awe-inspiring demonstration of fanaticism, mob hysteria, and violent hate. Goebbels, who could always hold a crowd spellbound, followed the usual route. The villain of all their speeches was the Versailles powers, who had "opposed the thousand-year-old desire of the German people for unity."

In Austria the secret police quietly and efficiently took over the press and crushed the small, hard core of resistance. Nazis who had been in Austria since the bungled coup of 1934 had the names of their foes all ready for the Gestapo. Men who had spoken out against the Nazis disappeared or were found murdered in alleys and in fields.

The average Austrian worker was wooed as he had never been before. Picked delegations of Austrians were

transported to Germany, where they were cheered and feted at every step. Thousands of photographs, newspaper articles, and radio broadcasts carried the news back to Austria. In Germany, Goebbels put on a grand show with Hitler reviewing Austrian troops.

More important was the work of the Nazi "Strength Through Joy" organizations. They brought more than 25,000 Austrian workers to Germany, expense-free, and took thousands of them on tours on luxurious German liners. Berlin girls draped flowers about the shoulders of the Austrian workers when they arrived. German workers were also sent to Austria. And winter-relief charity funds were sent to Vienna, auxiliary trains fed free meals to the poor, and army kitchens distributed meals to the working quarters in the name of Adolf Hitler. Even Goebbels gave 30,000 marks to save the struggling Vienna theatre.

In brief, the Nazis pulled out all stops to seduce the people of Austria with wine, women, food, money, and phoney promises—to show the world how everyone loved them.

It was no surprise to the world when Hitler proudly announced, on the night of April 10, that the greatest turnout of voters in Austrian history had given him the largest majority of his career. More than 50,000,000 men and women had marched to the polls, or been carried there, or had the ballot box taken to them. Of these, 48,799,269 had voted "yes," in approval of Germany's annexation of Austria. (Of course no Jews had been allowed to vote.)

Hitler now had Austria in his pocket. Mussolini was forced to face the fact that Nazi troops would soon be stationed at the Brenner Pass, severely restricting his independence. Il Duce could no longer dream of antagonizing Hitler, but would have to be dependent on him. The day after the Austrian vote was the first of Mussolini's long term as a prisoner of the head keeper, Adolf Hitler.

Hitler's victory also meant that he now could become boss of the Balkans and their great supply of raw material, such as the oil from Romania. But it meant, above all, that once more it was unnecessary for Nazi Germany actually to employ the mighty weapon of her new army. She needed only to threaten to use it in order to get what its commander, Adolf Hitler, wanted.

Czechoslovakia was next on his list.

The Man Who Thought He Was the Law

"I AM THE LAW."

This phrase would haunt Mayor Frank Hague for most of his late years and return again and again to sit on the footboard of his bed at night and leer at him. It became the rallying cry of all liberals and unionists across the nation, when the powerful Democratic boss of Jersey City opened war on the CIO—in its attempt to "invade our town," as Hague put it.

Hague, a ruthless political tyrant, had ruled Jersey City and New Jersey politics for years. In his sharply creased black suit, topped off by a high celluloid collar, he looked like an old-fashioned bartender dressed for Sunday services. He had helped elect FDR, and in return had received an enormous amount of federal patronage, which welded together his unbeatable machine.

In the winter of 1938, the CIO decided to test Hague and his machine. When they entered Jersey City to unionize the city's workers, Hague turned his police force on the union agents and "deported" them.

He followed this action with a monster rally in which he described the CIO as communist-dominated. It was like a scene from *All the King's Men;* the armory was jammed with loyal city workers, whose jobs depended on whether or not they attended; bombs burst outside; mounted police, dressed in striking white cord, kept the overflow crowd orderly. Veterans' groups matched sternly into the armory, determined to keep the "Red foe" out of their crumbling, grimy city that was burdened with one of the highest tax rates in the nation. Bands in shining brass hats and khaki trousers bore placards which read, in effect, "Mayor, we're behind you in this fight to keep the Reds out of Jersey City." They paraded up and down among the wildly cheering crowd of seventy-five thousand. The political hacks made their pitiful, crawling speeches. They had been put into office by Hague; now they had to lick his boots.

More rallies were held. Hague even went on a nation-wide broadcast to warn the whole country "it had better wake up" and ban the "CIO Reds."

When the American Civil Liberties Union denounced the Jersey City mayor for the tyrant he was, Hague, pounding his desk in his rundown city hall, warned Morris Ernst, counsel to the group, not to come to Jersey City "or his friends [wouldn't] see him for a long time."

William J. Carney, CIO regional director for the state, angrily denied he was a communist or a left winger. He said: "I am a Roman Catholic and was an altar boy for nine years and attended the Ursuline Sisters school. How could I be a communist and be a Catholic?"

Carney and the CIO replied to Hague's rallies and police-state methods by filing in Federal Court an injunction in which the entire Jersey City situation was made the basis of a constitutional issue which would find its way to the United States Supreme Court. In essence, the CIO was asking the high courts if Hague or any city, town, or village official in this country had the right to restrict union activity under the guise of state's rights.

A historic trial was held before Federal Judge William Clark. Hague was the star witness; his "evidence" was based mostly on sensational "Red exposé" newspaper clippings and his own opinions. One of his suggestions was to exile the CIO heads to a concentration camp in Alaska.

The result was a sweeping order to Hague from the court not to interfere with the union. It was one of the CIO's greatest victories.

Hague's defeat by the union was the first of many troubles which finally toppled his political empire and sent him into oblivion. In the end he discovered that he was not the law, after all.

Mayor Frank Hague welcomes President Roosevelt and his son Elliott to Jersey City, ruled for years by the Hague machine.

WRONG WAY

THE NINE-YEAR-OLD, nine-hundred-dollar plane had been patched and repatched more times than a college freshman's runabout. Although it was capable of high speeds, it had no safety device and carried no radio and no beam-finders. But it did carry oil and gas. In fact, as some experts told its owner, freckled-faced Douglas Corrigan, it was really a flying gas tank and not a plane.

But Corrigan just grinned and went on building extra tanks. There was one directly in front of his single seat that made it impossible for him to see ahead. Another was jammed so tightly in his back he had to sit ramrod straight.

"It's like an alarm clock," he told his friends. "It won't let me sleep."

In 1937, Corrigan had asked the federal authorities for permission to fly the Atlantic. It was refused. "We don't approve of suicide," an agent told him after looking over his plane.

In July, 1938, Corrigan took off from California, heading for New York. He was carrying 320 gallons of gas and 16 gallons of oil. He made the flight nonstop in just 27 hours, but his arrival was unnoticed in the excitement of Howard Hughes' round-the-world takeoff. Uncommunicative and boyishly shy even at thirty-one, Corrigan went to sleep on a cot in a hangar. He rose at midnight, filled his gas tanks, and told Kenneth Behr, manager of Floyd Bennett Field, that he wanted to take off for the West Coast so that he could have the cool of the desert.

Behr, who had seen many historic takeoffs, refused to let Corrigan leave in the darkness with his heavy gas load.

The young flyer shrugged and went back to bed. "Call me when it gets light," he said.

Just before dawn, with flares lighting the 4,200-foot runway, Corrigan rumbled off. The plane went 3,200 feet before rising into the air. Preceding the takeoff he had torn some maps from an atlas and borrowed a Boy Scout compass. His food supply was two chocolate bars. His total finances—fifteen dollars. Behr noticed that instead of heading west, Corrigan's plane pointed for the Atlantic Ocean.

Twenty-eight hours and thirteen minutes later, the daredevil pilot stepped from his ship after it creaked to a stop at Baldonnel Airfield, Dublin, Ireland.

His first words to the startled airport personnel: "I've just flown from New York."

"My God, not in that thing!" an amazed official exclaimed.

"Isn't this Los Angeles?" Corrigan asked innocently.

"Los Angeles! This is Dublin!"

Corrigan grinned. "Well, what do you know! I must have flown the wrong way."

Corrigan's "wrong way" non-stop ocean hop captured the imagination of the world. When he returned to the United States in August after receiving tumultous receptions in Paris and London, he was greeted by one of the largest ticker-tape parades in New York's history. Still wearing the brown leather flying jacket, he rode up Broadway waving to the cheering thousands.

Lindbergh's flight was epic, but Corrigan's was magnificent. And all it cost him was $62.26, the price of his gas and oil.

Douglas Corrigan before he became "Wrong-Way" Corrigan.

Corrigan being greeted by Ambassador Joseph P. Kennedy.

John Warde on a hotel ledge 17 stories above Fifth Avenue.

John Warde's death dive.

A remarkable picture of Warde's body bouncing off the marquee of the Hotel Gotham, seconds before he crashed to the street.

Man on the Ledge

ON THURSDAY, July 26, 1938, the traffic at Fifth Avenue and Fifty-fifth Street was tied in a hopeless snarl when Patrolman Charles V. Glasco of the Traffic Division Summons Squad arrived.

"What's happening?" he asked a sergeant.

"Up there." The sergeant pointed.

Glasco looked up. On a ledge just below the roof of the Gotham Hotel stood a man, arms outstretched, his back to the wall. He was hatless and coatless.

"He's been up there for a half-hour," the sergeant said, mopping his face. "They better get him off soon or there won't be a car moving in this part of town."

"Maybe I can do something," Glasco said.

The sergeant shrugged. "Maybe you can, Glasco. Go up to Room 1714 and tell the lieutenant I sent you."

High above the sergeant and the cursing drivers of trucks, cars, and buses, John Warde, twenty-six, a slender, good-looking young man with curly black hair, stared down. Two years before, he had tried to commit suicide and had been sent to Central Islip Mental Hospital on Long Island. Shortly before Patrolman Glasco appeared, John had told his married sister, Katherine, "I'm going out the window," and before she could stop him had stepped out on the ledge, just eighteen inches wide and 160 feet above the sidewalk.

Warde had told the first policeman who leaned out of the window, "I'll jump if you come near me."

The structure of the building made it impossible for the emergency squad to use any of its orthodox methods. All they could do was wait out John Warde.

Patrolman Glasco, before entering the room, borrowed a waiter's white coat. Getting the harassed lieutenant's permission, he tried his luck in persuading Warde to come in. With a noose around one leg he sat on the window ledge for most of the afternoon, talking to young Warde about everything from baseball to poetry, trying to get close enough to grab him.

Below, the crowd on the ground had grown to thousands. Radio networks had set up shop on the street or in offices around the Gotham Hotel, and before three o'clock the entire nation listened breathlessly as announcers reported every move of the dark-haired young man on the ledge.

Patrolman Glasco continued to talk to Warde as the night dragged on. He quit his post to make way for a boyhood friend of Warde's when suddenly there was a wave of sound from the crowds below. Warde had jumped. The body whirled end over end, struck the hotel marquee and landed in the street. Warde was dead before he hit the sidewalk.

243

Peace in Our Time

THE STALKING of the victim had begun many months before, but the actual rape of Czechoslovakia was accomplished at teatime in Hitler's Berchtesgaden, with the help of England's Prime Minister Neville Chamberlain and Premier Edouard Daladier of France.

In April, Konrad Henlein, leader of the Sudeten Nazis, declared in a speech that Czechoslovakian foreign policy had to be revised because it had led the country "into the ranks of Germany's enemies." All that summer the German press kept in high gear a campaign against the Czechs, speaking of "intolerable provocations." In midsummer Britain and France rejected Germany's proposal of a four-power settlement of the Sudeten problem. But in early September the National Socialist Party opened its meeting in Nuremberg with a week of incredibly inflammatory speeches, Teutonic ceremonies, and a mock war that revealed to the world some of Germany's latest war machines. It was climaxed by Hitler's beating the war drums in a violent anti-Czech address.

Chamberlain asked Hitler for a meeting and the Nazi head graciously granted an audience: the British mountain

Chamberlain's famous night visit to Hitler at the Hotel Dreesen, Godesberg, in September, 1938.

Here are the principal conferees in the historic Munich conference: (left to right) Prime Minister Neville Chamberlain of England; Edouard Daladier, Premier of France; Adolf Hitler, Chancellor of Germany; Benito Mussolini, Il Duce of Italy; and Count Ciano, the latter's son-in-law.

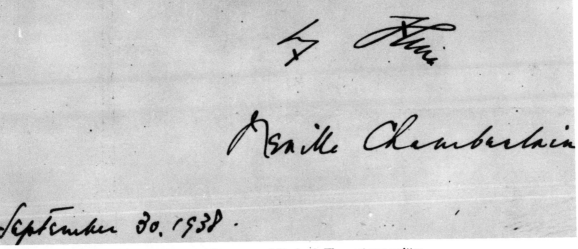

We, the German Führer and Chancellor and the British Prime Minister, have had a further meeting today and are agreed in recognising that the question of Anglo-German relations is of the first importance for the two countries and for Europe.

We regard the agreement signed last night and the Anglo-German Naval Agreement as symbolic of the desire of our two peoples never to go to war with one another again.

We are resolved that the method of consultation shall be the method adopted to deal with any other questions that may concern our two countries, and we are determined to continue our efforts to remove possible sources of difference and thus to contribute to assure the peace of Europe.

September 30, 1938.

The famous pact of nonaggression between Germany and England. The pact was written on notepaper of the British Consulate in Munich.

would come to the Nazi Mahomet. The supreme commander of the world's greatest army and the prime minister of the world's greatest empire were to stand face to face in the tiny village to decide the fate of all Europe. In Berlin, Goebbel's vast propaganda machine was pouring out stories of "Czech outrages." A hundred miles away from the idyllic Alpine mountain retreat, arrogant Sudeten Germans and sullen Czechs were at rifle point, looting and burning each other's farms. Embassies and state departments all over the world were buzzing with the latest speculations about the meeting, and from the protection of the German borders Konrad Henlein was now issuing proclamation after proclamation declaring that Germany must annex the Sudetenland in Czechoslovakia.

The gaunt, trusting old man with the black umbrella was whisked between a guard of steel-helmeted giants to Hitler's car and driven to the mountaintop villa.

"How swiftly the car climbs," the tragic appeaser murmured to Foreign Minister Von Ribbentrop as they sped up the long, twisting road.

Tea was served in Hitler's villa. The historic meeting lasted for two hours and thirty-five minutes. That evening Prime Minister Chamberlain, tired but smiling, retired to his suite. He would return to London the next day to consult with the British cabinet, the terse press announcement said.

Chamberlain did return to London and met with his cabinet; he also met with Daladier. They agreed to put pressure on Czechoslovakia to give in to Hitler's demands, and a few days later, the Czech cabinet accepted the ultimatum.

On September 22, Chamberlain flew

Chamberlain returns with the "peace" pact September 30, 1938.

to Godesberg to inform Hitler of the successful outcome of his efforts, but Hitler at once increased his demands on the Czechs. Chamberlain, weary and heartsick, agreed to submit the new terms to them. But the Czech government notified London and Paris it could not accept Hitler's proposals. On September 28, Chamberlain reported to the House of Commons on the Czech situation. His speech was interrupted by a message from Hitler asking him to come to Munich at once.

Next day in Munich, Hitler met with Mussolini, Chamberlain, and Daladier, no Czech being permitted to be present. In a conference lasting some twelve hours, they agreed to give Hitler all he demanded. Czechoslovakia had been dismembered.

That afternoon Chamberlain arrived home to receive a roaring welcome from hundreds of thousands of peace-loving Britons. When his American Lockheed arrived at Heston Airport, the prime minister read the text of his agreement with Hitler, and said: "This is the second time in our history that

there has come back from Germany to Downing Street peace with honor. I believe it is peace in our time."

Despite the drenching rain, thousands and thousands packed the pavements around Buckingham Palace long before the prime minister drove up, accompanied by his wife. While the throngs waited patiently the dark clouds which had hung over the city broke, letting the sun pierce through like a great spear of golden light.

"It was the sign of hope," the London *Times* said solemnly.

In Prague that night, the crowds gathered quickly. By twilight there were more than 100,000 violently shouting men, women, and children. The air quivered with their cries of "Long live the army," "Down with Chamberlain," "Down with Hitler," "Long live Sirovy."

"Who is Sirovy?" a correspondent asked.

"The one-eyed inspector of the army," was the answer.

"In the fifteenth century the Czechs had a one-eyed king who never lost a battle. He lost his other eye but went on

fighting blind. He is a Czech legend, for even blind he never lost a battle. Sirovy was a legionnaire. He made the march to Vladivostok. With his one eye he, in the tradition of the one-eyed king, is the symbol of national survival . . . he is our hope. . . ."

But not even Sirovy could help the Czechs. The restless crowd listened to the clear, calm voice of the London announcer telling how France and England had sacrificed Czechoslovakia to Hitler. The government announcement added:

"It is not cowardice which has moved our leaders to their decision, a decision which has pierced all of our hearts. Even the bravest of men must retreat before an avalanche. God knows that it often requires more courage to live than commit suicide. . . ."

The great throng continued to shout slogans and carry army officers on their shoulders, but when Sirovy himself finally appeared and begged them to go home and trust their government, reason undermined passion. The crowd thinned; before dawn there was no one left—only papers and cigarette ends blowing about in the September wind.

Hitler drives through a victory arch in Asch, Czechoslovakia, in the fall of 1938.

GERMAN FEVER

EMOTIONAL fever ran very high in Germany in 1938. Hatred, bitterness, arrogance, and ruthless ambition marked the behavior not only of the Nazi leaders but also of the German people. Even the youngsters took pleasure in the famous book-burnings. Because of the slaying of Ernst vom Rath in Paris, attributed to a Jewish youth, German rioters wreaked terrible vengeance on the Jews and on the remaining Jewish stores in German cities.

Colonel Charles Lindbergh attending a Lilienthal Society meeting in Berlin in 1938.

A street scene in Berlin in 1938 after anti-Jewish demonstrations resulting from the slaying of Ernst vom Rath.

Hitler's youthful followers burning the books in Salzburg, Austria, April 30, 1938.

This picture of the Kennedy family was found without precise identification. President John F. Kennedy, who is not in the picture, identified the members of his family (reading around the table) as: Ambassador Kennedy, (at his left) Bobby, Patricia, Jean, Miss Dunn (a governess), Mrs. Kennedy, Kathleen, Rosemary, and Teddy. Those not present were Joe, Jr., Jack, and Eunice.

AMBASSADOR
and
FAMILY

JOSEPH P. KENNEDY, appointed by Franklin D. Roosevelt in 1937 as American ambassador to the Court of St. James, brought to England probably the largest family in American embassy history. They made friends wherever they went, and the adult members of the family created quite a stir in English social circles. Quite possibly, two of the ambassador's sons gained some experience in foreign relations.

Dr. Salomon's candid-camera shot of Jack Kennedy and his brother, Joseph, Jr., who died in World War II.

Mrs. Joseph Kennedy with her daughters and two of her sons at the coming-out party of Eunice Kennedy in London.

A candid camera shot of John F. Kennedy in London in 1938-39.

Highlights and Sidelights: 1938

IN SPAIN, Barcelona underwent a massive bombardment by Rebel planes. . . . In Washington, the Small Business Men's Conference at the White House gave FDR twenty-two proposals for repeal or modification of many New Deal measures already enacted and the rejection of others now being considered. . . . William Green, president of the American Federation of Labor, "reluctantly" resigned from the Mine Workers after more than forty-six years of membership. It was the first big break between Green and John L. Lewis. . . . Richard Whitney, former head of the New York Stock Exchange, was sentenced to Sing Sing on charges of grand larceny. . . . Thousands of men and women enrolled in England's newly formed anti-air-raid corps. . . . Orson Welles created a sensational panic by broadcasting on radio a play about a mythical invasion of the U.S. by Martians. Many listeners thought they were hearing a true news bulletin. Some called police or military posts. Some gathered a few possessions and fled from their homes. It took considerable explaining to set the matter straight.

. . . The steamship *Acadia* struck the excursion boat *Mandalay* in New York's Lower Bay. After the 247 passengers climbed aboard the steamer, the excursion boat broke in two and sank. . . . Joe Louis, a silent, stalking fighting-machine, knocked out Max Schmeling in the first few seconds of a scheduled fifteen-round championship bout. . . . More than 1,800 Civil War veterans met at Gettysburg seventy-five years after the great battle. . . . Howard Hughes, with a crew of four, flew around the top of the world, establishing a new world record. He was given the Harmon Trophy. . . . Father Divine and 2,000 of his flock took over "Krum

The Wind from Hell: The 1938 Hurricane

ONE OF THE worst hurricane disasters in history hit the northeast coast on September 21, 1938. It pounced on Long Island, Connecticut, Massachusetts, Rhode Island, New Hampshire, and Vermont with unprecedented fury (wind-velocities were estimated as high as 200 miles an hour). This is some of the damage done by the killer-hurricane (they didn't give hurricanes girls' names in those days):

488 dead.

100 missing.

1,745 injured.

100,000 homes lost.

2,605 boats destroyed.

Deep permanent channels carved out of Fire Island.

Clam and oyster beds almost all ruined.

⅔ of Vermont sugar maples lost. ½ of New Hampshire's stand of pine destroyed.

63,000 sheltered by the Red Cross.

Countless trees, telegraph poles, gardens, shrubs, lawns washed away.

Many areas flooded with swirling water up to 25 feet deep.

"It was a wind from hell, that's what it was," a Connecticut man cried as he dug in the ruins of what had been his home, for the remains of his wife and three children.

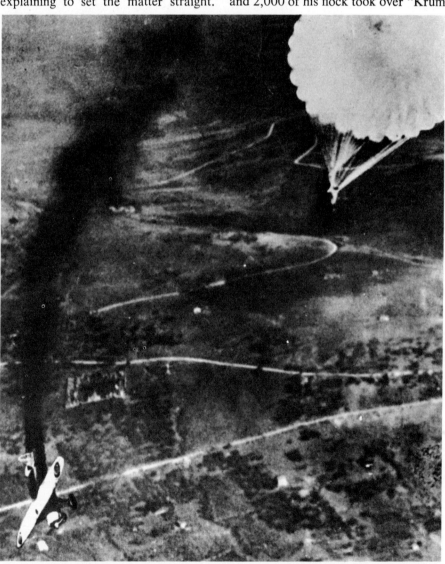

A Spanish Loyalist flyer floating earthward while his plane plunges to earth.

Joe Louis slaughters Max Schmeling in their famous re-match.

Elbow" on the west shore of the Hudson River, directly across from President Roosevelt's Hyde Park estate. . . . Patrick Cardinal Hayes, Roman Catholic Archbishop of New York and internationally known churchman, died in a summer cottage near Monticello, New York. He was in his seventy-first year. . . . In China, Japanese troops entered Canton and a few days later occupied Hankow. . . . Kemal Atatürk, president of Turkey, died at fifty-eight of a liver ailment. He had survived thirteen wounds received in battle and seven assassination attempts. . . . Anti-Jewish violence was at an all-time peak throughout Germany, with Jews being beaten, their homes wrecked, and synagogues burned and destroyed. In

Munich all Jews were ordered to leave the city, and a horrified world led by the United States protested to Adolf Hitler, who ignored them. . . . There was trouble in Palestine, too. The Jews were trying to establish a homeland there, but Arab terrorists took possession of a section of Jerusalem and there were frequent disturbances. The British troops guarding Palestine tried to maintain control. . . . The sharecropper problem reached a crisis, particularly in Missouri, where many such families were evicted by landlords. The Farm Security Administration's rehabilitation program did much to improve the sharecropper's lot. . . . In Vatican City, Mother Frances Cabrini was canonized. She was the first American citizen to be

so honored. . . . In Pittsburgh, John L. Lewis was elected first president of the newly formed Congress of Industrial Organizations. . . . The state of Alabama, in a surprise move, dropped charges of rape against six of the nine Scottsboro defendants. . . . William Buckner, a handsome young man-about-town, was jailed by the government on charges of manipulating Philippine railroad bonds, causing a loss of more than a million dollars to the public. During his sensational trial, society and Hollywood beauties testified how the dashing confidence man entertained congressmen, senators, and judges. . . . In New York, John Harlan Amen, appointed special prosecutor to investigate law enforcement agencies, exposed extensive corruption among officials. ... The Yankees won the World Series, beating the Chicago Cubs 4-0. ... This year death stilled the great trumpeting voice of Thomas Wolfe. It was now obvious that no mention of literature in the thirties could be complete without including Wolfe, whose huge works were alternately described as rich in poetry, powerful in description, lyrical in anger or vastly over-written, inchoate, and over-dramatized. ... His novels appeared at a time when members of the hard-boiled, naturalistic school of writing, led by John O'Hara and James M. Cain, were pruning their literary style, and other young writers were vainly trying to imitate Hemingway's lean prose and simplicity of expression. ... Both the audience and the critics at the opening performance of *Leave It to Me* stood and cheered a girl named Mary Martin, who stopped the show with her rendition of "My Heart Belongs to Daddy." Even veterans like Sophie Tucker, Victor Moore, and William Gaxton were forgotten when Mary came on stage. ... Robert Sherwood's *Abe Lincoln in Illinois,* hailed this year as a modern classic, would bring him his second Pulitzer prize for drama, in 1939. ... Milton Berle continued to star in radio, and a young announcer named Mel Allen began to attract attention. ...

Sharecroppers on the move on U.S. Highway #61 south of Hayti, Mo. More than 1,000 men, women, and children huddled over camp-fires this bitter January night.

By now Ernest Hemingway, the man and the legend too, began to emerge. He followed the Loyalist troops in Spain, and even before 1938 most Americans, even those who weren't interested in books, were familiar with the brawling, hard-drinking novelist. The legend of his prowess with his fists had not been hurt by his brawl (in the summer of 1937) with the noted editor and writer, Max Eastman. Hemingway, supposedly angry over something Eastman had written, tore some hair from Eastman's chest. Like many Hemingway legends, this story was slightly exaggerated. A few hours after it appeared on page one of all major metropolitan newspapers, this writer found Ernie in an East Side bar, and until the early hours of the morning was held fascinated by the story of the fight, and how to hunt lions in Africa, why I should leave the newspaper business to write, how to out-curse an editor, and why fine bourbon should never be mixed with water or ice. That helped me to understand the Hemingway legend. ... In another part of the literary world, space flight was virtually controlled by a small group of young writers of sci-

British troops in Jerusalem on guard against Arab terrorists.

Father Divine dines with his followers in his Harlem "heaven."

Father Divine leads his "angels" to their estate at Krum Elbow, N. Y., located directly across the Hudson River from President Roosevelt's Hyde Park estate.

Milton Berle.

Max Eastman.

Mel Allen.

(Left to right) Elmer Rice, Raymond Massey, and Robert Sherwood discuss Abe Lincoln in Illinois.

Orson Welles, whose Martian broadcast alarmed the nation.

A smiling young girl from Texas made Broadway history in 1938 when she stepped out on stage in Leave it to Me and sang "My Heart Belongs to Daddy." Before the song was finished she had the hearts of the audience in her hand. The chorus boy standing at Miss Martin's right has also come a long way since that night. His name is Gene Kelly. This is one of the Van Damm photos.

Red Rolfe scoring the second Yankee run in the third inning of the 1939 Series. Joe Di Maggio is on the left.

John O'Hara

ence fiction. Although their works were labeled "escapism," it is amazing today to turn back the yellowing pages and read a story built around a test that released a "nuclear ball" and when "power siphons" failed to reduce it, a huge "nuclear blast" resulted. Or a novel woven around U.S. development of atomic weapons which were used to end a monstrous world war. The readership of these novels and magazines was a small but faithful group. They were delighted by the tales of rocket ships, expeditions to the moon, propulsion belt flights, and small sets with screens on which you could see shows and movies and which also could be used to watch an enemy's movements from afar.

John Harlan Amen, who led the famous investigation of crime and corruption in Kings County in the late thirties. With him is J. Edgar Hoover. Amen later assisted at the Nuremberg trials.

The Man Behind the Mob

Lloyd Paul Stryker, the tall, dignified attorney with the white crew-cut and the booming voice, stood up in the high-ceilinged courtroom in New York's Criminal Courts Building and announced in a firm voice: "The defense rests."

A gasp went up from the packed courtroom. Many spectators rose to their feet to stare at Stryker and his client with open-mouthed surprise. Their amazement was caused chiefly by James J. Hines's failure to take the witness chair and repudiate in his own words the charge made by District Attorney Thomas E. Dewey that he had

Jimmy Hines and his attorney Lloyd Paul Stryker.

been the chief guardian angel of the Dutch Schultz policy mob and had protected its members from interference by the police and the courts.

A few minutes later Dewey rested the State's case, thus bringing to an abrupt close the testimony in one of the sensational trials of the decade.

A previous trial had ended the preceding year when Supreme Court Justice Ferdinand Pecora ordered a mistrial on the grounds that a question Dewey had asked a witness was prejudicial.

Huge crowds had packed the courtroom and the corridors during the six weeks of the second trial, eager to listen to the witnesses describe how the man who once had been one of the most powerful political figures in the county had accepted weekly sums of from $500 to $2,000 over a long period for his services in getting cases against Schultz's mobsters dismissed in magistrate's court, removing conscientious police-

men from the mob's scene of operation, and protecting the mobster's twenty-million-dollar policy racket in other matters. Former Tammany Hall leader John F. Curry had testified for Dewey that Hines had sent him requests for the transfer of patrolmen and that these requests were always favorably acted upon in the Police Commissioner's office.

Dewey also tried to show how former District Attorney William Dodge had been hand-picked by Hines and how Schultz had contributed to his campaign. For three days the former prosecutor had denied that he had been

dominated by Hines. One of the dramatic moments of the trial came when Dodge shouted his denials to the jury.

Another dramatic moment came when the former racket lawyer, Dixie Davis, took the stand and told about the inside workings of Schultz's underworld empire.

In summing up, Stryker put on one of the most emotional performances ever seen in a courtroom. In contrast, Dewey was cold and factual as he ticked off the evidence, page by page, witness by witness. As he went over the testimony about the frequent meetings between Hines and Schultz, he turned and leveled a finger at Hines. "These meetings announced to the world that the greatest gangster of his

Racket-buster Thomas E. Dewey, who broke the back of New York's organized underworld.

day was the pal and intimate of a powerful politician who made it possible for him to exist and operate in New York State."

Hines listened to Dewey's relentless attack with a wooden, expressionless face. Early in the day he had sent his wife away with these words: "Go home, Go to a matinee. Go anywhere but don't stay here. You've stood enough."

Hines was found guilty and sent to prison. The case further enhanced Dewey's fame as the racket-buster of the decade and paved his way to the governorship and later to the Republican nomination for President.

One wonders what would have hap-

Former District Attorney Dodge.

pened to the career of the former Michigan choir-singer had there been no Jimmy Hines, no Luciano, Dutch Schultz, or Dixie Davis in his day. But there had been, and for Tom Dewey it was the old cliché of being the right man at the right time in the right place.

THAT WONDERFUL, WONDERFUL FAIR

The opening day of the World's Fair. In the center is Paul Manship's sculptured sundial, "Time and the Fate of Man." Beyond is James Earle Fraser's giant statue of George Washington.

THE NEW YORK World's Fair of 1939, designed as an exposition of man's finest achievements and an illustration of how these might be used in the World of Tomorrow, became a reality on a beautiful May morning when President Roosevelt declared the fair opened to all mankind.

As he stood in the Court of Peace, FDR's rolling voice carried over a chain of loudspeakers, echoed and re-echoed among the tall structures of the vast exhibit area on Flushing Meadow. Behind him towered stone figures of "Peace" and "Unity." Before him were the builders of the fair and those who had come to see this evidence of America's faith in the future. Also attending the ceremony were numerous high government officials, members of FDR's cabinet, the Supreme Court, Congress, and representatives from every state in the union.

The dedication was preceded by a parade of twenty thousand from the Trylon and Perisphere down Constitution Mall and into the Court of Peace. It was a colorful parade, with each foreign delegation dressed in native costume.

Long before the official ceremony, huge crowds had lined up at the gates. So great was the press of almost a million persons that the gates were opened far in advance of the scheduled time.

Once inside, the visitors were caught up in the sweeping panorama of the fair and its twenty-five miles of broad walks. Spread out around them were

the visible and audible manifestations of the finest that had been achieved in every form of human endeavor, arranged to show the forces and ideas at work in the world of 1939. One designer of the fair explained, "It is the intent of the fair to make it say to each visitor: 'No superman is going to build the world of tomorrow for you. You

Billy Rose's Aquacade.

257

must build it yourself. Here are the tools with which it is to be built.' "

That thought was perhaps expressed best in the central figures of the fair, the great white Perisphere and its towering companion, the 700-foot Trylon. From the top of the 200-foot ball the visitor looked down upon Democracity, a model city of the future. Dominating the Court of Peace was the United States Government exhibit, erected at the cost of 3.5 million dollars.

The fairground covered 1,216½ acres, divided into sections devoted to amusement, communications, business systems, community interests, food, government, production, distribution, and transportation. The main exhibit covered 390 acres; within that area were 1,500 exhibits representing every major industry on earth. Almost every nation of the world had its exhibit. Saddest of these was that of Czechoslovakia, prepared for the fair before the German take-over, and now representing all that was left of the country's freedom.

The first night was topped off by what was then considered a fantastic science-fiction triumph. Shortly after darkness had fallen, the fairground, especially the Lagoon of Nations, was lighted with fire, water, light, and color, making an impressive display of the streamlined architecture and varied colors of the fair buildings. The demonstration was followed by an explanation by Dr. Einstein, who described how cosmic rays "captured" by scientists at Hayden Planetarium had been transmitted by wire to the Theme Center of the fair and used as electrical impulses to create a series of ten flashes in the Trylon and ten units of sound in the Perisphere, which were seen and heard within a radius of twenty miles. The cosmic rays lighted bulbs in the Trylon equivalent to more than a million lamps, powerful enough to turn night into day. With the final flash, trees, shrubbery, flower beds, and buildings glowed with light from the new capillary mercury vapor tube and the fluorescent tube.

The most popular ride in the fair, figures showed at the end of its first season, was the parachute jump. More than 550,000 persons paid to take the 250-foot drop. The best-paying show in the amusement area was Billy Rose's *Aquacade,* staged in the huge New York State Amphitheatre. Other hit shows of the amusement area were Frank Buck's *Jungleland,* The Swing Mardi Gras

The famous World's Fair Parachute Jump. Today it's at Coney Island.

Casino, Old New York, and numerous restaurants. Almost every national exhibit had its own restaurant featuring the national cuisine.

General Motors Futurama, designed by Norman Bel Geddes, was the most popular industrial show at the fair; more than 5,800,000 visitors took the ride "Across the America of 1960." It was estimated that 8,000,000 saw the Rail-roads Exhibit. A total of 32,786,521 people visited the fair between May 31 and October 31.

"We will be here for a long time," said a delighted Grover Whalen, president of the fair, at the end of the first season.

His boast was lost in the rumble of tanks and the screaming of the Stukas over Poland.

An aerial view of the 1939 World's Fair.

259

The Devil's Alliance

WITH meticulous punctuality, the two huge Focke-Wulf Condor planes landed at the Moscow airdrome at noon, August 23, 1939. For the first time the swastika was publicly displayed there; five banners hung in the sticky heat from the front of the airdrome building. When the door of one plane opened and the red-carpeted steps were put into place, the dapper, arrogant German foreign minister Joachim von Ribbentrop, stepped to the doorway, surveyed for a moment the waiting officials and military, naval, and air attachés, then started down the steps.

The German Embassy staff lined up like troops at parade. As each was presented to Von Ribbentrop, he sprang to attention and clicked his heels, gave the Nazi salute, shook hands, and concluded with more saluting and heel-clicking.

From the airdrome the party drove to the city through streets where police in white summer jackets were stationed every ten paces. Soon Von Ribbentrop, accompanied by the German ambassador Count Friedrich Werner von der Schulenburg, was passing through the gates of the Kremlin, and within three

hours the terms of a nonagression pact had been agreed upon. Within a few more hours, the pact that was supposed to bind Germany and Russia for ten years was signed. For Von Ribbentrop it was the peak of his career; he had prevented —as he thought—the conclusion of a three-power pact of mutual assistance between Russia, France, and Great Britain, which would have blocked completely Germany's dreams of European hegemony. Von Ribbentrop boasted that the world must recognize Germany knew how to do the right thing toward Russia, which Prime Minister Chamberlain had steadfastly refused to do.

During that summer the whole world was conscious of what Churchill later called the Gathering Storm, yet everyone wanted peace and tried to believe it would continue.

Was that why Russia signed the pact that summer's day twenty-odd years ago? Ivan Mihailovich Maisky, now in retirement but then Russian ambassador to the Court of St. James, revealed more than two decades later in a Moscow magazine that the pact was signed because he had told his government he

Winston Churchill, then First Lord of the Admiralty.

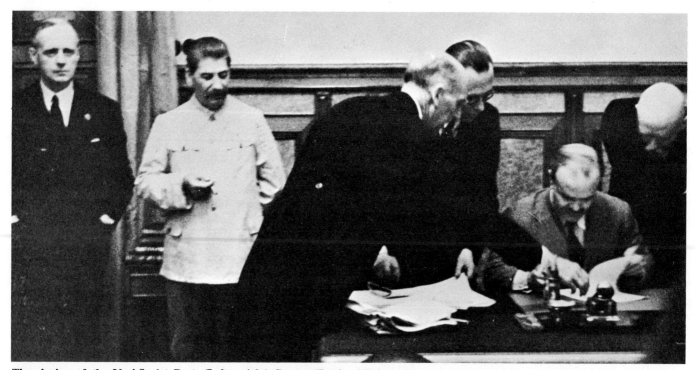

The signing of the Nazi-Soviet Pact. (Left to right) German Foreign Minister, Joachim von Ribbentrop; Josef Stalin; Undersecretary of State Friedrich Gaus; Counselor of the German Embassy in Moscow, Gustav Hilger; Molotov, and German Ambassador Count von der Schulenberg.

believed Prime Minister Neville Chamberlain actively wanted war—a war between Germany and Russia with Britain abstaining and profiting from the outcome. He had first believed that Hitler's onrush to world war could be stopped "by a formidable coalition of states, particularly by a concert of France, Russia, and Great Britain." However, as the summer dragged by, he became convinced Chamberlain would not cooperate to that end.

It would be monstrously cynical to discount Maisky's genuine effort for peace based on the three-power coalition, yet it would also be monstrously naïve to accept the hero-and-villain terms in which Maisky viewed the situation some twenty years later. In his description of that historic drama, the dark-mustached Chamberlain and French Premier Daladier were the villains, supported by their entourage of menacing English aristocrats. At no time, Maisky wrote, did Chamberlain want a triple alliance: "It would be difficult to find in the annals of diplomatic history another instance of duplicity and hypocrisy like the conduct of Chamberlain and Daladier in the tripartite negotiations of 1939."

Maisky admits in his memoirs that there were Englishmen who did view his fight for peace favorably. He revealed that on May 18 he had received a call from Churchill—then not in office —who said he intended to speak in Commons the next day on the subject of foreign policy, and wanted to know what the Soviet proposals were that Chamberlain would not accept. Maisky said he gave Churchill the information "and he listened very attentively."

The following day Churchill made a speech in support of the alliance. He said: "It is said, 'Can you trust the Russian Soviet government?' I suppose in Moscow they say: 'Can you trust Chamberlain?' "

The diplomatic talks dragged on, and their very slowness, Maisky insists, aroused his suspicion. Chamberlain himself, as one of his biographers states, was taking the view that the Russians "are chiefly concerned to see the capitalist powers tear each other to pieces whilst they stay out themselves."

When Lord Halifax, the Foreign Secretary, was unwilling to go to Moscow to take part in negotiations on collective security, Anthony Eden, a former Foreign Secretary, volunteered his services but was turned down by

Historic background. In 1935 Hitler played host to prominent Britishers and established friendly relations. He is shown here with Anthony Eden (left) and Sir John Simon.

the Chamberlain government. Maisky, in a footnote, claimed that later, during the war, Eden told him about his offer to fly to Moscow.

That July, Halifax summoned Maisky to his office and informed him military talks would begin immediately. Maisky then approached Arthur Greenwood of the Labour Party, with whom he was friendly, and asked him to let his government know unofficially that it was Russia's hope the British delegation for the military talks would be headed by a very prominent military man, preferably General Gort, chief of the British General Staff.

Instead, the delegation was headed

Lord Halifax.

But early in 1938 Eden, disagreeing with Chamberlain over appeasing Mussolini, resigned as Foreign Secretary. Sir John Simon supported the Government's stand.

by Admiral Sir Reginald Plunkett-Ernle-Erle-Drax, who went to Russia not by plane but by boat. According to Maisky, "Five days were wasted on the trip when every hour and every minute counted."

The talks later broke down over the question of the right of Russian troops to enter Poland and Romania.

The Russian-German pact followed.

Maisky, in his memoirs, is very defensive about the pact. His government, he points out, had no illusions about the Germans and they expected that sooner or later German Panzer divisions would be rumbling over Russian soil and Hitler's Stukas would be bombing Russian cities. But he says, "The pact gave us nearly two more years of peace and preparation."

There are holes in Maisky's story of the pact. A glaring omission is his failure to comment on the dismissal of Maxim Litvinov, a Jew, as Foreign Commissar, thus clearing away one obstacle to negotiations with Hitler. This was early in May. Neither does the veteran Communist touch on what Churchill has pointed out in his memoirs, that while the Drax mission was in Moscow, the Soviets agreed to give permission for a German negotiator to come to Moscow. Maisky's version, of course, is the Soviet's. There is little doubt that even in his twilight years he has not forgotten his diplomatic training; throughout his entire memoirs he never once mentions his former boss, Stalin.

The Royal Hot Dog

Mrs. Eleanor Roosevelt, King George, Mrs. Sara Delano Roosevelt, the president's mother, Queen Elizabeth, and the President in June, 1939, just before the "hot-dog picnic."

THE PICNIC luncheon was served on the Roosevelt grounds. When King George VI was handed his paper plate, he held up the roll and studied it for a moment.

"We call it a hot dog," said the grinning FDR. He passed over a jar. "You might want some mustard."

The King of England slid the knife down the gleaming hot dog. He gingerly took a bite, then smiled.

"It is good, my dear," he said to the Queen.

She nodded. "They're excellent."

The waiter came with a tray of glasses of cold beer.

"They go well with beer," said FDR.

The King took a beer and downed it with relish.

"I say, can I have another—er—hot dog?" he asked.

He had a second helping. It was quite evident that the King and Queen of England enjoyed their introduction to the American hot dog and cold beer. The picnic lunch was the highlight of their triumphant tour from Canada to the United States.

On June 8, a 21-gun salute boomed as the royal couple left Union Station for the White House. It was one of the most momentous welcomes the capital had ever seen. A solid mass of people crowded the streets and the roofs and windows of buildings, overflowed the grandstands, and hung on statues and public monuments at every possible vantage point along the royal route to the White House. More cannons boomed salutes, fleets of planes roared overhead, and smartly uniformed troops, rumbling tanks, and dashing cavalry units also took part in the impressive demonstration. It was a human as well as an official welcome; all up and down the route of march a waving mass of American and British flags signaled welcome to the first reigning British monarch ever to visit the United States. Flags and applause rippled like a rolling wave along Delaware Avenue to the Capitol and on down Constitution Avenue and Pennsylvania Avenue as the party proceeded.

Later that day, a historic garden party was held at the British Embassy. An estimated fourteen hundred elect had tea with the King and Queen, while the uninvited gathered in hordes outside the gates. No more immune than any other male guest from the sartorial idio-cies requiring formal attire under a blazing summer sun, the King sweltered and steamed in cutaway coat and striped trousers, but the Queen, in the thinnest and whitest of fabrics, looked as if she might have stepped from a Watteau painting as she greeted her guests.

Later, the royal couple were received by the combined Congress; then they went on to tour Mount Vernon like any other tourists. They topped their expedition with a visit to a CCC camp.

In New York the entire city, gaily bedecked with thousands of American and British flags, was bright with bunting as the greatest crowd in the city's history greeted the King and Queen. Hotels were filled with an influx of out-of-town visitors. More than a million school children lined the route along Central Park to the World's Fair. After the city's welcome, the royal couple took a four-hour walking tour of the fair. The luncheon at Hyde Park followed.

The grace and charm of the royal couple completely captured the nation. As the *New York Times* observed, the city would never forget them.

Death of a PONTIFF

THE FRAIL old man in white stood before the portraits of the English Catholic martyrs, Sir Thomas More and John Fisher, and told Prime Minister Neville Chamberlain in clear, scholarly English on that February day in 1939, what were the evils of totalitarian regimes, what were the duties of democracies to combat them.

"I often think of the English," he told Chamberlain and his delegation as they sat on the edge of their chairs like attentive schoolboys. "I am happy to believe that these two Englishmen"—he pointed to the portraits—"stood for what is best in the English race, in their courage, their determination, their readiness to fight and die if need be for what they knew to be right. I like to think—indeed I am sure—that these qualities, courage and readiness, still belong to the English. You agree with me?"

No one spoke. The silent statesmen seemed gripped by the strong words of the Pontiff, who had virtually risen from his deathbed to tell them of his thoughts.

With a quiet smile, his blue eyes twinkling behind rimless glasses, Pope Pius XI talked on, not lecturing but rather leading their thoughts to the problems and struggles which lay before them. The problems were great, perhaps greater than any other age had had to face, he said. He told Chamberlain and his men they had a hard task, "but you know better than I do what is in the English race."

Then he turned again to the portraits of More and Fisher.

After a moment a priest came and whispered in his ear.

"Well, I must say good-bye to you now," he said. "They are bringing me more work—and there is so little time."

There wasn't much time left for the aged Rock of the Church. The following month he died, mourned as no other pope of modern times ever was.

Pius XI was the 261st pontiff to occupy the chair of St. Peter. At the time of his coronation in 1922, his reputation as churchman, linguist, scholar, diplomat, and also as an Alpinist had been mostly confined to Italy and to politico-ecclesiastical circles in Poland. But the world soon came to know him as a great statesman, churchman, and humanitarian. He became head of a church having 250,000,000

Pope Pius XII being borne on his thronechair through the Vatican to St. Peter's for the ceremony of his coronation, March 12, 1939.

communicants, 17,000,000 of them in the United States. At his death it had 333,000,000, of whom 20,000,000 were in the United States.

At the beginning of his pontificate Pius was faced with a multitude of distracting problems, some of international importance, others vital only to church discipline and organization. Among the most important were the Roman question, the Mexican problem, French separation, the Anglican Church overtures, and the authority of the Church in the Near East and Soviet Russia. The end of his pontificate was marked by even more vexing problems in Germany, Austria, Spain, and Italy itself. A man of wisdom, deliberate in meditation, quick in action, and extremely placid and kindly, he wrestled with them to the end, and his encyclical utterances were among the most outspoken of any modern pope's. His condemnations of communism and of German fascism were couched in vigorous language. Under him the Roman Catholic Church attained an influence hitherto unknown in modern times.

From the time of Pius IX, it had been customary to compare each successive pope with his predecessor or predecessors. But in the case of Pius XI there were no achievements of his immediate predecessors comparable to his; in fact, from Pius IX onward, each reign in turn had added to the problems that finally confronted Pius XI early in 1922.

In the summer of 1934, strained relations between the Vatican and Nazi Germany neared the breaking point when a papal letter refused patronage to the Hitler Labor Front because of the organization's alleged anti-Catholic attitude. Later, the Pope took a very strong stand against German theories of eugenics and sterilization. He declared that if the German program of unmistakable paganism were extended to and accepted by other nations, incalculable harm would be done to the whole world. He was to continue his attacks on Hitlerism in the following years.

On June 29, 1936, Pope Pius issued an encyclical letter—"Vigilanti Cura"— in which he made an impassioned appeal for a ban on all motion pictures that were indecent or morally unsound. The letter was addressed particularly to "our venerable brethren, Archbishops and Bishops in the United States of America," and was the culmination of many appeals from the Vatican for reforms within the motion-picture field. In April, 1936, the Pope had told the Cinematographic Congress, in session in Rome, that thoughts of the harm done by evil pictures moved him to tears.

Pope Pius roused the wrath of the Soviet government when, in the spring of 1936, he denounced communism as "the enemy of all." He declared that communism was the destroyer of individual dignity, the sanctity of the family, civil order, security, and, above all, religion, and referred to it as "the great terror which threatens the world."

Even after the infirmities of age and his weakening heart had begun to show their effects upon the Pope, he continued his attacks upon atheism and communism, which he consistently joined together. Although a sick man, he summoned strength, early in 1937, to indite a bitter excoriation of those who had fallen so far from Christian ways as to embrace communism in any form. This was issued from the Vatican as an encyclical in March, and it bristled with vigorous language. The gist of it will be apparent from the quotation.

Reverberations of this encyclical were heard in the United States when the Knights of Columbus and other Roman Catholic organizations began a campaign against the "Red menace," despite the poor showing of the Communist Party at the elections of the previous November.

Pope Pius was also deeply worried over the conditions facing his flock in Nazi Germany and in war-torn Spain, but a short time after he issued his famous encyclical, he slipped into a coma and a few days later he died. Eugenio Cardinal Pacelli succeeded to the papal throne as Pope Pius XII.

From the Encyclical of Pope Pius XI — March 19, 1937

[According to communism] Even human society is nothing but phenomena and a form of matter evolving in the same way. By the law of inexorable necessity and through the perpetual conflict of forces, matter moves toward the final synthesis of a classless society. In such a doctrine there is no room for the idea of God; there is no difference between matter and spirit, between soul and body; there is neither the survival of the soul after death nor any hope of a future life.

Thus, man's liberty is destroyed. Every right of the human person is denied. Man becomes, as it were, a mere cog in the collectivist machinery which alone has unlimited control over the lives of men. All hierarchy, all authority is nullified. Religion is dubbed the opiate of the people and assailed with any weapon at hand. The very idea of God is rejected and condemned. . . . Communism is subversive to the social order because it means the destruction of its foundations, because it ignores the true origin and purposes of the State and because it denies the right, dignity, and liberty of human personality."

The FALL of MADRID

The Condor Legion passes the reviewing stand in the victory parade in Madrid shortly after the last Republican stronghold surrendered, to end the Spanish Civil War. As they marched by, officers and men gave the Nazi stiff-arm salute, which was answered from the reviewing stand.

WHEN THE symbol fell, the rest of the nation collapsed. Once Madrid, shell-torn symbol of Republican resistance, passed into the hands of Nationalist Generalissimo Francisco Franco, Valencia and the remaining cities had to fall.

After holding Nationalist forces at the edge of the war-weary, hungering capital for twenty-nine months, the Central Army withdrew from its trenches and hoisted the white flags of surrender. The fall of the city was regarded as the virtual end of the savage conflict that had unnerved Europe for so long.

Early in the afternoon of March 28, Franco's troops marched into the city by the Toledo Bridge while the *"Arriba España* [Up Spain]" populace cheered and danced in the streets. The brilliant sun glittered on the passing rows of bayonets. The balconies of the houses were draped with bright shawls and re-

General Miaja directing the government's defense of Madrid during the siege.

ligious and monarchist insignia, and the old red-and-gold monarchist flag was unfurled atop the fourteen-story telephone building, the largest structure in the city. A short time after the arrival of the troops, six thousand trucks began distributing food.

Occupation of Madrid by Franco's troops ended the longest siege of a major city in modern history, a siege of slightly more than two years, four months, and three weeks.

No fighting since World War I had been so fierce as the hand-to-hand combat in the Madrid suburbs, particularly in University City, during the tremendous offensive that had begun in the winter two years before. On one side of the city were government legions who had passionately resolved to die rather than lose their beloved city; on the other were the reckless members of the International Brigade. Finally General Franco decided to surround the

Government troops in a front-line trench in defense of Madrid.

The people of Madrid welcoming Franco's victorious troops.

Nationalist soldiers advancing over a trench during the siege of Madrid.

city, or at least cut off the road between it and the Mediterranean coast, to deprive the city of food and ammunition.

That too failed; a violent attack from the city smashed the Italian columns on the Guadalajara front. In the late spring of 1937 Franco decided to abandon the direct effort to take the city, and capture the cities on the north instead. By autumn the situation of Madrid's defenders again seemed impossible as Franco's victories continued on all other fronts. In October the government moved from Valencia to Barcelona. Then in 1938 Franco broke through the lines of the Republican army, cutting off Catalonia from southern Spain. Finally, early in 1939, Franco's forces took all of Catalonia and cut off all means of communication by land.

It was then just a matter of time before disease and starvation joined forces with Franco's troops to bring about the surrender of Madrid. But there was also another force. General Mola, it is said, gave that force a name—the fifth column, referring to the Franco sympathizers inside Madrid, at a time when he was leading four columns against the city. The phrase he coined was adopted all over the world, to designate a subversive force within an area, that is working with and preparing the way for an invading external force.

Street scene in Madrid after an air raid.

DER TAG

IT WAS like a nightmare. A feverish-eyed man with a Charlie Chaplin mustache, wearing a field-gray tunic and black trousers, stood on the rostrum of the Kroll Opera House in Berlin and announced he had brought war to the world.

The date was September 1, 1939. Inside the opera house it was hot and humid. The very furnishings of the place —the thick red carpets, the dark walls— seemed to hold the stagnant air. The faces of the listeners glistened with a sheen of perspiration; only the silvered beak of the lighted eagle above the rostrum was dry and cold-looking. The diplomats and the foreign dignitaries flanking Field Marshal Goering stared as if hypnotized at the violent man under the fierce eagle.

"Since 5:45 o'clock this morning," Adolf Hitler was telling the world, "enemy fire has been returned."

This then was war.

The previous night, wire services all over the world had clattered with reports that German patrols had "penetrated" Poland from several points. But there had been only silence from Berlin. From Paris and London had come stories that Hitler was backtracking in his demands, that the Nazi government was split and the leaders fighting one another. Now Hitler was showing that that confusion was only part of the nightmare.

The fierce words filled the opera house. It had been the same voice over Austria, the same over Czechoslovakia. First it damned the Treaty of Versailles. Then it spoke of Danzig, which should belong to Germany. Then the Polish Corridor question. Then the Poles — he had warned the Poles! And they had attacked and mutilated German citizens!

The dynamic, piercing voice softened a bit as it came to the question of West Europe. Of course he would make no claims on West Europe. As he said: "I have formal assurances and I repeat, that we demand nothing from the Western Powers and that we shall never demand anything."

Italy, of course, was thanked for standing by in Germany's great hour of

Hitler announcing to the Reichstag the invasion of Poland, September 1, 1939.

crisis and then Germany itself was dwelt on for three minutes; there would be privations, from which he himself would not be exempt, sufferings which he would also endure.

"My whole life belongs to my people from now on in a new sense," Adolf Hitler said. "I wish nothing other than to be the first soldier of the German Reich. . . ."

In thirty-four minutes the speech was over. The violent man with the comic mustache had told the world he had just summoned down on it the jagged lightning.

Two days later, on a lovely, sunny Sunday, a radio announcer interrupted Liszt's "First Hungarian Rhapsody" to tell his listeners that England considered itself in a state of war with Germany. Even as the announcer was speaking, the church bells were ringing out the Sabbath services on the Wilhelmstrasse and crowds were packing the sidewalk cafés along Kurfürstendamm.

In London, Mr. Chamberlain spoke long and earnestly to a gallery that was not filled. He spoke with indignation about Munich and broken promises, but his speech touched no chord among the listeners. It would never be recited by schoolchildren on graduation day. The applause was formal and polite. The thunderous words and phrases to match the occasion were left for Churchill.

Fifteen minutes after Chamberlain formally announced that a state of war existed, the sirens screeched. It was a false alarm, but the citizens of London had their first taste of air-raid shelters, which were then far from complete.

The streets of London that day were filled with newly uniformed service men and the auxiliary firemen, looking dashing in their blue uniforms and tin hats. Taxis proudly displayed stickers of the fire service, and signs everywhere implored the citizenry to fill the sandbags. Huge silver-gray balloons, which the High Command hoped would helplessly entangle enemy aircraft, waved gently on their guy wires, and below, in the railroad stations, mothers wept as they kissed their children good-bye.

General mobilization was ordered. Parliament rushed new defense laws and arranged new credits as the government took over control of the railroads. A White Paper containing the text of the notes passed between London and Berlin was published. These documents revealed that late in August Chamberlain had told Hitler Great Britain would aid Poland in case of an attack, and had pleaded for a peaceful solution of the German claims to the free city of Danzig, which had been a part of Germany from 1914 to the end of World War I. But Hitler insisted on dictating terms to the Poles, and demanded that within twenty-four hours Poland have an envoy in Berlin who was empowered to sign an immediate agreement—an obvious impossibility. This was the same maneuver he had used against the Austrians and the Czechs before seizing those countries. Great Britain continued until the last moment to seek a truce, but Hitler was in reality only stalling, attempting to build up a case against the Poles which could be used as propaganda in pinning the blame on them. On August 31, Foreign Minister Von Ribbentrop read to the British ambassador in Berlin the text of sixteen proposals to Poland. Among these were proposals that Danzig be returned to Germany, that Gdynia remain Polish, and that the fate of the Polish Corridor be decided within twelve months by a plebiscite under international supervision. Evidence of the Nazis' deceitfulness in the matter was the fact that although the Polish ambassador succeeded in reaching the German foreign minister that day, he found that his telephone had been cut when he attempted to send the German plan to Warsaw. The proposals had been broadcast by the German government, and when the Poles did not accept them immediately, Hitler launched his invasion.

France followed Great Britain's lead and dispatched to Berlin an ultimatum identical with the one from London. Martial law was established throughout France, and the government rushed plans for the evacuation of Paris. Australia and New Zealand declared war the same day and Canada automatically entered the war when the British ultimatum to Germany expired.

Meanwhile, Germany issued its own White Paper, charging that Great Britain had "sabotaged Premier Mussolini's effort to preserve peace and was responsible for the start of the war."

The Council of Ministers in Italy had announced, on September 1, that their country's stand was nonintervention. There followed declarations of neutrality from the nations of Europe and throughout the world, including one by the United States and another by Japan.

The cause of the war can be traced to Hitler's takeover of Czechoslovakia

Children, many of whom have been evacuated from London for safety, watch a cavalry troop—yes, there was cavalry then—pass by on their way to war. Note the gas masks carried by the children on their backs.

269

in March, 1939, breaking his promise of September, 1938, that the Sudetenland was his "last territorial claim in Europe." After the absorption of Czechoslovakia, Memel also was taken under Nazi rule. Still Germany and her Axis partner, Italy, aspired to more territory, to political and economic domination of the European continent through the control of the Baltic, the Adriatic, and the Danube. But Poland and the Polish Corridor stood in the way, and the Poles refused to relinquish any territory to Germany.

In mid-September of 1939, the British government, seeking to pin the guilt for the war on Germany, issued a 200-page Blue Book containing memoranda on five talks between Sir Nevile Henderson, the British ambassador to Berlin, and Adolf Hitler. In one section, Sir Nevile reported that on August 16, a week before the announcement of the German-Russian nonaggression pact, more than a month before Soviet troops invaded Poland, Baron Weizsaecker, state secretary in the German Foreign Office, had informed him that Russia would give only "entirely negligible" help to Poland and that in the end Russia would "join in sharing the Polish spoils."

The memoranda showed that Hitler was bent on war with the Poles, even at the cost of a world war, unless he could have his way with a settlement "imposed" upon Poland.

Ambassador Henderson reported in the Blue Book that his last interview with Hitler was "the most unpleasant of all." Hitler, according to the ambassador, "was far less reasonable." Sir Nevile never left his superiors in any doubt that he was dealing with an abnormal man.

He also disclosed he had warned Field Marshall Goering that Great Britain and France would go to war if Germany invaded Poland. Goering told him he did not doubt Britain's readiness to fight, but tried to contrast conditions of 1939 with those of 1914. "No power can overcome Germany in Europe," he boasted to the ambassador. "A blockade this time would prove unavailing. France cannot stand a long war, Germany can do more harm to Britain than Britain can do to her. The history of Germany is one of ups and downs, and this is one of our ups."

The German government issued in November a 3,000-word reply to the British Blue Book, charging that Great Britain had forced Germany into a war with Poland.

The war in the beginning was centered on the campaign against Poland. Along the Maginot Line of France, and the West Wall or Siegfried Line of Germany, troops waited in readiness but there was little action. On the sea, German submarines attacked ships carrying food supplies to Great Britain and the British fleet blockaded Germany. On the diplomatic front, accusing papers issued charge and countercharge.

While London waited, Poland resisted the invaders. But she had little defense against what was then the latest in equipment for making war. The Stukas, which froze a man in his tracks with the terrifying sound as they dived, reduced Warsaw to rubble, and the German army, mobile as Stonewall Jackson's "foot cavalry," swept over the so-called impregnable Polish Narew fortifications in only forty-eight hours. Within a week, the back of Polish resistance was broken, the air force destroyed, and remnants of the defeated army caught in a great pincers movement around Warsaw and further east.

On October 5, the first correspondent to enter the Polish capital reported most of the buildings demolished by the fury

Barrage balloons over London.

of the German bombardment. Starving Polish soldiers in the city had been forced to eat dead horses. The dull steel armor of the Nazi Wehrmacht had scarcely been dented by its first blitz campaign.

In the midst of the Polish fighting, the Soviet government notified the Polish ambassador in Moscow that Soviet troops were about to cross the frontier into Poland to protect Russian interests. Moscow declared that she considered the Polish-Soviet treaties nonexistent, since the Polish state no longer could be presumed to be functioning.

German and Soviet troops met at Brest-Litovsk on September 18. In the resulting partition of Poland, Germany and the Soviet Union established a new borderline. By the terms of the agreement, Germany took approximately the western half of Poland and the Soviets the eastern half. Germany absorbed a population of about 22,000,000, mainly hostile, and Russia 13,000,000.

The conquest of Poland illustrated and confirmed some frightening facts: Germany's overwhelming superiority in tanks, plus an overwhelming superiority in the air from the very beginning; the effectiveness of the dive-bomber as a form of super-artillery; the complete coordination between the German army and the air force; and most important, the success of Hitler's military strategy —lightning attack to gain the advantage of surprise, and the use of the swift, overlapping spearheads to split the enemy, encircle him, and crush him in an iron ring from which there was no escape.

With the campaign in Poland closed, Germany began moving her war-seasoned troops from the east to the west, where a stalemate had developed. French troops had taken their stations in the Maginot Line and the Germans had manned the West Wall, but no big battle or "over the top" onslaughts like those of the First World War had developed. Early in the campaign the French had occupied some German territory, approximately 155 square miles between the Moselle and the Rhine, near Saarbrücken beween the Luxembourg border and Lauterbourg. When the Germans pressed for this section later, the French forces withdrew.

Observers on the Western Front reported that the British and French indicated every intention of waiting until

Clerks and office workers place sandbags on the roofs of London office buildings.

spring to start an offensive. What fighting there was on the Western Front was mostly attacks by small groups.

"It is a war of patience," one French general observed.

To the north, neutral Netherlands and Belgium also prepared for war. In the Netherlands the dikes were set to release a flood in the path of the invaders. Belgium devised a portable steel wall to be used to repel tank attacks.

On the naval side of the war, Ger-

many launched a massive submarine campaign to cut off British war supplies. Great Britain charged Germany was conducting unrestricted submarine war, and then proclaimed a system of contraband control which comprised a long-range blockade of the Third Reich. In answer Germany declared a counter-blockade. The British Admiralty established convoys for merchant shipping, and the British air force was called into action to patrol the skies around the British Isles; British cruisers and destroyers roamed the seas in search of the U-boats.

The British Ministry of Economic Warfare announced that in the first twelve weeks of war the contraband-control system had detained 463,000 tons of cargo, including more than 100,000 tons of petroleum products.

In November of 1939, the third month of the war, shipping losses to the allies and neutrals mounted, as a result of contact with mines at sea. Great Britain charged that Germany was violating international law by having her U-boats and planes release floating and magnetic mines at sea. In retaliation, Britain ordered the seizure of German exports on the high seas. France joined in this action.

The German *Graf Spee,* after exchanging broadsides with the British cruisers *Exeter, Ajax,* and *Achilles,* put into Montevideo, Uruguay, with 36 dead and 60 injured. A few days later the *Spee* left at twilight, steaming down

Stuka dive-bombers over Poland.

German light tanks halt on a Polish road. Note Polish machine-gun cart and dead horse on left. Combat car of the commanding officer is at right.

Blitzkrieg sample. Though bridges are destroyed, German troops advance over streams and rivers on quickly constructed pontoon bridges.

German infantrymen advance cautiously around streetcars in the outskirts of virtually destroyed Warsaw.

the River Plate. She halted three miles offshore while the crew and Captain Hans Langsdorff went aboard barges. At 7:25 the captain set off an electric charge and blew up the ship. Two days later Langsdorff committed suicide.

The diplomatic front was extremely active in those early days. Although Italy was Germany's Axis partner, she did not enter the war but remained a neutral. The cabinet was reorganized and the pro-Nazis were replaced. Italy

also attempted to form a neutral bloc in the Balkans after Turkey had completed a mutual-assistance alliance with Great Britain and France.

Germany and Russia agreed to a "practical cooperation pact," but its scope was never defined. The Soviets pledged economic aid to Germany, but doubt was expressed that this would amount to much, since Russia needed most of her raw materials. While Germany was invading Poland, Russia had

negotiated "protection treaties" with Estonia, Latvia, and Lithuania, thereby gaining military and naval bases. She had now strengthened penetration of the Baltic states in her drive for control of the Baltic and for an outlet to the Atlantic. Of all the small countries, Finland was the only one to resist Soviet demands. On November 28, Russia denounced her nonaggression pact with Finland and the next day severed diplomatic relations. Premier Molotov demanded that a new government be set up in Finland and announced that the Red army and navy were on a war alert.

An offer by Secretary of State Hull to mediate for peace was refused. Russia's land, sea, and air forces moved against Finland on the thirtieth, Helsinki, the capital of Finland, being bombed without a declaration of war. On December 1, the Finnish cabinet resigned and the Finns began formation of a new government.

By mid-December the Red army had penetrated deeply into Finland, but the Finns fought bitterly for every foot, every mile. Many times the warfare was primitive; hand-to-hand combat on snowshoes and skis was not unusual. Long knives were sometimes the weapons resorted to, in the below-zero cold.

In the United States, Congress was called into special session and passed the Neutrality Act of 1939, which was immediately signed by the President. This act lifted the arms embargo (1937) which had placed commerce between the United States and belligerents on a cash-and-carry basis and barred American travelers and ships from belligerent zones. The Neutrality Act was hailed in London and Paris, but Berlin greeted it angrily and Moscow caustically.

Activities on the peace front in 1939 met with no success. Moves designed to pave the way for peace discussions were waved aside by the belligerents with a restatement of their aims: Germany's, the destruction of the British Empire; Great Britain's, the destruction of Hitlerism.

As the war continued President Roosevelt asked the belligerent governments to ban the bombing of civilian population in undefended cities. Hitler replied the following day that his air force had been ordered to bomb only military objects. Great Britain and France, in a joint communiqué, pledged themselves to wage a humane war. Pope Pius XII urged all nations to conform to existing international agreements, and expressed the hope that civilian populations would be spared the horrors of war and that poison gas would not be used.

President Roosevelt wrote the Pope, as the bitter year was fading, that he had selected Myron C. Taylor, president of U.S. Steel, as his personal representative at the Vatican. While Taylor was en route to Rome, the Pope outlined a five-point program for world peace to the College of Cardinals, but the proposals were lost in the thunder of war over Poland and Helsinki.

On December 10, 1939, Joseph P. Kennedy, our ambassador to Great Britain, in an address in Boston, warned the United States in strong terms to keep out of war in Europe. In an interview after the address, he said: "There is no reason to justify the United States entering a war."

At the year's end Hitler ate dinner with his troops in a bunker before Saarbrücken, taken by his army a few hours before, and proclaimed that the Third Reich would last a thousand years.

FDR signing the "cash and carry" neutrality bill, which lifted the arms embargo and opened Europe's war market to American industry on a cash-and-carry basis.

274

FAREWELL, LOU GEHRIG
The Passing of the Iron Horse

Lou Gehrig, the Iron Horse of baseball, saying good-bye at Yankee Stadium.

Lou Gehrig in 1925, the year he joined the Yankees.

The immortals of baseball, Gehrig and Ruth, at Lou Gehrig Day at Yankee Stadium, July 4, 1939—the day Gehrig said a sad good-bye to 61,000 fans. His career was ended when he was stricken with a strange paralyzing disease and his days were numbered, though he may not have known that. He had played 2,130 consecutive games for the Yanks from June 2, 1925, to May 2, 1939. He died on June 2, 1941.

The baseball world bids farewell to Gehrig.

Highlights and Sidelights: 1939

THE JAPANESE continued to press their invasion of China without arousing too much protest from the rest of the world, which had assumed an angry indifference to that informal war. . . . In May, the *Squalus,* a U.S. submarine, sank in a test dive 240 feet to the ocean floor off the New Hampshire coast, 12 miles from Portsmouth. Rescue efforts began almost immediately, and attempts to raise the submarine continued all summer. Though 33 crewmen were saved by means of a diving bell, 26 men remained entombed; their bodies were finally recovered when the *Squalus* was brought to the surface 113 days later and the water pumped from her hull at the Portsmouth Navy Yard. . . . In a much-publicized award ceremony in Washington, Mrs. Roosevelt greeted Marian Anderson, the famous singer who had been the center of a heated discrimination controversy. . . . Erskine Caldwell, author of *Tobacco Road* and *God's Little Acre,* married Margaret Bourke-White, artist-photographer. . . . Powel Crosley, Jr., introduced an inexpensive compact automobile, but the American public did not seem to be ready for it yet. . . . On radio, a young announcer named John Charles Daly, Jr., seemed headed for a big career. . . . By the latter part of the decade it was clear that the theatre had been revitalized. Plays like Kingsley's *Dead End* and *Men in*

Japanese mounted troops and infantrymen move in on Chinese troops at Yicheng, China, in the spring of 1939.

White had brought flaming dialogue and contemporary themes to Broadway. Theatre history had also been made during these years by Moss Hart and George S. Kaufman, with their hilarious *You Can't Take It With You, Merrily We Roll Along, I'd Rather Be Right, The Fabulous Invalid,* and the long-playing *The Man Who Came to Dinner.* . . . Other established dramatists had been busy too; Maxwell Anderson gave us *Elizabeth the Queen, Mary of Scotland,* the Pulitzer Prize winner *Both Your Houses,* and the poetic *High Tor* and *Winterset.* Eugene O'Neill, the master of them all, wrote *Mourning Becomes Electra* and *Ah, Wilderness.* Thornton Wilder's *Our Town* was a hit which would be revived again and again, and Robert E. Sherwood's *The*

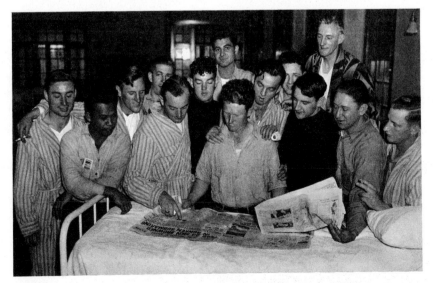

Fourteen of the lucky 33 survivors of the Squalus in the Portsmouth Naval Hospital.

Petrified Forest was not only a major play but also a major motion picture which helped boost Humphrey Bogart to movie fame.... By 1939, Hollywood had an audience of more than fifty million Americans who attended the movies once a week. The double feature was standard. Local admission was ten, fifteen cents, then a quarter. Midweek was featured as Bank Night, Dish Night, Keeno, or Screeno. On Dish Night the moviegoer was handed a dish as he went in ("Get a complete set of this genuine, gold-bordered china in only six weeks"). For Screeno, Banko, or Keeno, the assistant manager would come out on stage between features and nervously announce that with the turn of the wheel (he had a carnival-type wheel at his side) some lucky person was going to win ten dollars or twenty-

Streaming spray, the conning tower of the Squalus bobs to the surface. The craft was towed to the Portsmouth Navy Yard.

The Squalus snapping cables and lines, during salvage, to sink back to the bottom of the sea.

Eugene O'Neill.

Novelist Erskine Caldwell and his photographer-bride Margaret Bourke-White the day after their wedding.

Mrs. Roosevelt and Marian Anderson.

five. He spun the wheel and you looked at your ticket, and either grunted with disappointment or yelled out that you had the winning number. . . . Hollywood was now producing annually an average of four hundred pictures. Some were good, some bad, many indifferent. But for the millions of men, women, and children who sat in the more than 15,000 theatres, large and small, across the nation, they were a wonderful escape from the grim world that awaited them outside.

279

"OUTRUNS the imagination of all the wizards of prophecy," one editorial said after President Hoover was seen on a small television screen speaking from the Bell laboratory in New Jersey. Viewers in Washington saw not only Hoover but the script from which he was reading as well.

That was in 1929. Ten years passed before an occupant of the White House spoke directly to the people via TV. FDR made the first presidential television broadcast on the opening day of the New York World's Fair. At the time there were only a few TV sets in the country. Only NBC's New York experimental station telecast the ceremonies.

Eight years later, President Truman became the first President to be seen from Washington as he addressed Congress.

Robert E. Sherwood and his wife arriving from Europe aboard the Queen Mary.

John Charles Daly, Jr., in 1939.

Powel Crosley, Jr., and the 1939 Crosley.

EPILOGUE

THE DECADE that started with the crash in the stock market ended with the crash and boom of guns and bombs. The decade that began with business depression and unemployment ended with mills, factories, and shipyards working around the clock. Instead of a shortage of jobs, there was a shortage of help. The specter of unemployment had been laid. The fear for economic security had been dissipated. However, now there were new fears. The dark shadow of the war was spreading, the lights were out over much of the world. But no longer were the American people desperate. They faced the threat of war and the enemies of freedom with courage and determination.

Bibliography

THE Desperate Years has many monuments and memorials. Only total war will wipe out the Grand Coulee Dam, the Hoover Dam, the TVA, the George Washington and Golden Gate bridges, and in Washington the beautiful National Archives and the Commerce, Labor, and Post Office buildings. In addition, on a humbler scale, are the thousands of highways, bridges, post offices, and lush woodlands across the land.

But the story of that historic decade is also told in millions of words and countless photographs.

The Civil War had its Mathew Brady and his corps of one hundred photographers, but a legion of cameramen, famous and anonymous, recorded the rapid flow of history from apple peddler to Adolf Hitler in those Desperate Years.

Now in the National Archives, the photographic library of the Paris office of the *New York Times* contains prints of thousands of American and European events. The Abbott Collection of New York City in the thirties, now in the Museum of the City of New York, captured the city and its people. Obviously the collections of Eva Braun and Heinrich Hoffman, Hitler's personal photographer, are priceless historic records of the rise and fall of the Third Reich. The photographic files of the various New Deal agencies are easily available in Washington and offer a fascinating pictorial record of those years.

BOOKS

ALLEN, FREDERICK LEWIS. *Only Yesterday*. New York: Harper, 1931.

ALLEN, FREDERICK LEWIS. *Since Yesterday*. New York: Harper, 1940.

BURNS, JAMES MACGREGOR. *Roosevelt: The Lion and the Fox*. New York: Harcourt, Brace, 1956.

COMMONS, JOHN R., *et al. History of Labor in the United States*. New York: Macmillan, 1921.

CONGDON, DON (ed.). *The Thirties*. New York: Simon and Schuster, 1962.

DOUGLAS, PAUL H. *Social Security in the United States*. Second edition. New York: McGraw-Hill, 1939.

DULLES, ELEANOR L. *Depression and Reconstruction*. Philadelphia: University of Pennsylvania Press, 1937.

HEIDEN, KONRAD. *Der Fuehrer*. Boston: Houghton Mifflin, 1944.

HOPKINS, HARRY L. *Spending to Save*. New York: W. W. Norton, 1936.

HOWARD, DONALD STEVENSON. *The WPA and Federal Relief Policy*. New York: Russell Sage, 1943.

ICKES, HAROLD L. *Autobiography of a Curmudgeon*. New York: Reynal and Hitchcock, 1943.

JOHNSON, HUGH. *The Blue Eagle from Egg to Earth*. New York: Doubleday, Doran, 1935.

LAWRENCE, DAVID. *Beyond the New Deal*. New York: McGraw-Hill, 1934.

LEIGHTON, ISABEL (ed.). *The Aspirin Age*. New York: Simon and Schuster, 1949.

LEONARD, JONATHAN N. *Three Years Down*. New York: Carrick and Evans, 1939.

LINDLEY, ERNEST K. *Franklin D. Roosevelt: A Career in Progressive Democracy*. New York: Bobbs Merrill, 1931.

LINDLEY, ERNEST K. *The Roosevelt Revolution: First Phase*. New York: Viking, 1933.

LUDWIG, EMIL. *Roosevelt: A Study in Fortune and Power*. New York: Viking, 1938.

MINEHAN, THOMAS. *Boy and Girl Tramps of America*. New York: Farrar, 1934.

MITCHELL, BROADUS. *Depression Decade: From the New Era through the New Deal*. New York: Rinehart, 1947.

MOLEY, RAYMOND. *After Seven Years*. New York: Harper, 1939.

PERKINS, FRANCES. *The People at Work*. New York: John Day, 1934.

PERKINS, FRANCES. *The Roosevelt I Knew*. New York: Viking, 1946.

RIESS, CURT (ed.). *They Were There*. New York: Putnam, 1944.

ROOSEVELT, ELEANOR. *This Is My Story*. New York: Harper, 1936.

ROOSEVELT, JAMES, with SHALETT, SIDNEY. *Affectionately, F.D.R.* New York: Harcourt, Brace, 1959.

SHANNON, DAVID A. (ed.). *The Great Depression*. New York: Prentice-Hall, 1960.

WECTER, DIXON. *The Age of the Great Depression: 1929-1941*. (A History of American Life, Vol. XIII.) New York: Macmillan, 1948.

MAGAZINES

GLASS, REMLEY J. "Gentlemen, The Corn Belt," *Harper's Magazine,* July, 1933.

HEFFERNAN, JOSEPH L. "The Hungry City: A Mayor's Experience with Unemployment," *The Atlantic Monthly,* May, 1932.

KAZIN, ALFRED. "The Bitter Thirties: From a Personal History," *The Atlantic Monthly,* May, 1962.

KAZIN, ALFRED. "Does Anyone Remember the Thirties?" *Saturday Review,* Oct. 13, 1962.

ROCHE, JOHN P. "Memo to Today's Young Radicals," *New York Times Magazine,* Oct. 14, 1962.

SITWELL, SIR OSBERT. "New York in the Twenties," *Atlantic Magazine,* Feb., 1962.

VANDERLIP, FRANK A. "Why the Banks?" *Saturday Evening Post,* November, 1932.

PAMPHLETS

BURNS, A. E., and WILLIAMS, E. A. *A Survey of Relief and Security Programs*. Washington: WPA, 1938.

The CCC at Work. Washington: 1941. (The records of the CCC in the National Archives contain such material as the CCC national weekly, *Happy Days*, started in 1933, which included items of interest from the various camp bulletins. Its files are rich in original material.)

The FERA'S Monthly Reports (May, 1933 to December, 1935)

Series of Hearings, Federal Aid For Unemployment Relief. Washington: 1932. (Hearings before a subcommittee of the Senate Committee on Manufacturers.)

The Sixteenth Census of the United States. Washington: Bureau of the Census, 1940.

Social Aspects of the Depression. New York: Social Science Research Council, 1937.

Unemployment in the United States. Washington: 1932. (Hearing before a subcommittee on labor, 72nd Congress).

WEBBINK, PAUL. *Unemployment in the United States, 1930-1940*. (Papers and Proceedings of the American Economic Association, Vol. XXX, Feb., 1941.)

ZIMMERMAN, C., and WHETTEN, N. L. *Rural Families on Relief*. Washington: WPA, 1938.

NEWSPAPERS

The newspapers of the thirties are a klondike for the researcher mining that decade. From the ads to the news stories they present a vivid picture of what it was like during those turbulent years. The *New York Times* Sunday Magazine section has several excellent articles written about the period and the men who made their mark during that time.

Atlanta Constitution
Chicago Daily News
New York American
New York Journal
New York Sun
New York Times
New York Tribune
New York World
New York World-Telegram
The Times (London)
Wall Street Journal

Picture Sources

NOTE: A number of the pictures in this book, not listed below, are from the author's own collection or from other private sources.

ABBREVIATIONS: *t* = top, *b* = bottom, *r* = right, *l* = left, *c* = center

American Automobile Manufacturers Association
35 *tr*, 35 *tl*, 35 *cl*, 35 *cr*, 56 *tl*, 56 *bl*, 56 *br*, 169 *br*, 219 *br*, 219 *bl*, 280 *b*

Associated Press
65, 85 *b*, 90 *tl*, 105 *t*, 107 *b*, 115 *t*, 153, 176 *b*, 178 *b*, 179, 200, 214 *t*, 227, 233 *b*, 236 *br*

Columbia Broadcasting System
193 *tl*, 193 *tc*, 194 *tl*, 194 *br*, 254 *tr*, 254 *tc*, 280 *l*

International News (UPI, United Press, Acme)
21 *t*, 24 *r*, 25 *br*, 37 *br*, 41 *b*, 48 *t*, 55 *c*, 59 *b*, 64, 68, 69, 70 *t*, 76, 82 *b*, 88, 96 *b*, 97, 101, 102, 103 *b*, 104 *b*, 105 *b*, 106 *t*, 107 *t*, 111, 117, 120, 155 *b*, 156, 162 *r*, 171 *t*, 177, 183 *t*, 188, 193 *b*, 203, 205, 205 *t*, 206, 207, 215 *bl*, 216 *t*, 216 *bl*, 217, 220 *tr*, 220 *b*, 222, 226 *l*, 232 *t*, 235 *t*, 236 *lc*, 237 *bl*, 238 *b*, 239, 240, 243 *br*, 244 *b*, 253 *b*, 255 *br*, 261 *b*, 263, 271, 273 *t*, 273 *b*, 274, 276 *b*, 277 *t*

Magnum Photos, Inc.

50, 51 *t*, 51 *b*, 52 *t*, 52 *b*, 53, 248, 249 *b*, 249 *c*, 249 *t*

Metro-Goldwyn-Mayer
89 *br*, 170 *t*

Museum of the City of New York
15 *l*, 19 *r*, 208 *t*, 208 *b*, 209 *tr*, 209 *tl*, 209 *b*, 210 *tl*, 210 *b*, 210 *tr*, 211 *t*, 211 *b*, 212 *t*, 212 *br*, 212 *bl*

National Archives (U.S.I.A., U. S. Signal Corps, Work Projects Administration, seized enemy records, etc.)
14 *b*, 81 *t*, 83 *b*, 91 *t*, 92 *b*, 119 *t*, 119 *b*, 137, 138, 139 *t*, 139 *bl*, 139 *br*, 140 *b*, 140 *t*, 141 *tl*, 141 *tr*, 141 *bl*, 141 *br*, 142 *t*, 142 *b*, 143 *t*, 143 *b*, 144 *t*, 144 *b*, 145, 146 *t*, 146 *b*, 147 *t*, 147 *b*, 148, 149 *t*, 149 *b*, 167, 168 *t*, 195, 196 *t*, 196 *b*, 197 *t*, 197 *b*, 198 *bl*, 198 *br*, 198 *t*, 213, 214 *br*, 216 *br*, 228, 229 *tr*, 229 *tl*, 229 *c*, 229 *bl*, 229 *br*, 230 *t*, 230 *bl*, 230 *br*, 231 *tl*, 231 *tr*, 231 *tl*, 231 *bl*, 265 *t*, 265 *b*, 266 *t*, 266 *b*, 267 *t*, 267 *b*, 279 *b*

National Broadcasting Company
90 *cr*, 90 *br*, 192 *bl*, 219 *t*

New York Journal American
136 *bl*, 15 *r*, 16 *b*, 17 *l*, 18 *t*, 19 *l*, 20 *t*, 21 *b*,

25 *t*, 25 *br*, 29 *t*, 29 *b*, 39 *t*, 40 *b*, 42, 43 *l*, 43 *r*, 44, 45, 57 *bc*, 60, 66, 67 *t*, 68, 70 *t*, 72 *b*, 74 *t*, 74 *b*, 74 *t*, 74 *b*, 77 *b*, 79, 80, 81 *b*, 84, 87, 91 *t*, 93, 96 *b*, 98 *tr*, 103 *t*, 104 *t*, 108 *b*, 110, 123 *l*, 123 *r*, 124 *tl*, 124 *tr*, 124 *bl*, 124 *br*, 152 *b*, 155 *t*, 172, 174, 175 *t*, 176 *t*, 190, 202, 256 *l*, 256 *br*, 275 *t*, 275 *b*, 276 *t*

Port of New York Authority
46 *t*, 46 *b*

Arthur Rothstein
164 *t*, 165

Van Damm Collection
125 *t*, 125 *b*, 126 *tl*, 126 *tr*, 126 *b*, 127 *t*, 127 *b*, 254 *b*

Wide World Photos
13 *t*, 23 *t*, 24 *l*, 27, 28 *t*, 30, 31, 47 *t*, 57 *tl*, 57 *tr*, 57 *bl*, 67 *b*, 73 *t*, 73 *b*, 75 *b*, 85 *tr*, 89 *bl*, 92 *t*, 94 *b*, 98 *tl*, 98 *b*, 99 *t*, 99 *b*, 100 *t*, 100 *b*, 109, 113, 122, 128, 130 *t*, 133, 135, 150, 151, 166, 169 *t*, 169 *bl*, 171 *b*, 191 *b*, 192 *tr*, 192 *tl*, 220 *tl*, 224, 225 *l*, 225 *r*, 235 *b*, 236 *bl*, 237 *br*, 238 *t*, 244 *t*, 245, 246 *l*, 246 *r*, 247 *b*, 247 *tr*, 247 *tl*, 250, 252 *t*, 252 *b*, 254 *lc*, 254 *tl*, 255 *bl*, 260 *b*, 268, 279 *br*, 280 *tr*

Index

285